SIGNS OF AUTISM
IN INFANTS

SIGNS OF AUTISM IN INFANTS

Recognition and Early Intervention

Edited by
Stella Acquarone

Foreword by
Joan Raphael-Leff

KARNAC

First published in 2007 by
Karnac Books
118 Finchley Road
London NW3 5HT

British Library Cataloguing in Publication Data

A C.I.P. for this book is available from the British Library

ISBN: 978-1-85575-486-7

Edited, designed, and produced by Communication Crafts

Printed in Great Britain by Biddles Ltd, King's Lynn, Norfolk

www.karnacbooks.com

To Ignacio and Isabel—my inspiration, my life

*This book is also dedicated to the International Pre-Autistic Network
(registered UK charity, number 1116398), in their effort to provide
screening, treatment, and help for infants and their families
and training for the professionals involved with them*

CONTENTS

PART **III**
Early psychoanalytic intervention approaches

PART IV
Theoretical contributions

ACKNOWLEDGEMENTS

Thank you:

—To the babies and parents who come to us and trust us to treat them. We are grateful that they allow us not only to intervene in their relationships, but also to study their home and treatment videos to further our various researches and to use them to help educate more professionals about "pre-autism".

—To all the spouses, partners, and families for their support (technically and emotionally) in the production of all videos, photographs, charts, and drafts of materials used not only in this book, but in our research, treatments, and careers as well.

—To all of the translators who have translated into English the various contributions from the original French, Italian, and Hebrew.

—To the institutions, medical centres, hospitals, universities, private practice, and research, training, and health clinics mentioned throughout the book for their resources and support in advancing parent–infant psychotherapy.

—To Eric and Klara King of Communication Crafts for their clear management of getting this book produced. They flawlessly handled the onerous thousand-and-one details of editing, correcting, indexing, designing, and shaping a mountain of materials into the accessible and readable book you hold in your hands. Although they make it all seem so straightforward and easy, no one underestimates their complete mastery in preparing books for publication.

—To Karnac Books and its managing director, Oliver Rathbone, for providing the enthusiasm, energy, resources, and sheer willingness to turn a body of multimedia and multilingual materials into a book launched to an international market.

—To the many colleagues who, through their feedback, discussions, debate, and peer reviews, challenged nearly all of the many ideas, premises, and conclusions presented herein.

Again, I say thank you.

ABOUT THE EDITOR AND CONTRIBUTORS

Stella Acquarone, PhD, is an adult and child psychoanalytic psychotherapist and founder of the Parent Infant Clinic and School of Infant Mental Health in 1990 and of the International Pre-Autistic Network (an international charity registered in the UK). Based in London, she has worked for 32 years with parents and infants in the NHS as well as privately, pioneering and laying the foundations of parent–infant psychotherapy. She has presented workshops and conferences and trained professionals all over the world and has published many papers and several books, including the recent *Infant–Parent Psychotherapy: A Handbook for Professionals*. She has been researching and working with infants with autistic tendencies since 1980, and her Special Child Focus programme offers an intensive early-intervention treatment approach administered by a multidisciplinary therapy team and based on psychoanalytic thinking.

Hanna A. Alonim, a family therapist in Rosh Pinna, Israel, is experienced in early childhood development disorders of the autism spectrum. She is the founder (in 1987) and director of the Mifne Center for Early Intervention in Autism in Israel and director of the Mifne School for Therapists, under the auspices of Bar-Ilan University. Founder of the Diagnosis of Infants at Risk Unit, Sourasky Medical Center, Tel Aviv, she is also Partner in Research into Autism in Early Childhood at the Schneider Hospital. Her special expertise is eating disorders in young children with autism, and she has presented and published papers about her research and her family concept treatment approach in Europe, the US, Australia, and Africa.

Graciela Cullere-Crespin, who was born in Argentina, is a clinical psychologist and psychoanalyst in Paris. From her work in infant psychopathology for the past 25 years she has developed her speciality as an autistic children's therapist. She is a Principal in the Association for the Prevention of Pre-Autism in France and a Member of the Association Lacanienne Internationale in Paris and of the World Association of Infant Mental Health. She works individually with adults, furthers research into the early detection of autism, teaches early signs of alarm to pediatricians throughout France, has published many articles, and also lectures at conferences in Europe and South America.

Laurent Danon-Boileau is Full Professor in General Linguistics and Language Acquisition at Sorbonne University René Descartes in Paris, a Member of the Paris Psychoanalytical Society and of the International Psychoanalytical Association, a Researcher at the French National Center for Scientific Research (CNRS), and a psychoanalyst and therapist at the Centre Alfred Binet working with children with communication and language impairment (from severe dysphasia, to autism, to congenital aphasia). He has published three novels in French, and his professional books—*The Child Who Did Not Speak* and *Children Without Language*—are available in English. His expertise is the "birth" of language in at-risk children, and his background and education make him particularly attentive to two different dimensions of language that are often considered to be mutually exclusive: language as a psychic and poetic creation, and language as a word-processing activity.

Marie Christine Laznik, who was born in Brazil, has been living and working as a psychoanalyst in Paris for over 33 years. She is a psychoanalyst at the Centre Alfred Binet in Paris and a Member of the Association Lacanienne Internationale and is the author of books and articles on the psychoanalysis of autism.

Sandra Maestro, MD, is a neuropsychiatrist and psychoanalyst for the Division of Child Neuropsychiatry at the Scientific Institute Stella Maris, University of Pisa, Italy. She is the Coordinator of the Infant Psychiatry Service within IRCCS-Fondazione Stella Maris, is a Member of the Italian and International Psychoanalytical Association, and coordinator of research projects of the Italian National Health Department focusing on valuation and assessment procedures for infant mental disorders. She has conducted a study through home videos of the early onset of autism and other pervasive development disorders, studied treatments of the mother–infant relationship, and researched models and methodologies for the evaluation of the efficacy of therapeutic processes.

Henry Massie, MD, is a child, adolescent, and adult psychiatrist practising in Berkeley, California, and was formerly a Professor of Psychiatry at the University of California School of Medicine and Director of Child Psychiatry Training at St. Mary's Hospital, both in San Francisco. Building on his Fellowship in Family Studies at the Albert Einstein College of Medicine in New York City, he has made a career researching the areas of autism and making longitudinal studies of emotional development in normal and at-risk individuals, focusing in both on the significance of the early infant–parent relationship for subsequent development. Among his many publications are *The Massie–Campbell Scale of Mother–Infant Attachment Indicators During Stress; Childhood Psychosis in the First Four Years of Life* (with Judith Rosenthal); and *Lives Across Time/Growing Up: Paths to Emotional Health and Emotional Illness from Birth to 30 in 76 People* (with Nathan Szajnberg).

Filippo Muratori, MD, a psychoanalyst, is a Professor of Child Neuropsychiatry at the University of Pisa, Italy, and Director of the Psychiatry Clinical Ward and of the Research Team in Child Psychiatry and Psychotherapy at the Institute of Research Stella Maris. He is a President of the Italian Association for Infant Mental Health and has conducted many research projects for the Minister of Health, for the University of Pisa, and for CNR in the field of infant, child, and adolescent psychiatry. His scientific writings consist of over 300 publications in national and international journals, including "A Longitudinal Examination of the Communicative Gestures Deficit in Young Children with Autism", "Study of the Onset of Autism through Home Movies", and "Early Behavioural Development in Autistic Children: The First 2 Years of Life through Home Movies".

Joan Raphael-Leff is a psychoanalyst and has specialized for 35 years in perinatal issues. She is Dean of the Anna Freud Centre Academic Faculty for Psychoanalytic Research and Visiting Professor at

University College London, the University of Essex, and Stellenbosch University, South Africa. She started her career as a psychologist researching autism with Dr Lorna Wing. As a psychoanalyst, she specialized in treating individuals and couples with reproductive and parenting problems and has over 80 single-author publications in this field.

Maria Rhode is Professor of Child Psychotherapy at the Tavistock Clinic and has a particular interest in childhood autism, language development, and infant observation. She is the co-convener of the Autism Workshop at the Tavistock Clinic and is co-editor of *Psychotic States in Children* and *The Many Faces of Asperger's Syndrome* in the Tavistock Clinic Book Series and *Invisible Boundaries: Autism & Psychosis* in the EFPP Clinical Monograph Series.

Catherine St Clair, PhD, is a Clinical Psychologist at Royal Holloway and a past Researcher in Early Signs of Autism, Department of Psychology, Edinburgh University, with Professor Colwyn Trevarthen.

Colwyn Trevarthen, a New Zealander, is Emeritus Professor of Child Psychology and Psychobiology at the University of Edinburgh, where he has researched and taught infant development since 1971. Trained as a biologist and psychologist, he has published extensively on brain functions of vision and movement, on brain development, and, in the last 30 years, on communication with infants and toddlers. He compares autism to normal growth of movements and communication, relating differences to development in the brain of motives for forming attachments and learning, and he is currently studying the rhythms of "musicality" in human movement, on which early communication depends. He is a Fellow of the Royal Society of Edinburgh, Vice-President of the British Association for Early Childhood Education, and a Member of the Norwegian Academy of Sciences and Letters.

Expectations and experiences
of parents with a pre-autistic baby

Joan Raphael-Leff

This book brings hope where despair has prevailed. It offers the prospect of early detection of signs of autism and the possibility of effective therapeutic mitigation of the painful predicament for parents of perpetually failing to engage a seemingly unresponsive infant.

The birth of a baby is not the beginning but the culmination of many hopes, wishes, and fantasies elaborated during pregnancy and long before. A pregnant woman is aware of the disturbing situation of housing two people in one body, of being cord-connected for the duration of the gestation, of responsibility for providing nutrients (or toxins) to the baby and removing its waste products through her own kidneys. This physiological system of the placental exchange provides a metaphor for the two-way transmission of emotional influences—postnatal nurture and metabolization of the infant's anxieties, deemed "containment".

In pregnancy, most women experience a mixture of feelings, based on healthy ambivalence. Others tend to focus on a particular aspect of the placental exchange. One blooms, super-confident of her internal resources. Another feels depressed by a sense of inner "emptiness" and inability to provide. One feels anxious about her "badness" affecting the baby inside her. Another feels endangered, fearing depletion. Yet another feels persecuted, exploited, or poisoned by the "parasitic" foetus. Each expectant mother (and father too, if he is included) conjures up images of fantasy babies and elaborates preconscious representations of him/herself as parent-to-be. These are amalgams of attitudes within the social environment as well as by-products of their own specific psycho-histories—the mother and father they had and wish they had had, the ideal baby they want, and the baby each imagines s/he was, as seen through the eyes of their own original carers. Clearly, such expectations are affected by each woman and man's self-esteem and the emotional, social, and economic circumstances accompanying this particular pregnancy. If complications arise during pregnancy or labour, these may be attributed by the woman or her partner to "fate", personal failure, ascribed to punishment for sexual activity or for previous "misdeeds", including abortion. Thus, intertwining physical, sociocultural, and internal world systems colour each parent's expectations and influence their interpretation of signs and symptoms.

As a group, babies later diagnosed as autistic are found to have had more complications during gestation and delivery than their normal siblings and others. These problems include bleeding in pregnancy and near-miscarriage, foetus small for gestational age, congenital malformations, artificial induction, labour of less than one hour, foetal distress, meconium aspiration syndrome, birth under anaesthesia or obstructed labour, and "deep forceps" delivery, Caesarean section resuscitation at birth, and clamping of the umbilical cord before the newborn has breathed.

In addition to all these complications, infants later diagnosed on the autistic spectrum have a twofold rate of residence in neonatal intensive care units. Over the past 50 years, ever younger previously non-viable very low weight babies are being kept alive, some born as much as four months before term. However, it is becoming apparent that miraculous procedures to counteract organ immaturity and prolonged incubation contribute to a new gamut of hitherto unknown forms of neurological damage. With curtailed pregnancy, prematurely separated mothers and their babies both experience a prolonged state of limbo, with the fragile infant being exposed to excruciating medical interventions and overwhelming stimulation.

A healthy newborn comes to reside in a network of transgenerational family expectations. The imaginary infant fades as the real one takes precedence. However, the incongruity between fantasy and outcome may be too great to reconcile, or, conversely, the correspondence confirms the parents' worst nightmares. The mother of an autistic child says: "Even before I became pregnant, I knew I'd have a disturbed child" (see chapter 7). Many pregnant women have such an anxiety, but heightened significance is retrospectively ascribed to transient thoughts.

Parents of a pre-autistic baby come to a gradual realization that something is wrong—a discrepancy between anticipated reactions and their lived experience with an unresponsive infant who rebuffs their efforts, cries inconsolably, or appears to lose developmental gains. Cumulative awareness in the early months may relate to the baby's appearance or behaviour (such as the features described by many authors in this volume)—flaccid body tone, specific motor lags or deviations, vacant, unfocused gaze with no direct eye contact, or mannerisms such as squinting, screwing up the face, or rocking. Parents may come to feel concerned about their "good" infant's extreme passivity, with almost no crying, minimal body movement, and lack of interest in the surroundings. Conversely, the baby may become irritable or seem rigid with physical tension, or hyperactive with unsoothable incessant screaming that drives the carers to desperation. Each primary exchange is unique, a function both of the baby's mood, temperament, and psychosocial needs and of the carer's expectations, receptivity, and sensitive recognition. However, when atypical communication contributes to chronic misattunement, the parent can no longer respond intuitively, and the baby fails to develop a smooth transition between emotional states, living in a state of hyper- or hypo-arousal with deficits in self-regulation. Defences such as extreme vigilance or dissociation are brought in as strategies to avoid unmanageable affects and ward off unpredictable intrusions. These, in turn, affect interaction.

Most parents stress the absence of enjoyment, feeling rejected by the baby's consistent avoidance of their gaze, hurt by the aversion to contact—the little body recoiling when touched, arching or withdrawing from close holding even during breastfeeding. Carers may give up attempts at playfulness, worn down by trying to engage the reluctant baby, who seems better served by distance. Rather than floundering with their own preoccupations, early intervention enables parents to receive guidance before their own reactive patterns become established.

Theories of autism have undergone many changes since it was originally defined by Kanner as an affective disorder caused by deficient parental interaction. As autistic features were deemed defences rather than deficits, Bruno Bettelheim and others recommended removal of the child from parents seen as under- or over-stimulating. Debates about emotional or organic origins determined subsequent plans of management. Each decade has brought its own contribution to understanding the condition. The prevalent focus in 1970 when I was involved in a Medical Research Council study of autism was on cognitive deficits and linguistic peculiarities such as echolalia, extreme literalness, and pronominal reversals. The sample I tested was extracted from a register of all births in the London Borough of Camberwell and included the entire cohort of those showing any classical defining characteristics of autism—social isolation, language impairments, insistence on sameness, and absence of anticipatory posturing on being picked up. Seeing these children in the familiar space of their own homes revealed a wide spectrum of abilities, from social unrelatedness and linguistic irregularities coupled with relatively normal cognitive development but absence of symbolic play, to profound interpersonal and sensory deficits, including emotional detachment, deafness, blindness, and fitting. Parents differed, too. Unlike the pathonogenic stereotype of perfectionistic aloof achievers defined by Kanner (on the basis of his 1943 sample of eleven sets of parents, all but three of whom appeared in *Who's Who*), the mainly working-class Camberwell parents displayed a variety of characteristics, from warmth, humour, and forbearance through anxiety to over-involvement or defensive withdrawal. A similar variety was apparent when siblings were brought into the equation—in a case of 5-year-old triplets I saw, one boy lay on a mattress on the floor immobile, passive, and doubly incontinent; one brother sat up unaided, rocking, flapping his fingers, and shrieking non-stop;

while the third triplet—a communicative, engaging, and lively child—seemed compelled to compensate for his brothers' non-responsiveness to me by literally climbing the walls for my benefit, wedging his feet either side of the narrow corridor, and calling out for me to watch as he rose rapidly to the ceiling.

Since then autism has been identified as a developmental impairment due to a variety of causes that may include genetic, neurological, infectious, metabolic, immunologic, and environmental factors, all contributing to atypical brain development, which in turn leads to the autistic child's "deficient experience of intersubjectivity", as Professor Peter Hobson has defined it. Neonatal research reveals that innate capacities for sociability, self-regulation, thought, and language are activated through intensely bidirectional emotional interactions with others, within critical periods. Each individual child's constitutional strengths and acquired vulnerabilities are expressed within the family matrix, the specific emotional seedbed of development in which the baby is embedded. Aetiology is thus a complex mixture of both nature and nurture, and, as some authors in this book suggest, early- and late-onset autism may constitute different syndromes. Because of the low statistical incidence of autism, epidemiological research (such as that reported here by Graciela Cullere-Crespin in chapter 5), which is to include 25,000 babies, will provide a database for further understanding of this relatively rare condition. Meanwhile, innovatory research is crucial. Retrospective studies conducting close analysis of home movies and videos reveal an interactive mosaic of infant behaviours and parental initiatives and reactions that differ subtly with each child, even twins, where one is destined to develop autism (see chapters 1–4).

Neonatal research confirms that even genetic endowment is modified or inhibited by the specific emotional climate of the family environment into which each baby is born. Similarly, evolution of functional MRI has brought major leaps in brain research, revealing not only specificities of brain malfunction (previously indicated less precisely by EEG), but the *interpersonal nature of brain development*. Neuroscience shows that the interactive behaviour of the primary caregivers influences growth of the very structure of the baby's brain. In this book, Stella Acquarone, Marie Christine Laznik, Maria Rhode, and Hannah Alonim build on both these

factors of early neuroplasticity and interpersonal influence by promoting prodromal identification of pre-autistic signs and very
early intensive intervention programmes that maximize parental
capacities. Although the prevention of autism still lies in the future,
this book offers hope of alleviating distress through psychodynamic therapeutic work—to enhance intersubjective communication within the family and to foster the infant's growth potential.

INTRODUCTION

Why this book?

The book I envisioned, and needed in my own practice, didn't exist. So I arranged a conference of experts, and their presentations are the chapters you now see. I wanted to organize an effective approach for babies who show early signs of autism, and I needed to know as much as possible about pre-autistic states. What could we do about preventing autism if we learned the early signs? Do we have the technical psychoanalytic tools to help treat this disorder?

Although I am an adult and a child psychotherapist, I am not a newcomer to the field of infant–parent psychotherapy. My skills in early psychotherapeutic consultations and interventions with infants and their parents experiencing difficulties come from the 3,700 cases I have seen or supervised over a period of 26 years. Some—like a baby with pre-autistic features I treated in 1982—today show no signs of autism. Unfortunately, the reverse is also true: I have followed up babies who showed early signs yet received no treatment, and they later developed into people with autism.

The early signs were first described by Henry Massie in *Childhood Psychosis in the First Four Years of Life* (Massie & Rosenthal, 1984). He was studying home videos of babies and children who later developed autism, and he confirmed that there *were* indeed early signs. In 1990, I founded the Parent–Infant Clinic, and Hisako Watanabe from Japan joined me while she was in London. We continued with the treatment of babies at the earliest signs of alarm. At the same time, we realized the need for training and so began the School of Infant Mental Health. We were pioneers in treating early signs of autism. Using a psychoanalytic approach modified for use with babies, we based our treatment on the parents' concerns about their child's difficulties in relating to them and in the expression of emotions.

Today, this psychodynamic work with babies is called "early psychoanalytic intervention", and it is proving to be the "big-bang" event among parents and professionals. In almost all cases and among all ages, this kind of early intervention gets better outcomes more quickly because it unites observation of normal and not normal babies from birth with psychoanalytic thinking, clinical practice, and the latest research, in different areas of medicine, psychology, and social work. It is a focused help using everything we know about the presenting problem to to decode the"enigma" in each infant that is getting locked in and not relating to human beings. We know a lot more today about exactly when and where to focus the intervention, in part because of the important work of the professionals presented in this book.

Autistic-spectrum disorders and early intervention are hot topics. Every week that goes by sees more magazine articles, television programmes, newspaper articles, and scientific papers touting the benefits of an early intervention, and those who are psychodynamically trained (particularly those who are psychoanalytically trained) are best positioned to handle the early intervention necessary to ease the heavy emotional burden that an untreated pre-autistic can be to family and society. The problem with the early intervention, of course, is dealing with the preverbal and the unconscious. Even those skilled in psychodynamics are stopped by these impregnable walls.

As in all of my "early-intervention" work, I have scoured the world to promote the work of professionals who make a difference.

From their research come the latest treatments. From their clinics come approaches that work—and they are substantive works from comprehensive points of view from professionals representing fields other than psychoanalytic.

At the Signs of Autism in Infants Conference, organized and sponsored by the School of Infant Mental Health, at University College London on 11–12 July 2005, international researchers and clinicians renowned for their work in the field of early autism came together to resolve queries around the long debate on the development and resolution of autistic behaviour—is it genetic or not? The conference aimed—as does this book—to bring awareness of the possibility of preventing the full development of autistic behaviour and to help professionals recognize early signs of alarm. New information was explored to verify early signs of alarm and then to consider early clinical interventions to halt this disorder while the brain is still growing fast. This was done from the evidence brought to us by analysis of home-made videos containing babies who were diagnosed as autistic by the age of 3 or 4 years, and by the outcome of early interventions with difficult-to-reach babies. Another aim of the conference and this book is the solidification of the International Pre-Autistic Network to further the study, research, and interventions of pre-autistic stages in the development of this disorder.

The contributors to this book were selected for their penetrating and pivotal work with parents and families whose babies present early signs of autistic-spectrum disorders. Each has made career and long-term commitments to the emerging field of "pre-autism", its recognition and treatment through early intervention. Brought together under the premise that the development of emotions is central to the treatment of autism, these contributors together represent the most promising in research, theory, assessment, treatment, and front-line care for a condition that, if left untreated, can be devastating to families, relationships, ambitions, and personal achievements and represents an enormous burden on societal resources. The contributors come from many different countries, their lives and work separated by national, natural, and professional boundaries and by language, culture, and areas of expertise. For the most part they work as pioneers, fuelled only by their own curiousity and determination and by their desire for better outcomes and lives for those they serve. Brought together first in London and then later in Los Angeles, their work and findings are coalescing not only in this book but in their respective fields of therapy and science, pushing the boundaries of what we know about the autistic spectrum to reveal how psychoanalytically based concepts can make a real difference in the treatment of autism and its associated communication disorders. Although their work has been described as bold, insightful, empirical, intuitive, refreshing, creative, meticulous, methodical, painstaking, and even brilliant, they were selected primarily because their work is sure to reverberate and be felt in all future developments in the field.

Nature or nurture?

Autism occurs in 1 in every 100 births (Baird et al., 2006). It is the third most-common developmental disability, after mental retardation and cerebral palsy, and currently there is thought to be no medical detection, treatment, or cure. The impact on family life can be devastating.

This is the backdrop to *Signs of Autism in Infants: Recognition and Early Intervention*. The premise of the conference itself—the efficacy of early intervention—is unsettling to some, met with scepticism by others, and, at the same time, held in hope by experienced professionals and worried parents. The reason for the tension is because the nature versus nurture debate lies at the core of the premise, with the usual battle lines and opposing camps that unfold. But all the evidence today points to a nature *via* nurture reality, which is changing the debate and accelerating the importance of early intervention. By all accounts, autism is a hairball, a communication disorder, addressed by professionals in many disciplines. But steady progress made in all the disciplines addressing what is now referred to as the "autistic spectrum" makes early intervention possible; although a cure is unlikely, the early-intervention approach is most promising. By bringing together experts across these key disciplines, a convergence on early intervention will start to emerge from the debate.

The *nature* approach goes something like this: Is autism a dysfunction in the neural structure—in the cerebellum, the limbic system, the cerebral cortex? Is it caused by abnormal biochemistry—abnormal serotonin levels, increased beta-endorphins, or faulty-immune system response? Is it a dysfunctional tactile system, a dysfunctional vestibular system, or a dysfunctional proprioceptive system? And those in the *nurture* camp may well ask: Is autism triggered by something in the environment: the quality of parental attachment, family, over-stimulation, diet, chemicals, or vaccines? But as Matt Ridley argues persuasively in his 2003 book *Nature via Nurture*, "Genes are designed to take their cues from nurture." Autism may be in the genes, but there's a lot we can do about it.

The truth about autism is that it is emergent *and* it is recursive. It emerges from the interplay of nature and nurture, because our genes and environment are locked into intricate feedback loops where small worries, concerns, effects, and tendencies felt and seen in the first years of life can get "set in cement", making treatment difficult and taking many years.

In an unlikely twist of science and treatment, psychoanalytic psychotherapy and its lexicon of concepts—sometimes known as the "talking cure"—is proving to be most useful in treating infants, the "non-talkers". The field of infant–parent psychotherapy is emerging because, today, professionals and parents alike know that more can be done for their baby. The field is emerging because professionals who are trained and adept at reading the matrix of emotions and "signs of alarm" can actually act on a mother's intuition or a parent's feeling that "something isn't right" with the baby. It is emerging from small steps taken by therapists, doctors, researchers, specialists, public health officials, and all the other professionals whose work puts them in front of under-3s. It is emerging because what is known about early development is being integrated into frontline training for primary teachers and caregivers.

The field will continue to emerge because the question "What can we do?" is finally replacing the outdated belief that "problems will take care of themselves". It will continue to emerge because it *is* possible to see the tendency of the child in early signs: the struggle, the initiation of a repetitive behaviour or of a comforting habit indicating retreat. Why not do something about it? Why not, indeed!

That is what this book is about. It is directed to clinical practitioners who must build bridges between theory and practice, combining what we know with what we know that works, all for the betterment of the babies and parents in front of us. *Early intervention* is the treatment, the tool of the clinician, because it sits somewhere between prevention on the one hand and acute care on the other. The advances you will read about in the chapters—from the medical, biological, and psychological sciences—have extended our reach for better outcomes into the preverbal, the unconscious, and the mental matrixes that define our behaviour. In other words—as the book is titled—*we can recognize the signs of autism in infants and intervene early*. The more we know about the primitive aspects to take into account for these early interventions, the more effective we can be in tracking down and understanding what is not working in the infant and/or in the parents and is preventing them from a relationship they can feel happy about, be passionate in, have fun in, be satisfying, and find enriching.

PART I

HISTORY OF EARLY SIGNS
AND INTERVENTIONS

CHAPTER ONE

The prodromal phase of autism and outcome of early treatment

Henry Massie

Although Kanner first described autism in 1943, its aetiology and treatment remained a mystery when I was training in psychiatry in the late 1960s and early 1970s. Today, in a new century, it still remains one of medicine's great challenges. Progress exists, however, in that many mental health professionals, paediatricians, nurses, and educators now know that treatment has the best chance of preventing autism from handicapping a child for life if it is begun very early—when the initial signs of autistic disturbance first appear, typically between 6 and 18 months of life, before the condition is fully established later in the second or the third year of life.

My own research in autism (by which I refer to the whole spectrum, from severe with little or no speech or relatedness to high functioning with considerable speech, interpersonal relatedness, and normal or near normal cognition but also marked oddities in social and emotional functioning and some motor mannerisms or stereotypies) has focused on identifying the earliest manifestations or prodromal signs of the condition in order to facilitate the earliest possible treatment.

My work began in 1971 when the family of a severely afflicted 5-year-old girl whom I was treating—though without an effective plan because none existed at that time—offered me the home movies they had made of the child as a baby before they suspected a problem. I spent hours viewing them, often in slow motion, and saw that until 4 months the child had a good, strong smile for her parents, and then lost it and started avoiding eye contact. The mother, when she did make eye contact with the infant, made little or no effort to sustain it—certainly not the vigorous effort that we now understand might have prevented the child's gaze-aversion and withdrawal. Unconscious of what was sadly transpiring—even unconscious of her own mounting tension and sense of failure—the mother sometimes turned away herself from the child. Her husband, less involved, was even more unaware, and the couple had nobody to guide them with this first baby. By the end of the first year, the films showed that the child no longer made eye contact and had many other symptoms of autism.

Developmental theories of the time suggested that the mother's failure to meet her baby's eye gaze may have caused the disorder, but we now know that parents do not cause autism. Current research indicates that a variety of rare physiological and neurological conditions, some genetically mediated, underlie autism. Potential underlying physical conditions include structural abnormalities of the brain, abnormalities of metabolism--, digestive-tract disorders that link to central nervous system hormones and transmitters, disturbances of activation of different central nervous system circuits, and allergic or autoimmune states (Courchesne, Townsend, & Saitoh, 1994; Vargas, Nascimbene, Krishnan, Zimmerman, & Pardo, 2004; Welch et al., 2005). Nonetheless, these findings are all still imperfectly understood, and they are not necessarily specific to autism. The underlying conditions may directly lead to an autistic syndrome, or they may render children vulnerable to environmental factors that precipitate the syndrome. Potential environmental precipitants are viral infections, vaccination reactions, allergens, and severe psychological trauma and emotional deprivation. These are bio-psychosocial events that would not necessarily produce autism in non-vulnerable children. It is likely that autism is multi-determined. That is, different factors or combinations of factors cause the condition in different children.

Without a precise pathophysiology for autism, treatment lacks specificity or predictable success, except for the inflammatory and allergic states present in some autistic children where biomedical treatment such as antifungals and dietary programmes such as gluten- and casein-free diets can bring considerable symptom relief. But we can be precise about three things. *First*, we need to recognize the infancy signs of autism. *Second*, we have to observe how they impair dyadic parent–child interactions. *Third*, we have to help parents respond to their infants' social deficits. If this three-step sequence is followed, a baby's development can often be stabilized so that it does not deteriorate. Sometimes treatment can prevent autism from crystallizing in the second and third years of life, thus allowing the child to develop normally.

The prodromal phase of autism

I now focus on the initial signs of autism prior to intervention, returning later to treatment approaches. Following my first case, in the 1970s, I organized a project that collected a series of 20 home movies of children with autistic-spectrum disorders. Each family typically provided several hours of 8-mm and 16-mm film of family activities, holidays, and birthday parties. The research team studied the movies in comparison with a control group of similarly made home movies of non-ill children. Later the film analyses were amplified with reviews of the case records, interviews with the family, and sometimes interviews with the therapists.

The initial case highlighted how the child began avoiding eye contact with her mother and had lost her smile for her parents by age 6 months. Films from another case in the series showed a child who did not mould his body to his mother when she held him in the first six months, and was struggling away from her after five months. His eye gaze was normal early on, but his smile was lifeless and never conveyed excitement or recognition in response to his mother's face or presence. Overall this child had less-than-normal activity, reaching, attention to, and excitement at objects and people. The parents responded to their child and did not block any of his gestures towards them. But they were relatively inanimate themselves, and they lacked playfulness. They were unable to compensate for their baby's flaccidity by accentuating their efforts to draw him into a relationship with them. Between the ages of 3 and 6 months, this child's placidity gave way to irritability and a look of depression. A depressed affect first appeared on the mother's face when the child was 6 months old. After this time the boy's expression constricted into impassivity and never matured into firm expressions that communicated moods, intentions, or meanings. Instead he gave the appearance of marked self-absorption. A hand-waving autism appeared at the end of the first year, and his illness was clearly established in the second year.

Other cases illustrated families becoming disorganized, even destructive towards their children, as they felt their babies not developing emotionally, relationally, or slipping away from them in the first and second years of life. Typically, at this early stage, the parents were not fully conscious of their own anxiety and reactions, nor were they yet receiving guidance from professionals. Thus, in another family, the mother and father competed with each other to draw the child into a relationship after they sensed him slipping away. Film scenes show the mother reaching for and interacting slowly and gently with the child. The father moved with an entirely different rhythm that was rapid and forceful, and, impatiently, he occasionally took the child out of the mother's arms. Caught in the middle, the baby appeared confused. Similarly, in another family an impatient grandmother (apparently succumbing to her own anxious pressure to get a gloomy infant to show signs of normal emotional life, to smile, and later to walk at an age before the baby was ready) repeatedly interferes when the mother and child are sharing quiet moments together. The mother was not able to fend off the intrusive grandmother.

A mother and father are seen in another family becoming desperate at the child's first-birthday party when he shows neither pleasure nor interest in his presents. His expression is immature and labile. The scene ends with the parents exasperatedly throwing the gifts at the child (though not so hard as to cause bodily injury); the toddler rolls away from them, grimacing.

Two other cases strikingly highlight the prodromal phase and then the initial symptoms of autism. For example, family-made films follow non-identical twin daughters from early infancy into childhood. The parents respond to both children in a straightforward manner that appears free of conflict or avoidance. The child who becomes autistic is less active than her sister in the first weeks and months and has less eye pursuit and exploration of her environment. In the second six months when she starts to crawl, and later when she starts to walk, she is unusually uncoordinated, and her body moves in a fragmented way that does not correspond to any specific neurological sign or pathology. During this phase in the second half of the first year, the child has only fleeting half smiles, and her primary mood is irritability. On the other hand, her sister has strong smiles for her mother, and by age 1 year shows a full range of well-formed expressions. By the end of the first year, the twin whose development is going awry has hand-flapping stereotypies, episodes of flailing hyperactivity, and pushes away from her parents when they try to hold her, in contrast to her sister and children in the control films.

The final vignette is of a child who was separated from her mother from 7 to 11 months of age while the mother was treated for tuberculosis. Prior to the separation the child had bright, ready smiles and responses to her mother. At times, however, the child appeared more self-absorbed than other children. During the separation this baby had the misfortune to have aloof and mechanical caretakers and a remote father. When she was reunited with her mother, the baby avoided eye contact, developed marked stereotypies such as rocking her body to and fro for long periods of time, and never developed the ability to communicate clearly with facial expressions or words. This history of a traumatic experience ushering in autistic symptoms and developmental regressions is not unusual in case reports of autism. For this child the trauma was separation from her mother and poor surrogate care-taking. In other cases, symptoms and regressions to symptoms from more advanced developmental stages have followed flu-like illnesses with high fevers, febrile vaccination reactions, the onset of severe food allergies, and emotional trauma such as a parent's absence.

The following tables and figures, adapted from earlier publications (Massie, 1978a, 1978b; Massie & Rosenthal, 1984), summarize the findings. Table 1.1 lists signs of unusual development that appeared in films of children who later received a diagnosis of autism in the second to fifth year of life. It is important to emphasize that *none* of the early signs in Table 1.1 are specific to autistic-spectrum disorders. They may also occur in children who go on to develop normally, or who develop conditions as widely varied as learning problems, anxiety, and hyperactivity. These first-six-month signs were, however, more frequently observed in children who became autistic than in control films of the infancies of normal children in our study.

Table 1.2 focuses on specific symptoms that appear from 6 to 12 months. Case reports indicate (Alonim, 2004) that if treatment begins during this period, it has the best chance of preventing fixed autism. Table 1.3, which presents symptoms of established autism, typically at 12 to 24 months, shows the indicators of continuing developmental failure. Nonetheless, the second and third years of life are still an age when intensive therapeutic intervention may reverse autistic symptoms (Acquarone, 2004; Alonim, 2004, 2005; Edelson & Rimland, 2003; Lovaas, 1987).

Table 1.1.   Signs of unusual development from birth to 6 months in children later diagnosed as autistic*

Flaccid body tone

Lack of responsiveness or attentiveness to people or things

Lack of excitement in presence of parents

Lack of anticipatory posturing on being picked up

Vacant, unfocused gaze

Less than normal activity (e.g. reaching for objects)

Specific motor deviations (e.g. head lag on being pulled to sitting, facial palsy, ptosis [eyelid droop])

Eye squint mannerism

Predominantly irritable mood, little smiling

More somnolent than typical child

*These signs are not specific to autism and may occur in children who develop normally or with other problems; however, they were more frequent in infancy films of children subsequently diagnosed autistic than in control films of non-autistic children.

The film study worked largely with home movies without sound-tracks because of the era in which the films were made, so it did not systematically study the speech and language of the children. The medical records, however, did indicate that all of the children had communication impairments that, depending on the case, ranged from absence of speech, to unpredictable verbal responsiveness with

Table 1.2.   First symptoms of autism, typically 6–12 months

Seeming hallucinatory excitement

Appearance of self-absorption

No visual pursuit of people

Repeatedly looking away from people

Avoiding mother's gaze

Resisting being held, arching torso away from parents

Autisms/stereotypies/motor mannerisms: hand-flapping, finger-dancing movements, rocking, spinning

Plastic expressions that do not communicate affect or intention

Labile facial expressions that shift from grimaces to squints

Fragmented, uncoordinated body movements

Episodes of flailing, aimless, unmodulated hyperactivity

Table 1.3.   Symptoms of established autism, typically 12–24 months

---

Child doesn't approach parents
Child keeps distance from parents
Constricted, flattened affect
Little or no purposeful activity
Facial expression that doesn't convey intention or meaning
Failure of normal language development

---

echolalia and perseveration, to relative fluency. When children had near-normal speech, they nonetheless spoke with a stilted, flat tonal quality; used some words idiosyncratically; and lacked emotionally spontaneous expressions.

Figure 1.1 shows the bimodal occurrence of mannerisms (motor tics) in infancy and toddlerhood in children who are developing normally or with minor mood disturbances compared to the gradually increasing incidence of marked autistic stereotypies from approximately 8 months on in autistic children. Approximately 9 months to 14 months is a period when many young children have motor tics, but typically they are transient and do not become a fixed mannerism or stereotypie that is part of the autistic syndrome.

Figure 1.2 plots the age of onset of significant signs of developmental disturbance against the percentage of children with autism that

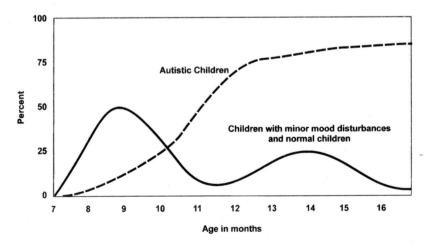

Figure 1.1.   Relative incidence of finger- and hand-waving and -grasping mannerisms in normal versus autistic children.

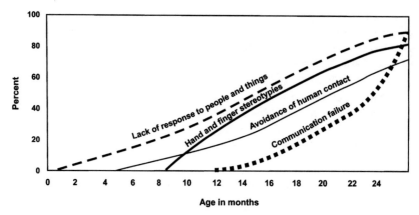

Figure 1.2.   Relative incidence of early symptoms in autism—percentage of children showing symptoms.

show them. Thus, at 2 months, a few children who become autistic lack response to people, but by 24 months approximately 90% have impaired responsiveness to others as well as unusual reactions to their environment.

In a related project (Rosenthal, Massie, & Wulff, 1980), we compared the cognitive growth of autistic children and normal children in control films through Piaget's (1936) six stages of sensorimotor development. Based on filmed scenes of their manipulations of objects in their environment, autistic infants were markedly delayed in progressing from Stage I, *reflex responses* (0–1 month); to Stage II, *primary circular reactions* (1–4 months: an infant's actions are centred on his own body); to Stage III, *secondary circular reactions* (4–10 months: an infant reproduces events discovered by accident); to Stage IV, *coordinated secondary behaviours* (10–12 months: an infant brings together two or more behaviours in goal-oriented play and manipulation of objects); to Stage V, *tertiary circular reactions* (12–18 months: a child shows curiosity, trial-and-error experimentation, coordination of spatial relationships, and an early sense of other people and objects as autonomous); to Stage VI, *invention of new means* (18–24 months: the child arrives at solutions mentally and can represent objects, events, and people symbolically, indicating the establishment of object permanence). In our study, none of 14 autistic-spectrum children traversed the sensorimotor stages to indices of symbolic thought, reflection, and object permanence by the end of the second year of life, as normal children do. Of the 14, only one reached Stage VI at 3½ years, the age when systematic analysis ended.

In recent years other investigators (Danon-Boileau, 2005b; Muratori & Maestro, 2005; Werner, Dawson, Osterling, & Dinno, 2000) have also carefully studied family-made films of children subsequently diagnosed autistic. The new studies, with soundtracks available, have revealed many of the early signs of autism we found, and they amplify details. For example, Werner and Dawson's most recent work (2005) suggests that there may be a subgroup of autistic children who develop normally, aside from modest difficulties with emotional regulation, until a regression to illness commences in the second year of life. And Danon-Boileau (2005b) demonstrates how a mother unconsciously establishes a different pattern of interaction with a pre-autistic infant from that with the infant's twin who develops normally. To my knowledge, however, the newer studies have not analysed the home movies systematically for strategies to help parents make their responses to their children's deficits as optimally corrective as possible in the ways to which we pointed, nor have they described how some parents of children with prodromal signs of autism may be impeding the child's attachment to the parents, thus putting the infants at further risk.

In a true prospective study, Zwaigenbaum et al. (2005) have followed 65 infant siblings of autistic children to 24 months of age. Of these, 7 have received clinical diagnoses of autism. In the first twelve months of life, these 7 pre-autistic children showed atypical eye contact and decreased orienting to their name, decreased social smiling, and less interest in their surroundings. They were more passive than controls and had less positive affect and fewer precursors of expressive and receptive language. Optimizing parents' interventions with children at risk for autism is the focus of the next section.

Treatment

Treatment for autism remains, in many respects, a wilderness. In fact, Thomas Insel, director of the National Institute of Mental Health, the lead agency in the United States for research on mental and behavioural disorders, has recently been quoted as saying that "parents are left with trial and error with their own child. The bottom line is that we need a lot of better science to test out some of these things to see what is helpful and what is not. As it is, every parent is left to do their own clinical trial" (in Seligman, 2005, p. 14). However, as more children with prodromal signs and autism are diagnosed at younger ages, increasing experience with the outcome of early treatment affords hope that some children can be spared what was formerly a very bleak prognosis. This optimism is derived from individual family's (Edelson & Rimland, 2003; Seligman, 2005) and therapists' (Welch, 1983) anecdotal reports of success and from a few series of cases using a variety of interventions. A selection (not exhaustive) of these reports is now reviewed to indicate the direction and possibilities of contemporary early intervention.

For example, Lovaas's (1987) now classic project using behaviour modification with autistic children at the University of California, Los Angeles, produced a significant rate of cure. In this study of 40 autistic children who were below the age of 4 years when treatment began, 19 (43%) improved to the point of no longer meeting criteria for an autistic-spectrum diagnosis, whereas children in a control group receiving traditional speech and physical therapy and special education showed very modest gains and none normalized. Terming his approach Applied Behaviour Analysis (ABA), Lovaas and his team used rewards such as food and praise to foster, enhance, and broaden children's signs of normal verbal and social interaction, and they used aversive conditioning or punishment such as a loud "no", mild slaps on the hands or knees, and withholding rewards to extinguish avoidant and stereotypic behaviours. The extremely intensive programme employed a team of therapists (usually including the parents) to work with the child up to 60 hours a week ("most of their waking hours") for up to three years. Attempts to replicate Lovaas's study have come up short in moving children out of the autistic spectrum, because of difficulty enlisting a study population of autistic children of comparable age and symptomatology, assembling a treatment team with the same skills, and sustaining the intervention with the same intensity and duration as the original project. A near exception is Sallows and Graupner's effort (2005) in which 7 of 23 children recovered after four years of rigorous treatment. Other new behaviour modification adaptations of ABA such as Applied Verbal Behaviour (AVB) and Pivotal Response Training (PRT) have shown sustained symptomatic improvement in young children, and one PRT report (Humphries, 2003) indicates that 10 of 51 children (mean age 4.1 years at treatment) escaped the autistic spectrum.

Recently Greenspan and Wieder (2005), using an interpersonal, relationship model, have created the Developmental Individual-Difference Relationship Based Treatment (DIB) for young autistic children. In this intervention (also known as Floor Time), the parents and therapists intensively engage the child in his or her physical and emotional space, sometimes gently obstructing autistic behaviours, and gradually expanding social, affective, and verbal interactions. It, too, is an arduous, home-based treatment, requiring up to six and a half hours per day of play, problem-solving, sensorimotor activities, and supplemental speech therapy for two or more years. Their results indicate that when treatment began between 2–4 years of age, 58% of 200 children followed up two to four years later were no longer in the autistic spectrum. Although their results are excellent, it is unclear how well other therapists have been able to replicate Floor Time.

An intensive, far briefer, relationship-based intervention—unique because of its use of residential treatment for the nuclear family to begin therapy—has been pioneered by the Mifne Center (Alonim, 2004) in Israel. Drawn from attachment theory (Bowlby, 1969), the Center brings the nuclear family into residence treatment, initially for approximately three weeks. During this time, the programme emphasizes strengthening and creating bonding between children from 6 months to 5 years and their parents when prodromal signs and symptoms of autism are occurring. The residential strategy employs day-long, relational play therapy, sensorimotor and physical therapy (focused on postural control) for the child, parent counselling to enhance the parents' understanding of the child's deficits and parent responses, and supervised parent–child engagement. When the family returns home, there is subsequent outpatient consultation. Independent analysis of the Mifne Center's results treating 56 children between 2 and 5 years of age found that 73% of the children were attending regular school classrooms without special assistance. The Center (Alonim, 2005) reports that 21% of these children no longer fall into the autistic spectrum. They indicate that intensive, residential family therapy and periodic outpatient follow-up successfully resolves symptoms in 80–90% of children if they are brought into treatment between 6 and 12 months of age. A caveat to the resolution of symptoms in 80–90% of children brought to treatment before age 1 year is that a significant percentage of these children may not have developed full-blown autism if they had been left untreated.

To obtain a contemporary sense of what works in treatment, Phillips and Schuler (2005) in the Department of Special Education at San Francisco State University recently reviewed approximately 60 cases seen over many years at the autism clinic in the child psychiatry division at the University of California School of Medicine, San Francisco.

With chart reviews and follow-up interviews, they found 7 cases (12%) in which the children normalized—that is, they no longer met criteria for autism and were attending regular school without special education.

In the cases where the children normalized, they found that there were six common elements in the successful treatment effort, as outlined in the next section. To their work I add my own review of 31 children whose parents described their treatment in great detail and reported it to the Autism Research Institute, San Diego, California (Edelson & Rimland, 2003). These children were treated with various strategies including behaviour modification, biomedical interventions (diet restrictions, supplements, antifungals, heavy-metal chelation), and interpersonal psychological psychotherapy. In this series of 31, many improved, and 6 children normalized (19%). In the histories of those who became asymptomatic there were the same six common elements that Phillips and Schuler described as well as two additional features of successful treatment, Points 7 and 8 below.

Eight common elements in successful treatment of autism

1. *Effective therapy begins with a theory of how the afflicted child's mind is functioning and not functioning.*   Although different treatment approaches (biomedical, behavioural, relational) have reversed autism in the first three to four years of life, no one therapy is consistently effective. But when treatment has been successful, there has been a theory or framework that guides it. For example, the hypothesis may be that exogenous biological factors precipitate autism. A contrasting hypothesis is that intrinsic genetic factors underlie the disability. The biological model emphasizes interventions such as gluten- and casein-free diets, supplemental amino acids, minerals, and vitamins and medicines directed at the digestive track to affect the balance of hormones that are secreted and active in both the central nervous system and the intestines.

In contrast to biomedical interventions, learning theory may be at the heart of treatment and utilize behaviour modification. Or the treatment may be rooted in an interpersonal, relationship-based psychological theory that draws on the psychoanalytic understanding of intrapsychic functioning. Elaborating on the latter, the treatment framework may derive from attachment theory (Bowlby, 1969) and ethological theory (Tinbergen & Tinbergen, 1983). Attachment-derived therapy seeks to correct both a child's problems with bonding to its parents and problems that parents may have in bonding. This is done through therapeutic guidance that focuses on child and parent external behavioural interactions and on internal psychic constraints that parents and child may experience against bonding and psychological attachment.

Furthermore, no one theory is exclusive of the other. Thus, an infant with an underlying genetic vulnerability may have undetected prodromal signs of autism. As appears in case histories not infrequently, the baby may then develop symptoms of a digestive disturbance and, concurrently, the prodromal autistic signs may accentuate into early symptoms. Not infrequently in case histories, a child with mild pre-autistic signs may experience a febrile illness (e.g. a viral or bacterial infection, a vaccination reaction) during its toddler months, suddenly withdraw interpersonally, and start exhibiting full-blown autistic symptoms over several days or a few weeks. In a further example, a genetically vulnerable child with mild prodromal signs may become symptomatic after a separation from its mother or an emotional crisis in the family.

In any of these illustrations, successful treatment may combine biomedical , behavioural, and interpersonal interventions to re-establish the threatened parent–child attachment. When treatment successfully resolves autistic symptoms, the theory or theories guiding the treatment organize and direct the therapeutic reaction to the child's disabilities in *all* of the child's environments—home, day care, even time with relatives such as grandparents.

2. *Parents who are successful with autistic children have in common a strong sense of autonomy, efficacy, mission, and sacrifice.*   When parents are guiding the treatment effort, they couple their sense of efficacy and mission with their theory of the child's mind. When parents lack autonomy and an inner sense of resourcefulness, professionals must help them to gain assurance.

3. *Treatment requires continuous engagement with the child.*   Parents described how everybody who was in contact with their children was integrated into treatment, twenty-four hours a day.

4. *Successful treatment is a team effort.*   Husband and wife work together and spell each other. Other children in the family model healthy behaviour; they must be interactive with their ill sibling, and they are a link for their brother or sister to peers. The treatment team also links

the child to key people in each of the child's other settings who know what is happening and what the treatment plan is. Conversely, treatments are not fully successful if parents cannot work well together, or when a single parent is overwhelmed by the demands of caring for the child.

5. *There must be a drive to normalize the child, to treat him or her like other children in the family and in the community.*   As a parent said, "I really pushed him out there. Swimming and dance were big parts of his early programme. I really did a lot of things with him in the community and with the preschool."

6. *Successful treatment finds and builds on a positive element in the child's characteristics.*   Highlighting this common theme, a parent said, "Once John started interacting even minimally with people, he was really nice, a real cute kid, and so people wanted to work with him. I think that made a difference."

7. *Treatment began early in life, by age 4 years, in reports of successful efforts that normalized a child's development.*   The age between 6 months and 4 years is critical, probably due to the massive reorganization of central nervous system connections (Courchesne, Chisum, & Townsend, 1994) that makes the brain plastic and amenable to therapeutic intervention during this time.

8. *Children with positive outcomes were not retarded.*   Even if psychodiagnostic testing was subnormal (often the case, because the handicapped child cannot adequately participate in testing), the children who normalized showed some signs of normal intelligence prior to treatment. Indicators of intelligence may be present in memories for past experiences, capacity for learning new activities, signs of symbolic representation in play and in the use of language, some progress towards object permanence (the mental representation of a person or object even in the absence of the person or object), invention of games, and rudiments of self-care.

Choice of treatment

Without clear evidence that one treatment is superior to another, parents have to pick the approach that is within their resources and with which they can collaborate the best. Some treatments require commitments of time, emotional resources, and money that are beyond many families' reach, and some treatments simply are not available in many communities. In some instances in the absence of professional resources, resourceful parents educate themselves and mount their own successful effort with their child.

Presently in the United States the most readily available interventions are biomedical and behavioural, for which the Autism Research Institute in San Diego (Edelson & Rimland, 2003) is a well-known clearing house for information. In my own work I have gravitated towards relationship-based treatments that emphasize creating or re-establishing the psychological bond between infants with prodromal signs of autism and parents, because my earlier film research showed disruptions in the basic components of infant bonding. Leading practitioners of interpersonal treatment for young children showing signs of autism are the London School of Infant Mental Health (Acquarone, 2004); the Mifne Center in Rosh Pina, Israel (Alonim, 2005), which commences with a residential stay for the whole family; the Martha G. Welch Center in New York City and Cos Cob, Connecticut (Welch, 1983), which employs a strategy of mother–child embrace to repair attachment; and the Greenspan and Wieder group in Washington, DC, who emphasize intimate engagement by joining the child in his or her play space. In addition, Danon-Boileau (2005a) at the Binet Center in Paris melds his background as a linguist and psychoanalyst to attend to very young children's specific language disabilities as well as their emotional life.

Based on the earlier film research, in order to facilitate early recognition of autism and intervention and to guide the progress of treatment, B. Kay Campbell and I constructed the one-page Massie-Campbell Scale of Mother–Infant Attachment Indicators During Stress (ADS Scale: Massie & Campbell, 1983, 1984, 2006, 2007; also reprinted in part in Acquarone, 2004). The scale describes problematic infant–parent responsiveness in the core bonding modalities of vocalizing, gazing, smiling, touching, holding, and maintaining physical closeness. These are interactions to which all treatment programmes must be alert, trying to build them if they are missing or bolster them if they are flagging.

PART II

RESEARCH ON EARLY SIGNS

Signs of autism in infancy: sensitivity for rhythms of expression in communication

Catherine St Clair, Laurent Danon-Boileau, Colwyn Trevarthen

The complex nature of the problem

There is no biological test and no single reliable measure with which to confirm a diagnosis of autism. Its relative "invisibility" (Midence & O'Neill, 1999) means that diagnosis does not usually occur until well after language has failed to develop—usually when the child is 3 or 4 years old. However, research suggests that parents are often aware of differences much earlier than this, to the extent that "50% of parents with autism report that they suspected a problem before their child was one year of age" (Werner, Dawson, Osterling, & Dinno, 2000, p. 157). What do these parents notice in the first twelve months that evaluation tools and practitioners cannot? Parents often have an instinctive understanding of what is normal and what is not, and they are an invaluable resource for practitioners. Gaining a better sense of what it is that triggers their concern seems to be a logical and fundamental way to maximize our ability to identify children who are likely to develop autism, and it should also give valuable information on how to help the parents and the child.

Current clinical assessment tools such as the Checklist for Autism in Toddlers (CHAT: Baron-Cohen, Allen, & Gillberg, 1995), the Autism Diagnostic Interview–Revised (ADI-R: Lord, Rutter, & LeCouteur, 1994), and the Autism Diagnostic Observation Schedule (ADOS: Lord,

Rutter, Goode, Heemsbergen, Jordan, Mawhood, & Schopler, 1989) all draw on Wing's "triad of impairments" (Wing, 1996; Wing & Gould, 1979) and are based primarily on the same social, communicative, and behavioural signs as were recognized clinically by Kanner (1943), who first described autism and who identified the main symptom as "an innate inability for interpersonal contact". The "triad" of signs focus attention on how the child interacts with the environment and other people, as defined by theories of developing psychological capacities of the individual. They are rarely used for children under the age of 18 months. They do not adequately address the fact that interaction with a person is, by definition, a joint dynamic enterprise, a reciprocal "two-way street" that engages the motives of more than one person and that may be active from birth. Autism is, in essence, a disturbance of the innately motivated intersubjective life of the child, and it must affect other persons who live with the child (Trevarthen, Aitken, Papoudi, & Robarts, 1998).

In trying to obtain richer data on the development of infants long before a diagnosis of autism is possible, researchers have resorted to analysis of home videos in which parents have recorded their infants in various activities and games (for references to these studies, see Trevarthen & Daniel, 2005) (see also chapters 1 and 3). Gradually a fund of evidence is being accumulated that suggests that subtle changes are occurring, even before age 6 months, in the way the child who is developing autism coordinates moving and perceiving and, especially, in how the child combines growing interest in exploring and manipulating objects with communicating to people and engaging with his or her changing psychological states.

It is likely that some fault in regulation of the fundamental motives for engagement with the world, one that particularly affects the development of imagination and expressive capacity for interpersonal contact, is the root cause of autism (Trevarthen, 2000). But the appearance and development of the condition will depend on how the human environment responds.

HOW PRODUCTIVE EXCHANGES DEVELOP IN PLAY, AND HOW THEY MAY FALTER: A CASE STUDY OF DEVELOPING AUTISM

While there many ways in which both mother and infant are adapted to support the infant's attachment for care of vital states of health and well-being, there are also intricate ways that experiences, purposes, and feelings may be shared (Trevarthen, 2005a, 2005c; Trevarthen, Aitken, Vandekerckhove, Delafield-Butt, & Nagy, 2006). The infant is ready to learn by participating in joint experiences of many kinds, using all senses and all the body.

The reciprocity of play forms an undeniably vital role in social development. Most free-play interactions contain a series of "moments" (Stern, 1977) or cycles, each of which consists of a number of discernible stages. Brazelton, Koslowski, and Main (1974) categorized these as follows: "initiation", "orientation", "state of attention", "acceleration", "peak of excitement", "deceleration", and "withdrawal or turning away". Essentially, a normal interaction consists of repeated cycles of attention and non-attention, in which each partner approaches the other participant, then withdraws and waits for a response. If parents regularly attempt to engage with a child who, for whatever reason, does not respond to social cues, they will adjust their behaviour accordingly and will eventually cease to expect or wait for such a response. This may effectively compound any other social deficits, and interactions will be characterized by a lack of behavioural cycles or reciprocity.

The effects of developing autism were demonstrated by detailed micro-analysis of a game played with monozygotic twin infant girls in separate free-play interactions with their father (Trevarthen & Daniel, 2005). Twin A was later diagnosed as autistic at age 20 months according to ICD-10 (WHO, 1993), while Twin B appeared to be developing normally at that stage.[1] Detailed evidence is given from analysis of videos made by the mother of the girls at 11 months. Time-coded videotapes were viewed repeatedly to gain a detailed microanalytic account of behaviours of the girls and their father in various playful situations in the home.

Here, further consideration is given of what the analysis of these videos revealed about the twins' ability to engage in the game, and we report other information obtained from different playful interactions between the twins and their father at home.

Sharing parts in the "Monster Game"

Two sections of home-video footage of comparable duration (Twin A, 52 seconds; Twin B, 65 seconds) were chosen as especially clear examples of how the father engaged in play with each twin, inviting her to share the mini-drama of a pretend "attack", like the "creep up and pounce" game that kittens and many other young mammals play. In

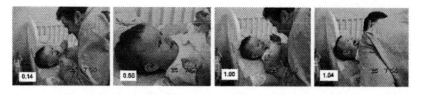

Figure 2.1.   The "Monster Game" with Twin B.

each section, the father enacts the "Monster Game" with the child—a repetitive routine of suspense and anticipation, in which the peak of excitement involves the father blowing raspberries on the girl's tummy. This closely resembles the routine described by Stern (1977), in which the parent uses an increase in length and pitch of vocalizations, repetition, eye-widening and eyebrow-raising, mouth-opening, timing, and pauses. The infant responds with a similar eye-widening and mouth-opening, smiling, face-brightening, and a twinkling in the eyes: "with each phrase the baby expressed more pleasure, and his body resonated almost like a balloon being pumped up, filling a little more with each breath" (Stern, 1977, p. 11).

At first sight the two pieces of video appeared to be very similar. The analysis has shown that Twin B's behaviour (Figure 2.1) was comparable to the "norms" expected of a 10- to 12-month-old in a free-play dyad. She and her father followed closely choreographed "dance steps": they responded to each other's social cues, and their behaviour was clearly interdependent. At the start of the game, when he got into position, placed the child in front of him, and lifted up her shirt, she looked with eager excitement at him and puffed up her stomach in readiness for his approach. The father maintained regular and consistent eye contact with Twin B, and this behaviour was reciprocal; their cycles of looking and not-looking are virtual mirrors of each other. Although the father was not totally attentive to his daughter's social cues, he was for the most part responsive and receptive. He watched Twin B's facial expression each time he growled at her, and he allowed her time to react and attend to his questions, although at one stage he moved too fast, and her face showed a mixture of fear and surprise. As he pulled her towards him in a sudden reorientation, the behaviours of both infant and parent were remarkably similar to a mother's misjudgement of tempo described by Stern (1977):

> Finally, she rushed forward again, perhaps a bit earlier and with more acceleration than the times before. His readiness had not fully

settled yet, he was caught a split-second off guard. His face showed more surprise than pleasure. His eyes were wide and his mouth open but not turned up at the corners. He slightly averted his face but still held his end of the mutual gaze. When she returned back at the end of that cycle she saw that it had missed somehow—not quite backfired, but missed enough. The pleasure had disappeared. [Stern, 1977, pp. 12–13]

However, in the case of Twin B and her father, he realizes his mistake in time, and instead of moving straight into a series of build-up growls, he slows down and lowers the volume and tempo of his vocalizations, allowing her time to adjust before resuming play.

Unlike her sister, Twin A (Figure 2.2) showed no pre-emptive anticipation or dramatic emotion, and her gaze was almost permanently directed at the video-camera (or possibly at her mother, who was operating the camera) or the ceiling, rather than at her father, who in turn looked at Twin A more regularly but for shorter periods of time.[2] Although he was constantly referring back to her, checking each time for a reaction, she consistently failed to return his gaze; instead of persevering, he resorted again to the game-play that appeared to be a tried-and-tested method of eliciting a response. The sequence seemed to be more rushed, without any shared build-up or suspense—presumably because the father had had little or no success with such tactics in the past. The given impression was very much that he did not notice any signals that Twin A may have been sending or been attempting to send. While the father does not use build-up growls with Twin A, he does kiss her, possibly as a way of maintaining contact while avoiding

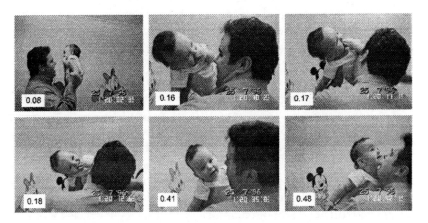

Figure 2.2.   The "Monster Game" with Twin A.

attempts at eye contact, which he knows are likely to fail. Even this strategy is unsuccessful, however, as each time he kisses her, she turns her head away in a manner characteristic of autistic children (Hutt & Ounsted, 1966; cited in Stern, 1971).

In summary, then, Twin B looked at her father more regularly and for significantly longer periods than did Twin A, who also showed fewer anticipatory behaviours. These findings were inherently tied to the behaviour of the father, who looked at Twin A more frequently than at Twin B but for significantly shorter periods of time. His lack of build-up growling with Twin A did not actually afford her any opportunity to anticipate the climactic raspberry-blowing on her stomach.

The pattern of behaviour in the father–Twin A dyad falls undeniably short of Brazelton, Koslowski, and Main's (1974) "homeostatic" or regulation model, which specifies that within a dyad, each participant "must be sensitive and ready to adjust to the other member in the envelope" (cited in Tronick, 1982, p. 22). The evidence suggests that an autistic failure to regulate interaction is effectively self-perpetuating. If a parent's social advances are met with an unresponsive face and non-reciprocal behaviours, the parent will alter his or her own behaviour patterns accordingly, and social actions start to lose their signal value (Beebe, 1982).

Emotional regulation

"In early development, the affective system is the primary means of regulating joint exchanges" (Tronick, 1982). The ability of an autistic child to regulate such exchanges of emotion, which guide the development of knowledge and skills in communication (Trevarthen, 1998, 2005a), is clearly deficient (Hobson, 1993; Loveland, 2005; Trevarthen et al., 1998). Although the findings presented here essentially deal with only two emotions—"enjoyment", which both twins show, though in different ways, and "anticipation", which is much more evident for the non-autistic twin—there is scope in these two interactions for investigating the expression of affect in much more detail.

It is evident that Twin A's enjoyment is expressed at a low level. She gives a short laugh only as a reaction to her father tickling her tummy, and it is not clear if she is laughing because she is enjoying the social interaction, and the game as a whole, or just because of the physical sensations of the tickling. Of course, it might be assumed that the laughter of infants might often be just an immediate response to sensation, but the clear evidence of anticipation in the father–Twin B dyad suggests that Twin B is also tracking his intentions and perceiving the link between interaction with her father during the build-up and the tickling event. Twin A also shows signs of enjoyment during periods when there is no tickling—it is interesting to speculate whether or not those signs of some happiness could be traces of an earlier laughter, recalling the previous physical sensations. Further study of early autistic pleasure in such situations could investigate the concept of "*Funktionslust*", Karl Buhler's (1934) word for "pleasure in the activity itself" in games or talking, although, as Bruner points out, regardless of, "whatever motivates such process pleasure [sic.], it serves the child well in keeping him at it" (Bruner, 1983, p. 47).[3]

Other videos showing developments in movements and attention

Three other video clips give us additional evidence on differences in the behaviour of the two girls and corresponding differences in the communications and actions of both father and mother. Running descriptions of the behaviour of the twins and the father were made by repeatedly viewing the tapes.

Video 3:   A family scene with toys

Video 3 was taken by the mother in the living room with a number of family members present, watching television. (Figure 2.3). The father is seated on the floor with the twins seated near him. A frame-by-frame narrative description was made of the postures, movements, and communicative behaviours and reactions of both girls, and of the father's actions and comments. The mother's comments recorded by the camera as she was making the video are also transcribed. This video covers 1 minute 20 seconds.

Videos 4 and 5:   The father encourages the girls to walk.

The father supports each of the girls, though in rather different ways, according to what the girls can accomplish as he tries to get them to walk for the camera (Figure 2.4). He tries to assist each girl's balance and forward progression. The tapes are of comparable duration: Twin B, 43 seconds; Twin A, 41 seconds. As before, we made a detailed, frame-by-frame account of the behaviours of each girl, including the father's behaviours and comments and the mother's comments.[6]

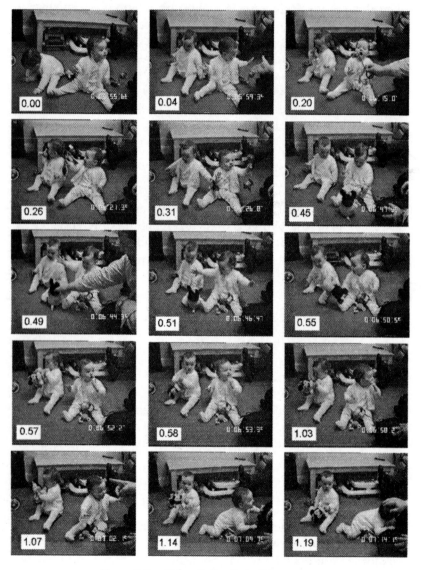

Figure 2.3.   Video 3: Family in living room.

28

TABLE 2.1. Descriptive analysis of Video 3: Family in living room.

Both girls are seated on the carpet
to the right of their father,
Twin B nearest him.
Film music is heard on TV.
F = Father, M = Mother

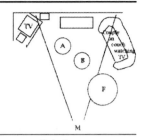

(Sec)	Twin B	Twin A
0–10	B sits with her legs in front of her, apart and straight with feet bent up, looking up to F on her left, hands held out expectantly with an interested look. She responds to F's outstretched hand, looking at it while holding her hands out wide to the side. F withdraws his hand. B reacts immediately to loud shouting and cheering on the TV, looks back to her left to couple on the couch, raising her hands. F reaches out to B again and she looks at the hand with her hands held out to side as before.	A bends over, looking at the floor, hands on floor, legs spread out and bent. She sits up slowly to look straight ahead, reaches behind her with the left hand without looking to feel a soft toy, right hand in air. She kicks her feet left–right–left, feet pointing down. stares ahead with mouth open, feeling the toy behind her with her left hand without looking She ignores the TV noise, grabs the toy from behind her with her left hand, without looking, lifts it slowly around to her mouth, still without looking and holds it with both hands there, then looks briefly to her right to TV. Snaps right hand to toy as she stuffs it in her mouth, looking down.
10–20	F holds his hand out to B, then flicks her on the mouth. B watches him and anticipates with her hands and mouth then holds her hands out afterwards, keeping oriented left to face F. F whispers something and takes up a toy from the floor near B who looks at him with a clenched mouth and forward jutting jaw. F holds out the toy to B who tracks and fixes it with her eyes, then briefly looks away with a smile. B opens her mouth to bite at the toy in F's hand, waving her right hand as if to catch it. Looks over to her right, away from the toy.	Turns away slowly to her right with toy to mouth, apparently looking at nothing. Turns slowly to front holding toy to nose and mouth with right hand. Amuses herself holding toy to her mouth with her right hand, staring ahead and swaying slightly. Wriggles slightly as she stares.
20–30	Looking away to right to TV with a playful grin. F tosses the toy he was holding out into the lap of B, who is still looking away to her right with a smile. Mother	B is expressionless as she mouths her toy and turns to her right. Holding toy to her mouth with right hand, slowly turns to face forward and then back to the

(continued)

29

(Sec)	Twin B	Twin A

clicks tongue 4 times and speaks, apparently to attract A's attention. B hits toy with right hand holding it out to right while watching to her right with a grin. Waves toy about in her right hand then brings it to middle and reaches to grasp toy with left hand as well, patting it several times, looking straight ahead.

Looks up with an alert, amused expression to F, holding toy in left hand, right hand extended, toes up.

right, apparently not looking at anyone. She stares right, perhaps at TV, while still mouthing toy.

Turns slowly to front still with toy to nose and mouth, snaps right hand round to grab the toy and releases hold with left hand. Grabs at toy with left hand staring ahead.

30–40 Holds up toy to F, waving it with a smile and an intent face. Right hand gestures to him with palm up. F says "Do what?"

Still looking at F, now a bit startled or confused, throws down the toy with her left hand and holds her right hand up. Without looking down, she grasps at the toy in her left hand and pulls it over her left leg, with right hand still up and looking intently at F who makes 4 popping sounds with his mouth. B is holding the toy with her left hand, grasping and ungrasping it, and holding up her right hand high to face F as she watches him, smiling.[4]

Pulls toy from mouth with left hand and holds right hand back beside her, feet still on floor; toes down, pulled in slightly. Wriggles and kicks spasmodically, part alternately and part synchronously, holds toy back behind her with left hand and drops it on B's right leg, staring ahead.

Sits staring. Turns to gaze at toy, expressionless, holding her left hand against her left leg.

Turns slowly to front apparently looking at floor, then quickly far right. Sits, swaying slightly.

40–50 B turns round to look over her left shoulder, toward the couch. Then she watches as F brings in a toy from his right, holding up her right hand as if to grasp. She follows as F brings the doll quickly round in front of her and sits it facing her between her legs. She stares down at the doll with right hand raised expectantly, left hand still holding toy.

Suddenly she opens both hands leans forward and makes a grab at the doll with a grin, knocking it over. Withdraws as F picks up the doll and places it between two girls next to their feet, B's left and A's right. B follows the doll and raises her hands up high, ready to pounce.

A turns slowly back looking down to front, hands down, head tilted to left.

Suddenly she jerks her arms up as F puts doll in front of B\was J: ok as changed?\, and turns in their direction looking at doll, perhaps with a slight smile, as F places it and bounces it 3 times on the floor. Snaps hands down and wriggles her whole body.

She then watches quietly as F takes the doll, then jerks back looking in front of her. Wriggles again and kicks, staring vacantly in front of her.

F bounces doll 3 times quickly as A turns and both girls watch.

50–60 A waves her right hand, then grabs for the doll, holding up her left hand. She seizes the doll and pulls it to her, lets go and raises her right hand high to pounce again.

With open-mouth smile looks right

B seems to be gazing vaguely in front of her, hands to herself.

She reaches for the leg of the doll with left hand without looking, grabs hold of it and opens her mouth, looking ahead and down. Whips doll away from B, pulls

	Twin B	Twin A
	holding doll, toes still up. Lifts hand while looking away to right without smile. B attempts to follow the escaping target. Holds left hand to mouth with a surprised, perhaps frightened expression, holding right hand up, looking at F, both toes up. M says a loud "OOOH!" for 5 seconds as F laughs. B has left fingers in her mouth, and grins, right hand pointing.	it up to her mouth, staring ahead, then turns right. Looks to her left possibly to M, surprised but expressionless, holding doll in both hands, still with dazed expression.
60–70	Still watching F, hands to mouth, not smiling, right hand up. F makes amused comment, and laughs. Hand in mouth, turns further round to left. F laughs. M says, "Who did that?" B takes hand from mouth as turns to look down in F's direction. Facing F she holds both hands out wide, and leans to him. M says again, "Who did that?" F points at B. and whispers to B "Look who took your toy!" B looks up at F's pointing hand, arms still out wide. M laughs. B leans whole body to F and he reaches to her. He reaches under her left arm to tickle her, and she grins.	A turns with a dazed expression to her front, then back to her left. She pulls the doll up to her mouth with both hands. With doll still in her mouth, she shakes her head vigorously then looks vaguely to her left, holding the doll in her right hand away from her mouth. She makes a wry expression, perhaps a smile on the left side of her mouth. She wiggles body again, mouth open, looks back to right, seemingly not engaged with anybody. She shakes her head with a slight smile as she pulls the doll to her mouth, looking away. Turns back to face camera holding doll to mouth in left hand, not smiling. Looks down and lowers hands, turning with left leg bent to get nearer F. Gazes blankly waving doll at mouth slightly.
70–80	A reaches with her right hand to F, crawling toward him. F holds her left arm. She looks up at him with a grin, leaning over folder left foot. F says, "Where are you going?" Still holding F's trousers, turns to back of room over her left shoulder. Sways back and forth a bit then brings head down on F's leg. F places hand over J's head, stroking her consolingly. B lifts her head as F withdraws his hand and looks away from camera over her left shoulder.[5]	B brings her right hand to the doll and pulls it to her mouth with a slight grin while she looks hard at the doll facing away from camera. She takes the doll from her mouth and looks right, then looks back to the camera holding the doll down, with a dazed appearance. She stares at the camera then slowly drops the doll on her knee. The doll falls to the floor and B sits up with a surprised expression, touching her right leg with her right hand.

31

Twin B

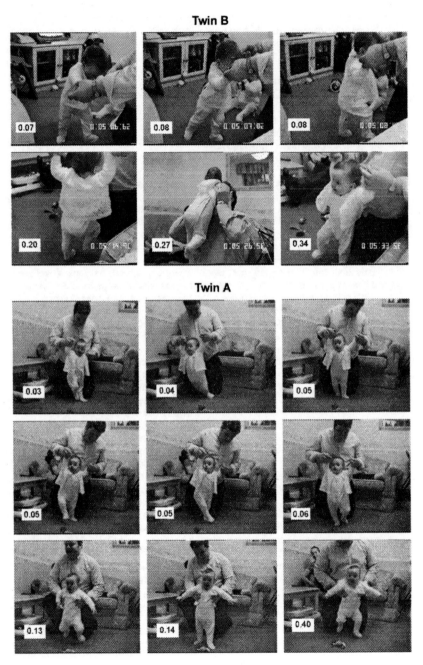

Figure 2.4. Father helps the twins to walk. Twin A can only jump.

32

TABLE 2.2.   Descriptive analysis of videos of father helping the infants to walk

Video 4 (Twin B). At the start (M 1), F is kneeling on the floor to the left of B, facing her and holding her right hand. (A is seen under F's R[ight] arm, sitting on the floor behind, self-absorbed, chewing toy, or looking vacantly in front of her).	*Video 5 (Twin A).* F, kneeling behind A, is holding her standing. (B is held by a woman who is lying on the couch in the background.
(Length of video clip = 43 seconds)	(Length of video clip = 41 seconds)

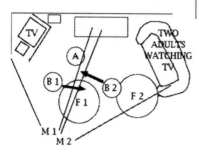

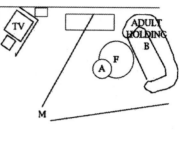

(Sec)	*Video 4: Twin B*	*Video 5: Twin A*
0–5	B 1 is standing close to the camera looking at it, R hand to chin, L[eft] arm held by F 1, who backs away, leaning her forward. She removes R hand from chin, pursed lips, still staring at the camera. M 1, watching her through camera, says "What are you thinking?" F 1 says quickly, "Come on, show your mum." B is moved back to stand more upright, still looking at camera. Looks away, R hand to mouth. Sways back in front of TV, looks back at camera, sways forward . Looks away to F 1, hand still to mouth. M 1 says, "Are you going to lead her?" F 1 says, "Hold the hand." B takes her R hand from her mouth as she swings round to approach F 1, and reaches out to him with her R hand. F 1 takes her R hand in his palm, leading her toward him. She looks down and ahead toward F 1's feet.	F says, "Move". A looks to her R, perhaps to TV. F pulls her hands up and says, "Do your wee dancin'". Her body is wiggling but feet stay planted in place on the floor, R facing forward, L foot turned out. She is swayed forward by father, brings R foot *back* beside L as he leans her forward with a twist, lifting her R hand forward while holding her L hand back at shoulder height, trying to help her step. F repeats at higher pitch "Do your wee dancin'" while leaning forward and pulling her body forward so her feet are dragging on the floor almost 30 cm. behind her head. She makes no attempt to step forward.
5–10	B 1 raises her R foot, pushing down with R hand against F 1's L palm, pulling back her L hand held by F 1. Looks down to her own feet as she lifts her R foot. Puts down her R foot and lifts the L, still looking down at own feet. Makes	As F sways her body to her L, lifting her R hand, A raises her R foot as if to step, but swings it back to beside her L foot. Mother "yelps" encouragement. A looks slightly to M's L, mouth open. F is watching A's feet. F pulls A's weight to her R so *(continued)*

33

(Sec)	Video 4: Twin B	Video 5: Twin A

big stride with L foot toward F 1 moving to the right of the frame (arrow).

She stands firm with two feet far apart, L foot ahead, looking down.

She lifts her L foot again and replaces it more in front of body, puts weight forward onto it and lifts her R foot, which is now extended back. Rotates toward F and strides forward with her R foot.

F says, "Come on then, show mummy walking. . . . Show your walking."

She places R foot near F. Shifts weight over R foot and lifts L foot. Completes stride leaning forward, both hands held up at head level by F.

she shifts her weight to her R foot, which is just in front of the L. She has increased her smile, still looking away to M's L. She steps forward on her L foot leaving the R behind. M "yelps" again, weaker, then as A swings her L foot forward, M "yelps" a third time, louder. She is vocalizing in sympathy with A's efforts to step. F has both A's hands up high suspending A's weight. Her feet drag behind. When she steps she does not reach forward to take her weight. F sways her to her R then far L to get her stepping. As he rocks her forward and to her L, she drags her feet behind. She is now on her L foot and the R is behind and raised. F says quietly, a little exasperated, "Come on!" He now suspends her by her hands on her L foot, leaning to her L.

M says, "Hold her under her arms", as F grunts, "Ooh!" and raises his R leg from kneeling on the floor, then says voicelessly and quickly, "Da-da-da-da-da". A shifts her weight to her R foot which is bowed, and she raises her L foot as if to step. She is looking ahead and down. F gets on L knee and R foot, holding A by her hands.

10–15   B leans far forward on her L foot, with R behind. Lifts the R foot and brings it past the L.

B sways sideways to R, held by F.

Has weight on R foot now.

Lifts L foot and steps toward F.

Rocks to keep balance as F moves.

A does not step, and F shifts hands to her waist pulling her back slightly over her feet. She has not stepped since second number 0.07\ok as changed?\. Her feet are still behind her hips. She is held upright by F, who shifts his hands above her waist, supporting her elbows.

F lowers his hands to her waist and moves her hips to the R. She lifts her R foot in an arc, pulling it sharply behind her while standing on her L. F lifts her as her R foot is raised behind her, then takes both her feet off the ground, and she is smiling, still looking to her M's L, probably to the TV. She pulls both feet together backwards and kicks them straight while F lifts and puts her down so they touch the floor. She springs and pulls her feet up in the first jump, the L leg more bent than the R. She is grinning slightly. She kicks both legs straight again, feet pointing out, but held by F

	too high to touch ground. She is smiling, and immediately pulls feet up high with hands out like wings. Kicks down a third time], still grinning, as F drops her.
15–20　F says, "Where are you going?" B lifts R foot, hanging body on F's L hand. Does not complete step. Brings feet together. Raises L foot 　F says, "Come on, lazy bones." As B completes big stride with L foot, F makes an encouraging comment. Lifts R foot, swings it round with F's help and places it securely on floor.	A finishes kick, touches the ground with toes and pulls legs up (L a bit ahead) with a big grin, as F lifts. Kicks again with open grin, legs straight, touches floor with toes. Lifts feet high again as F lifts and kicks down, R ahead slightly. Lowered to touch floor with R foot. Lifts feet, R ahead, then heels together, then immediately shoots them out straight, feet turned out. Touches floor. Jumps high still grinning. Feet at climax of lift, arms wide, big grin. M laughs. A kicks out as she is dropped. Lifts feet high and kicks again. Starts next lift and 　F laughs. A pulls her L leg high and kicks hard down. A is looking eagerly to L of camera. Pushes both feet, toes out, on floor. This is her 10th jump. Lifts feet high back together, L slightly ahead, at beginning of F's lift, She is grinning. Completes two more bounces with feet touching floor. She makes a two-syllable baby vocalization.
20–25　B lifts her L foot and completes a stride. 　F steadies her under her R arm with his L hand as she stretches back on her R foot. He lifts her, saying, "Yea!"	A makes four jumps in 2 seconds as F holds her far over to his R to look at her face. F continues bouncing and brings her round in front of him again. She jumps high and kicks out four times, now looking more ahead and down. She is no longer grinning. Then she looks up and grins again as her body rises in the lift. She makes 2 more kicks at 24 seconds.
25–30　F holds her high in air and brings her to his face, laughing. She curls her legs up. 　F continues to hold her over his face and hugs her, gives her a kiss, lifts her away, questioning, "Ay?" Smiling broadly, he says, "And back again." He lowers B over his L arm and turns her round to face the camera (M 2). She is looking down to floor. 　He turns her to face away from him (F 2).	Looking up with a grin, she makes 2 jumps. F makes gruff hoot, then says in a whisper in time with her jumps, "Dance, dance, dance." Another two jumps with vigorous kicks. M laughs. Five more jumps and A stops smiling, F grinning away to L, sharing the game with someone off camera. 　M sings first line of a traditional fisherfolk song with a strong rhythm, "Dance little lady, dance for your daddy." A completes 2 jumps.

(continued)

35

(Sec)	Video 4: Twin B	Video 5: Twin A
30–35	F 2 releases B 2 as she reaches the floor, holding her R hand in his R and taking his L arm away from her front. She is standing free, supported only by his R hand. She reaches out with her L arm and F grasps it (saying "Woop!"), to support her with both arms facing away from him. Her legs are splayed on the floor behind her body. She lifts her L foot and makes a small step to bring it under her. As she reaches the ground F says softly, "There". She lifts her R foot and steps forward a short distance to put it down, vocalizing one sound.	A makes two jumps, with smaller lifts. F bends down and kisses her on the L cheek, giving her a squeeze. A looks mildly startled. This interrupts her jumping. F makes a small lift and drop, but A's feet stay on ground. M sings the second line of the song, "Dance little lady, till your boat comes in." A bends knees and goes low for another jump, grinning again, and makes two further jumps with F's help.
35-end	F 2 sways B 2 over her R foot and she lifts her L foot. She steps out looking ahead toward the TV and where Twin A is sitting on the floor (arrow). She tries to get her balance and completes this step, raising her R foot. Moves her weight forward with F 2's assistance over her R foot and makes the next step with her L foot. She is looking down and smiling slightly. She stands for a couple of seconds, then seems to be making another L stride. F says, "Come on then."	A makes 10 jumps in 5 seconds. She is kicking out vigorously like a frog each time she is bounced by F, sending her legs out sideways to touch the floor with her toes facing out. M says, "What a jumping bean you are!" The couple on the couch peer round from behind F to enjoy the spectacle.

Independent reflections by Laurent Danon-Boileau on the video extracts of the twins

General observations

First, neither of the twins appears to present according to the classical description of autism. Even Twin A is normal in much of her behaviour.

She smiles, she can communicate with expression, she addresses her gaze to the person she is relating to. I think it is important to emphasize the apparent normality of Twin A at this stage of her development. In fact, when looking at the film for the first time, it is difficult to say which child will become autistic.

Concerning the rhythms of interaction, it is difficult to say anything, for there are no rhythmic dialogues in which the adult is matching a gesture or a smile or a sound made by the child, and the child matches it in turn. However, when father interacts with Twin B, his bouts of speech are separated by regular silences, as if he anticipates a reply from Twin B in these silences. These regular pauses do not seem to occur with Twin A.

In my opinion, the areas where subtle differences can be noted are as follows.

- *On the side of the child:*
  —communication or anticipation of communication (quite classical)
  —posture and coordination of movements.
- *On the side of the parent:*
  —the attunement in play and in speech; the motor and verbal behaviour of the father is different with Twin A and Twin B.

Observations on the "Monster Game"

Both children have, to a certain extent, normal behaviour. They manifest pleasure by smiling or laughing, and they do so at the right moment in the game. But this moment is not the same for Twin A and Twin B.

Twin A is held in her father's arms (Figure 2.2). Her smile is very brief. She does not look in her father's eyes or at the camera: she looks at the light or in front of her. Her manifestations of pleasure (short laughs) come after the peak of excitement when the father kisses her stomach making a lot of noise—that is, after physical contact. This expression corresponds to an easing of tension or relaxation; it is not a communicative sound (contrary to what we find with Twin B).

Twin B is lying on a bed: she does not have to concentrate on her muscle tonus and balance (Figure 2.1). She can easily devote her attention to the exchange with her father. In this she can be said to have an advantage over Twin A. She constantly looks in her father's eyes when her father's face is not too close to her body. When she cannot see her father's eyes, she looks towards the camera, trying to catch her mother's look. In fact there is a moment [0.27] when she has looked towards her mother (because father's face is not visible) and then, as her father starts a new episode and his face becomes visible once more, she turns to look in his eyes again. This proves that she has an anticipation that the game is going to start again. Now B's manifestations of pleasure also take place when father pretends to attack her, not only when there is physical contact. And the sounds she emits are more modulated than those of her sister. They are of a communicative type, not only of an expressive type. With B, her laugh is an expression of joy, not the mere effect of a relaxing of tension. Twin B is also able to show fright on two different occasions in the course of the game. Her facial expression (eyes and mouth) shows fear or incomprehension, and she then tries to pat her hand against her father's face, after which she becomes more peaceful and smiles again. The expression of uneasiness appears again [0.53] when the father changes her game and says "Oh, oh . . ."

(It would be useful to compare spectroscopically the sounds of pleasure of Twins A and B and to identify where differences appear. When the cry of a baby is expressive, the intensity of sound is distributed through all the harmonics of the spectrum [formants]; when it becomes a call for something and becomes communicative, then all the intensity gathers on F_0, the fundamental formant of the voice. My impression is that those of Twin A are not as nicely shaped as those of Twin B—they sound louder, and less harmonious. They appear with Twin A only after the peak of excitement, on relaxation. With Twin B, a vocalization is made every time she is happy—even with herself, as is shown in the film where she succeeds in walking.)

The father's behaviour in the "Monster Game" differs with the two girls. With Twin A, in addition to holding her constantly, he makes frequent physical contact with her against his face and mouth. The end of each bout of the game is emphasized by the mouth contact on the child's stomach and a loud monstrous sound. The father completes his tickling attacks; he touches his daughter and persists—there is no pretending.

With Twin B the father can pretend that he is *going to* tickle and attack, and this phase in the game lasts longer than the actual monstrous "attack". This pretence offers a long phase of preparation.

When the father speaks to Twin B, his voice is much lower pitched and less varied, and when he calls her he leaves silence between calls or words, so the child may answer in his silences. He is acting as if he imagines Twin B will reply. He is addressing a possible answerer.

Observations on the "family" film)

Again, at first glance (Figure 2.3), both infants seem normal. They both can sit, and their postures and general attitude seem well developed. They are also capable of active exchanges in interaction, and they are expressive. On closer inspection, differences appear. The posture of Twin B is good, but she holds her legs wide apart extended straight from her thighs.[7] She expresses her interest in the interaction with her father with a direct look towards his face, and she has a definite sign of interest on her mouth when she interacts. Yet, sometimes she goes off the track, as when she turns away from the interaction and her father holds out his palm to attract her attention. She then looks at the hand, but is distracted by a noise and looks away again.[8]

During the second period of the interaction [0.16], when the father hands her a toy in the form of a stick with a cloth star at the end, she opens her mouth as if she wanted to put it in her mouth, but when she takes the stick in her right hand she does not put it in her mouth, as if she had forgotten about it. While busy with the stick after transferring it to her left hand, her right hand is extended with palm vertical, and the fingers are extended as if forgotten. This hand is kept in a stiff position while the rest of the body is busy holding and touching the stick and waving it about. She stays with her right hand like that for a long time, until the father puts a doll (Mickey) between the two twins. Then she bangs on the Mickey doll with her right hand while her left hand is held up inert and stays like that until her sister catches Mickey. When this happens, although she was playing with the doll, B does not seem to worry—she does not look at the Mickey she has just lost, not even when her father points at the sister saying, "She stole your toy!"[9]

Twin A is sitting with both legs bent in a semicircle, not like Twin B whose legs extended straight from the thigh. She inclines her head forward, and seems to explore the carpet just in front of her with her hands, bending her trunk towards the floor. When she takes an object, she puts it in her mouth and holds it there, either with the hand that seized the object or with both hands, which is different from her sister. When she steals Mickey from her sister, she does it with her left hand, without looking, but she coordinates the capture with putting the doll in her mouth, and then she brings both hands to the task, putting the right hand on the toy against her mouth.

This seems to prove that while Twin B devotes a part of her body to an intentional action, another part of the body may remain stiff. Twin A seems better able to coordinate two hands and a hand-to-mouth movement. In other words, in this scene, as far as motor skills are concerned, it looks as if A, strangely enough, were *more* coordinated than B as regards hands and mouth, though not, of course, as regards eyes and hand. Perhaps this is due to Twin B being in interaction with her father, while having to maintain a seated position and trying to catch objects at the same time. Twin A is acting for herself and on her own.[10]

Observations on the "walking" film

Twin A jumps but cannot balance on her feet (Figure 2.4). She does not address her glance to anyone, but just looks in front of her. Her reactions of pleasure (smiles and laughs) are part of physical reactions associated with the jerks and tosses of her body. She does not smile when her father stops making her jump and kisses her.

Twin B has an unsteady equilibrium, but, notwithstanding this difficulty, she constantly maintains her look in her father's eyes when he talks to her; when he does not, she looks at her feet, which is the source of her problems. One can see, from the expression of her mouth and her eyes, that she looks at things because she is concentrating on what she is doing. She is not merely being excited and then relaxing. She is concentrating on trying and succeeding to do the difficult activity of walking. When she utters sounds of pleasure, they do not correspond to an easing out of tension, and I suspect that they are different in their form, which should be investigated with the appropriate tools—the intensity should be more concentrated on F_0 than for the grunts of satisfaction of her sister A. In this film Twin B's sounds of pleasure do not occur after a peak of excitement: they appear while she is walking. They seem to be little cries of victory when the child is pleased to be successfully achieving her walk.

The father holds Twin A under her arms. His voice is quite shrill, varied, loud, and actively pulsed with the jumps he is helping his child achieve. He speaks as if he were playing with a puppet, making it speak while moving it with his hand.

With Twin B he sustains and follows the autonomous movement of the child; he is not the origin of the movement but is supporting it. Besides, the movement is more complicated: he guides B. There seems to be a common and complex plan built up between child and father—that of walking along a path on the floor. It is not a repetitive two-phase routine of moving up and down as it was with Twin A. Besides, when the movement has come to an end, he says, "Back again" before guiding her to walk in a different direction. His tone of voice with Twin B is communicative. He speaks as he would speak to a young child he would like to encourage or help. His voice is gentle, and he does not speak continuously. He leaves silences, as if the child will answer. What he says sounds like an invitation addressed towards the child, inviting her to speak between his words. His speech is not, as it was with Twin A, a way of provoking the reflex excitement of the "jumping bean", with his imposed ups and downs of the child's body.

The father also talks as if B could understand an intention to show something to a third person, saying, "Show your Mummy." He addresses B as a potential partner in an interaction with someone different from himself, and therefore he considers B as an independent actor. This proves that he is convinced of the existence of an inter-subjective contact with B, and not just of a physical contact like the winding up of a mechanical clock. In this situation, the mother also makes an "aside" comment to the father, when she says "I can't see", not referring directly to the child.

My conclusion would be that with A the father uses his voice as a sort of incentive for movement, whereas with B he uses language to share plans with someone whom he credits with a sort of rudimentary "theory of mind", and common purposes.

CONCLUSIONS: HOW SHOULD WE LOOK OUT FOR EARLY SIGNS OF AUTISM?

The failure of the father–Twin A dyad to conform to a homeostatic model of mutual, inter-mental regulations between persons is confirmed in the "Monster Game" by the disparity in behavioural cycles between the two interactions. While the behaviours of Twin B and her father can be quite neatly "pigeonholed" into cycles, those of the father and Twin A are more difficult to judge. The above findings prompt the conclusion that communicative deficits are not only latent, but are overtly manifest in an autistic child at the age of 11 months, at least six months prior to the age that delays in linguistic development normally become apparent.

Free-play dyads provide an ideal arena for observing the interactions between parents and infants, as they are richly varied and incorporate the core elements of attention–non-attention cycles (Brazelton, Koslowski, & Main, 1974), anticipation, and parent–infant reciprocity (Prechtl, 1963; Thoman, 1975). In addition, they do not require any specialized equipment and can take place in any situation.

Practitioners—preferably trained in observation with the aid of video to pay attention to details of expression and reciprocal engagement—should be encouraged to note whether or not there is evidence of good eye contact and anticipation and of reciprocity in looking, vocalizing, and touching between child and parent. If not, why might that be? Does the parent's behaviour encourage or inhibit the child's initiatives for communication? Is it possible to see easily anticipated cycles of interaction? Is there any clear and enjoyable pattern to the interaction—does it seem to resemble a "game" or a "dance" in any way (Stern, 1977)? Is more intrusive physical stimulation (tickling, kissing) often substituted for social and emotional interaction? What do the parent's expectations for the child seem to be? And if there is a pattern of avoidance, who is avoiding whom?

At the same time as making these observations, practitioners should try to view the child and parent as a system and be alert to all possibilities, whether positive or negative in their implications for development. Each dyad is different and should not be immediately categorized, as the initial aim is not to diagnose but to develop an understanding of the patterns of interaction and how development might be supported. A child's style of interaction might vary greatly depending on who the partner is, so, if practical, it would undoubtedly be helpful to observe the child with more than one parent or carer. In addition to close observation of dyadic interactions, parents' own observations and concerns about the child's enjoyment of all social encounters should be taken into careful consideration, and appropriate and thoughtful questions should be asked.

Formal criteria, such as those of the DSM-IV (APA, 2004), are invaluable in helping clinicians to reach firm conclusions regarding the presence of autism, but a diagnosis by these means is unlikely to be made before a child starts to display delayed or impaired language development and "restricted repetitive and stereotyped patterns of behaviour, interests and activities" (DSM-IV). In the meantime, throughout the first year of life, the child who is already having trouble perceiving and communicating with people is missing out on potentially helpful interventions, and the parents will not be receiving the practical and psychosocial support that could be invaluable to them. If there are early warning signs, and if it is possible to identify them, why wait?

We should be careful, however. Although the benefit of hindsight makes it tempting to leap to such conclusions, evidence of communicative problems at a prelinguistic stage must not automatically be taken to signify the onset of autism. Development of communication and language in children varies widely, and definite early deficits could be indicative of the later problems identified with many disorders considered to be outside the "autistic spectrum", such as Rett syndrome or Williams syndrome. Intervention could involve working closely with parents to understand how maladaptive traits manifest themselves in everyday social interactions and to investigate whether a change in the parent's responses and feelings can effect a change in the child's own behaviour (cf. Gutstein & Sheely, 2002). If parents are encouraged to regulate their own behavioural style when interacting with their autistic child, they can then guide the child through social development using sympathetically aware, positive reinforcement rather than conditioned, often negative interactive behaviours or coercions. If the autism is detected early enough, then it may be possible to use a practical scaffolding paradigm to pre-empt the potential derailing that Tronick (1982, 2005) suggests can disrupt the developmental process, and to help the child anticipate and enjoy the "dance steps" so necessary for getting at meaning through social interaction (Bruner, 1990; Rogoff, 2003; Trevarthen, 2004).

Taking all our observations together on these very informative videos of the twins with their father, we would draw particular attention to the differences in the quality or form of expressive movements—in body, hands, and voice—and how they show the difference between self-consciousness and intention to communicate. Direction of regard, face expressions, movements of the hands and how they are oriented or aimed, and rhythms and tone of voice all give evidence of emotions. Twin A is certainly aware, at times, of other people, and she does show emotions of interest, surprise, and pleasure, but her interest lacks enthusiasm, her surprise is confused or astonished, and her smiles or chuckles are more expressions of self-satisfaction. Often she does not look to monitor what her hands are doing, and she does not watch her feet like her sister when her father prompts her to step forward, which she evidently cannot do. She seems dis-coordinated in her "body image". All these features of her motivation and imagination and self-image affect the way her father engages her in play, what he expects her to do. The rhythm and phrasing of his speech and the tone of his voice are less subtle and cooperative than with Twin B—less communicative. These indices, which show how he feels with the two girls, promise to be rich fields for future analytic research on the early stage of autism.[11]

We believe that investigation of behaviours to reveal evidence of changes in the child's perception, cognition, and learning alone is too limited in its scope. A search for early signs of autism will be more fruitful if direct attention is given to the expressions of motives and emotions and to how they regulate communication in familiar situations, between infants and those persons they know best.

AFTERWORD

Since this report was written, Twin A and Twin B, now 10 years old, have been seen by CT, and their medical records and psychological reports have been studied. They are beautiful, and, despite their difficulties in movement and attention, are happy, in good health, and developing well, with excellent care and attention from their family. The parents have provided valuable comments and made some corrections to our interpretations. Laboratory comparison of nine polymorphic markers confirmed that the girls have identical genotypes.

The twins were born early, at 34½ weeks. Twin A was the smaller of the two, with a birth weight of 4 pounds 5 ounces (2 kilograms). Twin B was the better developed through gestation and at birth weighed 5 pounds 8 ounces (2.5 kilograms).

Twin A was an alert infant, but her attention became fixated on certain objects, notably bright lights, and she was inattentive to persons. Her father was the first to suggest, before she was 18 months old, that she might be developing autism. She was slow to smile and was often inattentive to both visual and auditory stimuli. She received a clinical diagnosis of autism at age 21 months. Her mother and father sought to aid her development by all possible means. They went with her for training at the "Son Rise" Program, Option Center, in Sheffield, Massachusetts, and then at Growing Minds in Jupiter, Florida, in the United States, and her communication improved. Twin A first spoke words and used pointing around age 3 years, but she did not show imaginative play with dolls as her sister did at this age. At 10, while delayed in attention, motor development, and communication, she has progressed well with the help of speech and behaviour therapies. She is sociable and affectionate, making progress at school, and beginning to read, but she has severe difficulties with visual selection and comprehension and coordination of large movements of her body.

Twin B appeared to develop well in the first two years, but the records and her parents' recollections confirm Danon-Boileau's reservations about her body awareness, posture, and attention at 10 months. Her vocabulary increased from 2½ years, but by 3½ years she was clearly developmentally delayed. She had trouble using language effectively and in coping socially with peers and understanding games. Her large movements were awkward, and she could not learn to cycle. She showed confusion in planning actions and refused difficult options. Despite these clear developmental difficulties, she is not judged to be autistic. She is much better at school than her sister but tends to be shy, and she resolutely avoids people or situations that confuse her.

Notes

1. See Afterword concerning Twin B's development to age 10 years.

2. Twin A's mother reports that her gaze was captured by bright objects—a red light on the video camera and a light in the ceiling. When the camera light was covered, Twin A ceased to look in her mother's direction. This is a clear symptom of a difficulty in directing attention away from salient features, which is linked to her inability to sustain engagement in her father's game.

3. See Afterword. At 10 years, the twins show differences in sociability and temperament. Twin A is friendly and comes up to strangers and touches them without fear. She is affectionate and lively, though often inattentive and obscure in her speech. Twin B tends to be shy and avoids people she does not know. She can act in a manipulative way with her parents and familiar teachers when she is avoiding tasks she dislikes or trying to redirect engagement with them.

4. Both girls have developed abnormal patterns of motor coordination. They had delayed walking and difficulties in learning skills such as running and bicycle riding. See Afterword.

5. See Afterword and note 3 regarding Twin B's timidity. She seeks contact with familiar adults when shy with strangers.

6. Twin B, though less affected than Twin A, was late in walking unaided, and she is not skilled in large body movements at 10 years.

7. The weakness of posture or motor coordination noted here became more evident in later development of Twin B. See Afterword.

8. While Twin A has a pronounced difficulty in attending to the actions of her father and anticipating his intentions, Twin B is merely confused by sudden changes, such as when Twin A snatches a toy from her, and she seeks reassurance from her father (see note 9)

9. Twin B is evidently confused here and cannot comprehend the disappearance of the toy.

10. These observations delineate subtle abnormalities and differences between twins in body awareness and in the coordination of their movements to outside events. Twin A is lost in her own world and tends to become fixated on isolated phenomena that distract her from the offers of communication made by her father. This restricted field of interest may help her to coordinate her movements better. Twin B is attentive to her father but cannot follow complex overlapping events or those that suddenly interrupt what she is doing.

11. See previous notes on differences in attention, motor coordination, and emotion between the twins; see also the Afterword.

CHAPTER THREE

Early signs of autism in the first year of life

Filippo Muratori, Sandra Maestro

arly identification of autism has become a "best practice", since it helps families gather information about their child's disorder and begin treatment (Volkmar & Pauls, 2003). In fact, several intervention studies have demonstrated significant gains in social and cognitive functioning for young children with autism participating in early-intervention programmes (Rogers, 1996). Early intervention is thought to be critical for preventing a cascade of effects that result from early deficits and interfere with later functioning. They are considered of great importance, given the current consensus that the beneficial impact of intervention programmes increases with earlier treatment as a function of early neuroplasticity and of the role of early experiences in shaping brain development (Hockfield & Lombroso, 1998a; Shore, 1996, 1998). However, the early identification of autism is not without its challenges: autism is a behaviourally based diagnosis, and there is often a lack of familiarity with its early behavioural manifestations among front-line professionals. For this main reason, delays in diagnosis are common.

Background

Although first described by Kanner in 1943 as an inborn disorder of affective contact, information on autism in infants and very young children is limited. The question of whether symptoms of autism are visible during the first two years of life is still an open one. We can consider three possibilities: first, core behaviours truly are not present in very young children with autism; second, core behaviours are present but difficult to recognize because caregivers compensate for the child's deficits; third, core behaviours are present, but not recognized as problematic until later, when expectations of caregivers grow higher or clinicians and parents become wiser. From a practical perspective, these three possibilities describe different types of young children with autism and different problems in early detection. From a theoretical perspective, a better understanding of these three possibilities can help both to understand the core and the secondary features of the disorder and to identify the precursors of the traditional diagnostic criteria. We try to explore these three possibilities through a research based on home movies of children later diagnosed with autism. The retrospective analyses of home movies provide a potential research resource. Up to now they can be considered the only instrument available to study the course of onset and development of autism in the first years of life before diagnosis. Such research has generally confirmed the early emergence of developmental differences in infants with autism (Adrien et al., 1993; Baranek, 1999; Losche, 1990; Mars, Mauk, & Dowrick, 1998; Massie & Rosenthal, 1984; Osterling & Dawson, 1994; Osterling, Dawson, & Munson, 2002; Sauvage et al., 1988; Teitelbaum, Teitelbaum, Nye, Fryman, & Maurer, 1998; Werner, Dawson, Osterling, & Dinno, 2000). Retrospective analysis of home movies makes it possible to overcome the methodological shortcomings that have been a feature of research involving retrospective parental accounts (Davidovitch, Glick, Holtzman, Tirosh, & Safir, 2000). In fact, home movies, in contrast to parental reports, may allow us to obtain data and information that are not influenced by time or by parent's recall and to study the natural history of autism.

Methods

In the different research studies described in this chapter (the original results are fully described in the papers quoted in the references), we have studied home movies from the first two years of life of children later diagnosed with autism. All children in the autism group were recruited among those referred from multiple community sources to a suburban public academic hospital providing care to patients of all socioeconomic levels (Department of Developmental

Neuroscience of the Scientific Institute Stella Maris at the University of Pisa). The home movies of the autism group were matched for gender and months of age with home movies of children with typical development recruited among those attending a kindergarten in the city of Pisa. The samples comprised Italian children belonging to middle-/upper-middle-class families. As far as the autism group is concerned, after a multidimensional five-day inpatient or outpatient assessment period (encompassing direct individual observations, psychological testing, group observation, and biological exams), the diagnosis was performed independently by two senior child psychiatrists through a checklist of symptoms composed of the twelve criteria for autism derived from the three impaired developmental areas according to DSM-IV (APA, 1994). The overall reliability for each item of the checklist was consistently high, with a Cohen's kappa ranging between 0.8 and 1; all of the children satisfied the criteria for autism diagnosis in accordance with DSM-IV criteria and the consensus of the two child psychiatrists (for some research we included the category Pervasive Developmental Disorder Not Otherwise Specified for cases in which the criteria were met in an insufficient number of criteria, other than merely on the degree or severity of abnormality). Additionally the Childhood Autism Rating Scale was administered. On this measure, all children in the autism samples received scores above the cut-off of 30 (i.e. the cut-off for autism). As regarding diagnosis, the more recent research has utilized the Autism Diagnostic Interview–Revised. The protracted assessment period allowed us to exclude children with expressive, receptive, or mixed language disorders and children with isolated mental retardation. We have excluded any type of Pervasive Developmental Disorders associated with medical disorder or second syndrome previously described and already well established in medical literature. Participants were excluded if they had Fragile X or Rett syndromes, Down's syndrome, a sensory impairment, cerebral palsy, or any central nervous system disease.

At the time of assessment, families were asked to bring their child's videotapes, and, after a complete description of the study to the families, a copy was made. The tapes were reviewed in detail and logged according to the child's chronological age during each scenario and to specific content. Chronological ages were calculated by full months, based on the child's birth date and corresponding dates appearing on the tapes themselves. To analyse the videos we divided the recordings into different age ranges: (a) 0–6 months; (b) 6–12 months; (c) 12–18 months; and (d) 18–24 months. For research aims we have included only videos without any editing by the parents, without any selection by the researchers, and running for a minimum of ten minutes for each age range. The various scenes were analysed and divided, labelling every scene in which the infant was visible and involved in human and object interaction. We coded only the scenes lasting more than forty seconds. All available footage was coded in order to prevent selection bias. The home movies usually consist of recorded sequences of normal daily activities like feeding, bathing, or playing, alone or in interactions with parents or siblings; the first birthday or several other important moments of early life, like breastfeeding, the first bath, and the first steps, appear in almost all videos. These scenes can be included in three type of events: (1) familiar routines (feeding, bathing, toilet); (2) special events (sibling's birthdays, infant's baptism, Christmas, Easter and other holidays); and (3) play situations (with objects or people). We provide samples of home movies with no significant differences between autism and typical groups with respect to the type of events and to the length of the analysed video recordings.

The films of the compared groups were mixed and rated by blind observers through the different instruments we have used in the different research described in this chapter. These instruments (The Grids) are composed of items referring to behaviour in everyday life situations that can be taped by movies. The items were chosen by a team of researchers and clinicians (supervised by Daniel Stern), and they were sometimes grouped in different developmental areas. The Grids have a high degree of face validity both for single items and for these developmental areas (i.e., social attention, non-social attention, etc.). The first version of each Grid was always revised after a study of a preliminary small group of normal and pathological children.

The raters had a Masters degree in clinical or developmental psychology. They were trained by experienced clinicians and a research consultant, using video samples of children not being used in the study. The aims of the training were: (1) to familiarize with the Grid glossary; (2) to achieve ability in detecting early developmental competencies; and (3) to improve the ability in focusing on infant's molecular behaviours from very naturalistic and sometimes overloaded situations. The training was in general three months long and continued until inter-rater agreement reached 80%. For the rating of these different Grids, after the presence/absence method, we used an interval scoring method and computed the frequencies for each item. Since the length of each video was different, we have calculated, as in other video studies, the frequencies of each behaviour for 1 minute (unit-time). These frequencies were then converted to a ratio number of behaviours per unit of time.

The search for symptoms

Our research on home movies was born from the conviction that the parents were not able to recognize the pathological signs of autism and that a more experienced eye could detect symptoms not evident to parents. It was considered that an overriding wish or belief that the child was normal may lead parents to the conviction of a skill being present when, in fact, it is not. To explore this idea, we applied to the home movies the Behaviour Summarised Evaluation (Barthélémy et al., 1992) to evaluate the symptom's appearance in children with autism (Maestro, Casella, Milone, Muratori, & Palacio-Espasa, 1999). Several findings emerged from this research. First, we did not find significant differences between the age of appearance of the first symptoms reported by the parents and the one recognized by the researchers in the home movies. Both of them became concerned about the child's development at an average age of 12–15 months (Rogers & DiLalla, 1990). Second, we were confronted with parents who, contrary to the stereotypical portrayal of mothers of children with autism as cold and non-expressive, appear in the film to be highly flexible and involved (Doussard-Roosvelt, Joe, & Bazhenova, 2003). Third, the most serious—and not totally surprising—finding was the length of time that passed between when the parents began to suspect that something was wrong in their infant and when they were helped to decide to take the child for a psychiatric consultation or treatment. This gap went from a minimum of 6 months to a maximum of 41 months. From this research onwards we are convinced that the mothers are correctly worried about their child and give their preoccupations—probably between the lines—to the paediatric clinical services: what is sometimes absent is the clinician's capacity to point out the risk for autism and provide a prompt diagnostic procedure and support service to address parental concern. Fourth, we became able to recognize two main forms of the onset and course of autism: the first is a slow, gradual, but progressive course. In the observed sequences, starting from age 3 months, there is not the progressive increase of vivacity and of capacity in modulating the affective states that should appear in typical infants of the same age. On the contrary, there is an amount of indifference, apathy, and lack of affects. Even though these children show the emergence of some primary communicative competence (like exchanging glances) of attention to demonstrated objects, and of good reaction in respect to environmental stimuli, the attention of the observer is drawn to the lack of vitality, of initiative, and of interactive exchanges. The emotional and intersubjective relationship fails to develop over time, and, by the beginning of the second year of life, there is an increased withdrawal of the child. The second pattern of the early course of autism is characterized by a "free period"—with normal or near-normal development—before the unexpected loss of skill and the onset of the first signs of autism. In the home movies of children with this type of onset, it is possible to see frequent glances towards the mother while feeding and changing the infant; prolonged peek-a-boo games with lively vocal interchanges with the mother; games in which the child attempts to catch a sibling; and short sequences of declarative pointing. The change takes place between age 12 and 18 months, and it mainly concerns the reaction to environmental stimuli, the development of communicative gestures, and interest towards people. The increasing social withdrawal bring the child to a "world of its own", with less gaze monitoring, a lack of interest, and a decrease of response to adult speech (Rogers, 2004).

The different timing of an early-symptoms constellation

Our research on early symptoms in infants with autism has brought to the surface some additional rated items that could constitute a typical symptoms constellation (Maestro, Muratori, & Cavallaro, 2005; Maestro, Muratori, & Cesari, 2005) to be considered as the expression of the early developmental symptomatic trajectory of both early- and late-onset autism. This constellation is characterized by withdrawal (expressed by the items: ignores people, poor social interaction, and abnormal eye contact), lack of initiative and hypoactivity, and lack of emotional modulation (which suggests an early mood disorder). Such a clinical constellation confirms Kanner's idea of an innate inability to form the usual affective contact with people. Moreover, it seems very close to prominent depressive symptoms, supporting DeLong's hypothesis (2004) that idiopathic forms of autism, not associated with clear brain damage, might be related to familial major mood psychopathology and could represent an early-life phenotype of major mood disorder. The fact that among the symptoms one of the more frequently rated was hypoactivity accounts for the emphasis recently placed on motor development in autism. Teitelbaum et al. (1998) have supported this point of view that movement disturbances play an intrinsic part in autism from birth. Moreover, we could consider that hypoactivity has an important basic role in the lack of initiative and seeking for contact that characterize these infants. The possibility to have an evaluation of symptoms during the first year of life has allowed us to observe how the frequency of the symptom constellation shows a remarkable growth from the first semester of life up to the second one. Symptoms increasing in the second semester of life have at least three implications. First, the identified constellation seems specific and continuous enough. Second, it makes these symptoms easier to detect, and confirms the existence of an opportunity for early diagnosis between 6 and 12 months, as suggested by Baranek (1999), who reported the presence of subtle sensorimotor abnormalities at 9–12 months and suggested that this period is a special window for early diagnosis. Third, the increasing of symptoms in most autism cases during the second semester of life can shed light on the pathophysiology of autism; in particular, it makes our clinical observational data closer to Courchesne, Carper, and Akshoomoff's (2003) report of two phases of brain-growth abnormality: a reduced size at birth, followed by a sudden and excessive increase in head size in the second semester. Finally we could hypothesize a different timing for the expression of the Initial Pathological Processes proposed by Mundy and Crowson (1997) as a cybernetic model of autism, where an initial functional developmental disorder feeds back upon itself to give rise to additional and pernicious neurobiological disturbances associated with autism. We suggest that this initial pathological process can be detected at an early stage through a clinical pattern characterized by withdrawal, hypoactivity, lack of initiative, and mood difficulties. The presence of a limited set of increasing symptoms during developmentally sensitive periods could orient early-intervention programmes tailored to modify the natural course of the disorder.

From symptoms to competencies

The still-open issues raised from our research is whether symptoms emerge at the same time as the regression of competencies (as if the former were the negative of the latter), or whether symptoms are responsible for the lack of appearance of some competence, or whether symptoms are present from an earlier age but do not inhibit the normal course of competencies until a certain age. For this reason we thought that it could be helpful to define these two aspects of variation in the early course independently rather than assuming that late onset of symptoms invariably implies loss of skills and vice versa. A better understanding of the reciprocal interference between development (and regression) of competencies and onset of symptoms can lead to the understanding of the core clinical problem in autism, which is how the potential operation of genetic or other factors might be expressed during different critical periods (Mundy & Neal, 2001). From the very beginning of our research we were surprised by the fact that all infants who subsequently were diagnosed with autism (both early and late onset) showed during their first year of life some sequences of good social performance, as recorded in the home movies. Sequences of protoconversations with adults made a deep impression on us, and these observations have modified our point of view about autism. We became less interested in recognizing autistic symptoms in home movies and much more curious about the presence of typical competencies showed by these children. According to infant research, we advanced our research starting from the assumption of a socially competent infant (Stern, 1985). At this point, we prepared a Grid for the study of typical behaviours, which we started to apply to the home movies of our children with autism. In this Grid we have grouped specific behaviours of the child into two developmental areas: social behaviour and intersubjectivity. In this way we have differentiated items referring to an innate interest towards social stimuli from items referring to infant's intentionality performed towards the control of other persons' subjectivity. This differentiation between social behaviour and intersubjectivity arises from Trevarthen's description of purposeful intersubjectivity as a fundamental item for human development (Trevarthen & Aitken, 2001). Intersubjectivity—where infant's intentionality is performed towards the control of other persons' subjectivity—is clearly distinguished from the infant's subjectivity, where infant's intentionality is performed towards inanimate objects.

The core deficit in intersubjectivity

In our first research (Maestro et al., 2001), we used a presence/absence method (in which the appearance of a behaviour in the home movies was sufficient to consider the infant competent, assuming that if the behaviour were present once, it meant that the baby would thereafter be able to use it competently in different situations), and we found an important difference between autistic and typical children in behaviours belonging to the area of intersubjectivity, but only very small differences for items in the area of social behaviour. This latter finding means that infants with autism also display many social behaviours; however, they show a lower number of intersubjective competencies (such as pointing comprehension, anticipation of the aims of the other, declarative pointing, or communicative gestures). We have described this finding as an early developmental disconnection between basic social behaviour and intersubjectivity. This developmental disconnection confirms the need for distinguishing the domain of intersubjectivity from the domain of social behaviours in early autism. According to this point of view, babies with autism could have specific difficulties in coordinating basic social competencies with intersubjectivity. They seem able to concentrate on simple social behaviour (i.e. to look at) rather than on the social behaviour as a part of a whole dyadic intersubjective interaction. The fact that infants later diagnosed with autism show, during the first year of life, the presence of basic social behaviours could be the reason for the difficulty for parents to detect a disturbance and for clinicians to propose a diagnosis. In fact, parents—and, even more, the clinicians—are prone to think that these social behaviours will develop into more complex dyadic interactions.

Difficulties in anticipation of others' aims

The presence/absence method applied in our research has showed two specific behaviours, belonging to the intersubjective area, that are able to differentiate, at a very early age, typical children from the pathological ones. The absence of such behaviours provides an early, temporal-specific index of developmental risk. "Anticipation of others' aim" and "Pointing comprehension" are, in fact, represented in significantly fewer infants during the first six months of life who are later diagnosed with autism. In other words, in the first six months of life, children with autism seem to have more difficulty in foreseeing the aims of other people, in anticipating others' intentions, and therefore they are less interested in the caregiver's actions. In the second six months of life, we found significant differences in the development of communicative social gestures like "bye-bye", "good", "clap". The lack of these communicative gestures maintains its significance throughout the second year of life, so that at 18 months of age it stands out as a specific major difficulty in addition to the deficit of joint attention.

The study of social and non-social attention

Despite these interesting results, the stage of our research characterized by looking for the presence or absence of specific behaviours
became more and more unsatisfactory for our group. In fact, during
the period when we were applying the presence/absence method,
we also pointed out that, while for typical children we needed only a
few minutes of home movies to codify the behaviour as present, for
children with autism much more time was necessary. We therefore
began to be less convinced about the assumption that it was enough
for the behaviour to be present just once to be considered established
and consolidated, as opposed to those cases where that behaviour was
displayed many times and in different situations. These numerous observations have moved the direction of our research to a quantitative
study of specific behaviours in the infant. We started to follow a more
complex frequency method instead of the simpler presence/absence
method. Taking into consideration the frequencies of these behaviours,
and not only their presence or absence, we expected to find greater differences between autistic and typical children during the first months
of life not only in intersubjectivity, but also in social behaviour area.
For this new research we adapted the Grid we had used in the previous research, and we chose eleven behaviours more representative of
the growing infant's social competencies. These behaviours were then
grouped into three developmental areas. The first two areas are composed of dichotomous items. The area of Social Attention is composed
of four items: *looking at people; orienting towards people; smiling at people;
vocalizing to people*. The area of Non-Social Attention is composed of
four specular item: *looking at objects; orienting towards objects; smiling
at objects; vocalizing to objects*. The third area is composed of items that
refer to more global Social Behaviours: *seeking contact; anticipating the
other's aim; postural attunement*. Carrying out of this new research based
on frequencies of typical behaviours has led us towards the exploration of the early competition between social and non-social attention
in early autism.

Less social attention

In fact, in the home movies these infants exhibited a specific qualitative pattern of attention, highly consistent with theories predicting
that children with autism have a specific deficit in attending to social
stimuli. Our first study in this direction was focused on the first six

months of life (Maestro, Muratori, & Cavallaro, 2002). At this very early age, we found a significantly lower interest in social stimuli in infants with autism compared to typical children. However, we did not find attention towards objects as a behaviour that would enable us to distinguish infants with autism from infants with typical development. These parallel results indicate that, in autism, attention is not implicated as a primary function, but as an elective function only towards social stimuli. Our results indicate that attention towards objects is not impaired during the first six months of life and that, instead of a more general problem with responsiveness to all types of sensory stimuli, in infants with autism there is a specific deficit in social attention from the beginning. This early selective difficulty in attention towards people could impair attention monitoring, and this impairment could be an essential factor involved in the pathway leading to autism. The specific deficit in social attention seems a primary feature of infants later diagnosed with autism, and it could limit the coordination of attention with affect. This coordination is essential for the development of the ability to engage in interactions involving emotional signals and motor gestures. The child's capacity to connect emotions to attention and action begins to become more apparent between 9 and 15 months of age as the infant shifts from simple patterns of engagement to complex chains of emotional reciprocity. We suggest that social attention has a central role in the building-up of these simple patterns of engagement and that its early deficit could prevent this critical shifting from simple to complex patterns of engagement.

Moreover, the early specific deficit in attention towards social stimuli may interfere in the expression of the innate primary intersubjectivity (Trevarthen & Aitken, 2001) that is an active and immediately responsive and conscious appreciation of the adult's communicative intentions. We suggest that the early deficit of social attention could be the basic mechanism for the well-known impairment of intersubjectivity in children with autism.

Longer span of attention to objects

Unlike intersubjectivity, attention towards objects is preserved. In fact, this type of attention does not distinguish infants later diagnosed with autism from typical infants: object exploration—involving a few activity patterns such as mouthing, waving, and banging—tends to be the same in both groups. However, it should be emphasized that there is an essential difference between a person doing things in relation to physical world and the control of communication between persons: two people can share control, each can predict what the other will know and do; physical objects cannot predict intentions, and they have no social relationships. By extending our research on social and non-social attention, we have had the possibility to examine early social and non-social attention at two points: the first and the second six months of life. Two most relevant findings arose from this research (Maestro, Muratori, & Cavallaro, 2005; Maestro, Muratori, & Cesari, 2005). The first consists of the decrease, during the second semester of life, in differences between children later diagnosed with autism and typical children as far as attention to social stimuli are concerned. The other finding consists of the increase in behaviours regarding attention to non-social stimuli, which is present in both groups but is more evident in infants with autism, so that by the end of the first year these children are significantly more attracted by objects compared to typical children, whose social attention always remains at a higher level. The increasing attention to objects between 6 and 12 months also involves explorative activity with objects, and the home movies of children with autism are not different in this respect from home movies of typical children. The latter data confirm that stereotypy with objects is not present from the beginning and is not useful as a predictor in the first year of life. It probably becomes more obvious after the second year of life, and we can hypothesize that it is a long-term consequence of earlier social dysfunctions, which do not allow enlargement of the knowledge of objects through interactive social actions.

Joint attention as a post-cursor

We have to consider that social attention is one of the basic functions for the development of joint attention that is known to be problematic in children with autism after 12 months of age (Sigman, Dijamco, Gratier, & Rozga). Joint attention is considered a pivotal skill in autism (Charman, 2003). Pivotal can refer both to "acting as a fulcrum" and to "being of crucial importance" or "the thing on which progress depends". In typical development, joint attention behaviours emerge between 6 and 12 months and involve the triadic coordination or sharing of attention between the infant, another person, and an object or event. The term encompasses a complex of behavioural forms, including gaze and point following, showing, and pointing. As far as pointing is concerned, the critical distinction may not be the imperative (where triadic exchanges serve an instrumental or requesting function) versus declarative (where triadic exchanges serve to share awareness of an object or event) level. Rather, the degree to which a child is monitoring and regulating the attention to the other person in relation to objects determines the severity of the deficit seen in autism. This does not mean that joint-attention impairments cause autism. However, it does suggest that joint attention is a critical "downstream" effect of earlier brain psychopathology (Charman, 2003). Much interest has focused on the role of joint attention as a "precursor" to later theory-of-mind development in both typically developing children and children with autism. Acting as a "precursor" involves joint attention growing or transforming into the later theory-of-mind abilities. However, recognition that joint attention is not a starting point but merely a staging post for early social communicative development—and hence a "post-cursor" of earlier psychological and developmental processes— focuses attention on what earlier impairments underlie the impaired development of joint-attention skills in autism. Therefore, studying the possible precursor of joint attention is of seminal importance for the comprehension of autism. This investigation is needed to clarify whether a deficit in attentional skills may serve as a precursor to difficulties in socially directed behaviours, such as joint attention, which involve a triadic coordination of attention between the infant, another person, and an object (Bakeman & Adamson, 1984). The specific focus on the frequencies of an infant's behaviours related to two types of attention—attention to people and attention to objects—could allow us to provide data about one of the most important candidate precursors to joint attention. The intriguing and counterintuitive finding of a decrease in differences in social attention during the second semester of life deserves special attention. It may seem somewhat surprising that early significant differences in social attention are not confirmed later on. One explanation could be related to the development, in typical children, of person awareness versus object awareness as an essential precursor to joint attention. As described by Trevarthen and Aitken (2001), infants are proved to possess an active and immediately responsive conscious interest for adult intentions (which was named primary intersubjectivity); during these earliest stages of postnatal development, faces are highly salient to typically developing infants. Around the middle of the first year, the baby's increasing interest in objects competes with this earlier interest in persons and, just before the end of the first year, leads, through shared and lively games with objects, to the development of joint attention. This has profound effects on infant development, creating a new form of person–person–object awareness (which was named secondary intersubjectivity). This is shown in our study through the clear rapprochement in typical children between the interest displayed towards people and that displayed towards objects. On the other hand, children with autism are seen to grow up in their social and non-social abilities, but with a totally different and divergent behavioural organization from that of typical children. We could hypothesize that while the rapprochement of interest in people and in objects represents a developmental process that allows joint attention to emerge, the deficit of early social-attentional skills we have observed during the first six months of life in children with autism, and the divergent pathway of social and non-social attention in the second semester of life, could prevent joint attention from emerging, even when social contact seems to improve. The very different pathways of social and non-social attention in very young children with autism allow recognition of joint attention as a "postcursor". Our findings suggest that the early decrease in the tendency to direct attention to social stimuli (together with an excessive attention to objects) may create in infants later diagnosed with autism an atypical developmental gap and a later deficit of integration of social and non-social attention during the second half of the first year of life. This deficit may be associated with a disruption of the early self-organizing process in social learning, and the resulting impoverishment of social information during the first year of life may be so significant as to contribute to disruptions of typical brain development through impairment of experience-expectant neuro-developmental processes. The early decrease in the tendency to direct attention to social stimuli in infants with autism, coupled with the secondary lower exposure to people, may create an atypical developmental gap and a later deficit of integration of social and non-social attention during the second half of the first year of life. This deficit may be associated with a disruption of the early self-organizing process in social learning; the resulting impoverishment of social information during the first year of life may be so significant as to contribute to the disruptions of experience-expectant neural development in the social brain, which comprises a diverse set of frontal, limbic. and temporal lobe circuitry. In fact, the early selective difficulty in attention towards people could impair attention monitoring and the coordination of attention and affect that is necessary for joint attention. The attenuation of the typical capacity of the child to attend to and process social information can deprive the developing child with autism of the amount of social information that is needed for normal shaping of neural connections involved in the early neuro-developmental processes (Dawson, Munson, & Estes, 2002; Mundy & Neal, 2001). Our findings (consistent with the home-movies research conducted by Osterling and Dawson, who pointed out that 8-month-old infants with autism are much less likely to orient when their name is called than normally developing infants) raise the possibility that a child with autism has a specific problem in orienting to persons. Children with autism have attentional problems in their ability to orient towards human voices, and this enables us to form the hypothesis that it is a part of a basic dysfunction regarding human relationships. Indeed, our data may suggest that children with autism have, instead of a more general problem with responsiveness to all types of sensory stimuli, a specific deficit in social attention, which appears from the beginning and does not depend on maturation to become apparent.

Recommendations for future research on early symptoms

As far as early-screening instruments are concerned, we should con-sider different temporal domains of an infant's development as critical targets during the first year of life. While in the first six months "to look at a person" remains a key item, after the first six months the de-velopment of some "human-being connecting" behaviours (looking, smiling, vocalizing) may mask the social deficit. At this age we should focus more on behaviours exploring the quality of infants' attention to inanimate objects: items such as "orienting, smiling, or vocalizing to objects" could be more indicative of a deficit in the infant's ability of discriminating social from non-social contact, and they should be bet-ter analysed. We should consider that early-onset children are charac-terized by a clearer and persistent early deficit in social attention. For these children, the early symptomatic patterns (mainly withdrawn, poor social interaction, hypoactivity, lack of initiative, and lack of emotional modulation) may involve a different early organization due to the interrelation between presence of symptoms and absence of ex-pected behaviours. Differently, early high rates in social and non-social attention could reduce in regressive cases the first emerging signs of autism and may mask the first deviations. Nevertheless, our research shows that both autism groups have the distinguishing feature of a higher non-social attention across the first eighteen months of life. The longer attention span for objects can result in an abnormal neural for-mation of the brain from the beginning and in an altered development of experience-expectant neuro-developmental processes. It is possible that the typical divergent and periodically competing development of object awareness and person awareness, during the first year, is derailed because of the clear preference for physical objects. This distinguishing feature has many clinical and theoretical implications. First, because physical objects cannot predict intentions and have no social relationship, the preference for physical objects can impede the development of both primary intersubjectivity (based on basic social motives of the infants) and secondary intersubjectivity (based on the person–person–object awareness). Second, the higher attention to objects may also further explain the core deficit of joint attention in autism. Our research suggests that joint-attention deficit in autism is twofold: in fact, besides the lower social attention of the early-onset group, in the whole autism group there is a clear and permanent prevalence of non-social attention, as opposed to typical children whose social attention is always higher compared to non-social attention. In particular, this pattern, characterized by the predominance of interest in objects, seems peculiar of regressive cases also when social attention grows up during the second semester of life. From this point of view, both early-onset and regressive cases are characterized by an altered competition between social and non-social attention, which probably means an altered organization of the brain area for face and object processing. Third, we can reason that the long attention span for objects can result in the deficit of central coherence in autism. According to this view, autism is suggested to be a state of retarded concept-formation (individuals with autism see the parts, not the whole; they see the trees where we see the forest). Concepts are groupings of the attributes of objects, deriving from the sharing of the experience of the objects with others. Once the brain learns such critical groupings, the "object" attributes are inhibited from conscious awareness; the details are inhibited when the concept network is activated (Snyder, Bossomaier, & Mitchell, 2004). We suggest that the formation of this concept network needs a sharing of object experience with the other. Without this social sharing, object experience remains limited to details with difficulties in the development of a central coherence.

Two final questions remain unanswered—namely, what the actual autistic process is and at what age it is detectable. Our studies confirm the hypothesis that autism is characterized by a specific pattern of positive and negative signs apparent from 18 months of life. This final step of autism seems to be a long-term consequence of earlier and less obvious dysfunctions. Our research show that this final pattern can be reached through two different pathways: one consists of an early lack of social attention associated with higher non-social attention and early autism signs; the other consists of an early and increasing prevalence in interest for non-social stimuli without a clear reduction of social attention and without the presence of positive signs of autism during the first year of life. Therefore, non-social attention—that is, longer attention span for objects—might be included as one of the items to investigate in screening tools for autism.

The impairment of social behaviours in the first semester of life may be considered a risk to development of early-onset autism, and this remains true during the first eighteen months of life. Besides, the period between age 12 and 18 months represents a second sensitive window to detect the emerging decrease of social attention and the appearance of the first autism signs in regressive children. However, also for these children, signs of autism may be preceded by the strong interest in non-social stimuli during the first year of life. This abnormal prevalence of interest for objects in late-onset autism leads us to believe that, for these subjects, the idea of a normal development before the regression is only apparent. We hypothesize that the particularly intense interest in non-social stimuli can be the first sign of an atypical development and could be considered a red flag in the first year of life.

CHAPTER FOUR

Early signs related
to posture and communication:
the child's attitude, and the mother's reaction

Laurent Danon-Boileau

The aim of this chapter is to point out a certain number of signs that could indicate future difficulties in the domain of communication and interaction. In this respect, it is clear that a sign is not necessarily a predictor of autism; it is only the possible mark of difficulties to come. And, of course, there are children who originally present with some of the signs we are trying to spot but who later come back to normal and no longer exhibit any disturbances.

The data on which we are working are family videos of children who have been diagnosed as autistic at the age of 4 years.

Research into early signs of autism is now commonly carried out. However, we have a certain number of specific ways of treating the problem. First, we are interested in very young children. And, of course, the younger the child is, the more the signs that the observer has to focus on are related to the child's tonus and posture, because when the child is very young, signs related to preverbal and communicative behaviour (gaze and smile) are restricted. Second, we think that the signs are not only visible on the child's part: a child whose

The research presented in this chapter was conducted in collaboration with Mary-Annick Morel, Marie-Michèle Bourrat, Anne Philippe, Marie Leroy, Caroline Masson, Florence Rouger, Justine Chillet-Krauss, Marianne Baudoin, and Carinne Leibovici.

interaction is problematic tends to alter his or her mother's gestures and speech (syntax and intonation). The communication of the mother is itself also very revealing, and, in fact, her reaction to the child's peculiarities is sometimes more visible than the peculiarities of the child him/herself.

In this chapter, we outline our research protocol and present the data that we have gathered from a comparison between two sisters, one of whom turned out to be autistic, the other normal. We have undertaken a thorough analysis of two parallel and contrasting situations, involving a mother giving a bath to her daughters: first, Julie at 5 months of age; and then, two years later, Tiphaine at 3 months of age. The "same" scene is therefore filmed with each child, and allows comparison. The difference in age is of no importance, as it is Julie, the elder one, who will later turn out to be autistic, and not Tiphaine.

The bath is a particular moment of intimacy in the interaction between mother and child. It is a daily event. However, from the point of view of the child, it is always slightly puzzling: the child is suddenly naked, plunged into water, and has to find its balance in a somewhat peculiar situation. From the point of view of the mother, the situation is, of course, different. While giving a bath to her child, the mother has, in fact, two goals in mind: the goal of care, which is of primary importance for the health and hygiene of the child; and the goal of play, based on pleasure and joint attention. This latter aim is, of course, decisive for good cognitive development, and it is much akin to a format. Ninio and Bruner (1978) showed that the rules of communication are set up in ritualized formats (bath, meal, cuddle, etc.). These situations are repeated thousands of times between the child and a restricted number of people. While getting involved in these episodes, the child comes to acquire the codes that govern human communication.

In our transcripts, we have taken into account the verbal and nonverbal elements of the communication between the child and its adult interlocutor. We have not coded these elements, as a plain description has eventually seemed preferable to allow the reader to measure the variety of indices involved.

We call "verbal" all sounds emitted by any of the participants. For each verbal item, we have noted the variations in prosody: variation of pitch, intensity, and syllabic lengthening. As a rule, we have focused our analysis on the child's behaviour (gaze, mimicking, posture, vocal productions) and on the mother's discourse (lexical and grammatical items, intonation). We name as *interaction* a set of *exchanges* between the two participants. An *exchange* is composed of an *initiative* and its corresponding *answer*. *Initiative* and *answer* do not necessarily imply deliberate intention on behalf of the participants; they are defined by their position in the exchange.

The mother's speech—the children's reactions. How interaction is carried on when the contact is deficient

The children's attitude

Three essential domains were taken into account and observed in the two children: posture, facial expressions, and gaze.

Posture

If we look at Julie's posture and general attitude (Figure 4.1), she seems to be clinging to her own self, with firmly grasped hands. Tiphaine, on the contrary, is quite relaxed.

Moreover, Julie seems to adopt autocentric behaviour: she is not interested in what occurs around her, nor even in her mother's gestures even when she is the target of these gestures. In comparison, when the mother touches Tiphaine, she is arched or she smiles. She lies in the water with her arms peacefully outstretched and sometimes touches her mother's arm .

Facial expressions

Concerning the children's facial expressions and mimicry, Tiphaine is smiling, as has just been said, but sometimes she also opens her

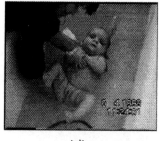
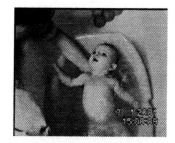

Julie   Tiphaine

Figure 4.1.   Posture.

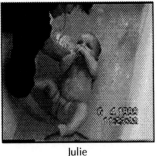 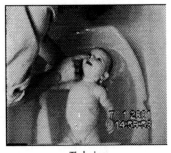

Julie   Tiphaine

Figure 4.2.   Facial expression.

mouth wide, which shows that she is quite attentive to what mother is doing (Figure 4.2). Julie, however, never smiles, and the only mimicry she carries out is a grimace when she is touched by her mother. This visible contrariness on her face is also reflected by her posture: it reveals an extreme tension, expressed by the clenching of her fists or through her putting both hands in her mouth.

Gaze

Unlike Tiphaine, who constantly looks at her mother, Julie makes infrequent and short eye contact. She alternates between moments when she looks at her mother furtively and moments when she looks towards the camera or does not even seem to worry at all about the cameraman or her mother. During these periods she seems to be looking elsewhere, sometimes at her hands.

A closer analysis of the gaze reveals that while the mother baths her daughters in the water, Julie looks her in the eyes, but not constantly (Figure 4.3). The gaze strays elsewhere when the mother takes the

Figure 4.3.   Gaze (Julie).

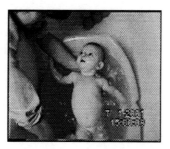

Figure 4.4.   Gaze (Tiphaine).

child away from her face, and the child's gaze goes back to her eyes when the movement brings her back to her face.

Tiphaine, on the other hand, makes constant eye contact (Figure 4.4); the movement of her body has no effect on her gaze. She compensates for the movements of her body through eye and head movements.

In conclusion, it seems that while being bathed, a child experiences a need to cling to something or someone. Tiphaine clings to her mother's gaze and her body is relaxed, unlike Julie, who cannot cling to her mother's gaze and therefore has to cling to her own self.

We would, of course, like to explain these observations, but what theory could make sense of them? In a way, what we see contradicts the provisions of the theory of mind. For example, Julie does not avoid her mother's gaze, contrary to the predictions of such a theory. In fact, she tries to catch her mother's gaze but sometimes cannot. She seems to lose her mother's gaze because she cannot adjust herself and produce the compensatory movement she should produce to counterbalance the up-and-down movements of her body in her mother's arms. Here, the idea of dissociation (or of lack of intermodality) would probably be a more adequate description of the facts: in effect, the explanation for Julie's loss of eye contact could be a failure to use her perception of the body movements induced by her mother to produce adequate compensatory movements of gaze adjustment.

Julie's poor eye contact, absence of mimicry, and queer posture (her clinging to her own self) clearly indicate—at least in this scene—that something is going wrong, that this is not ordinary behaviour. The comparison with her sister's bath in that respect is quite revealing: Tiphaine is smiling, relaxed, and constantly looking in her mother's eyes. She produces signs that can be clearly interpreted by the mother and the observer as signs of pleasure.

This difference, of course, explains why the mother cannot behave in the same way with both children. This is also clearly revealed by objective features in the language and communication she addresses to each of them.

The mother's language

The frequency of speech depends on the child

We noticed that the mother speaks more to the child who later turned out to be autistic than to the child who has no problems.

The nature of the mother's statements mainly depends on what the child does and the behaviour she adopts. With Julie, mother seems somewhat at a loss (Extract 1). She cannot interpret the attitude of her

Extract 1. Frequency of speech: Julie

Time (min/sec)	Nonverbal mother	Verbal mother	Verbal Julie	Nonverbal Julie
02'23"		M22: t'éclabousses? (↑) t'éclabousses avec tes pieds, chérie (↓) ["you're splashing around with your feet, dearie !"]	J31: throat sounds	J31: looks towards C and moves her feet
02'27"		M23: <laughs> (−)		J32: switches off eye contact (with C) and clings on to her own belly with her two hands
02'28"				J33: puts both hands in her mouth
02'30"				J34: puts both hands in front of her eyes
02'32"	Smiles	M24: <laughs> (−)		
02'33"				J35: turns down her hands and looks towards C
02'34"		M25: mm mm mm :::: (↑ +)		J36: puts both her hands in her mouth
02'35"			J37: / o :: o :: e::/	

Note: See Appendix for explanation of abbreviations and symbols used in these extracts.

daughter. Julie does not make intense and long eye contact; she groans, she looks at her hands, and so forth. Mother tries to make sense of all these disturbing manifestations. She tries to put a name to her daughter's behaviour, but, in fact, she cannot guess what is going on, what the child wants or feels. And this is clearly revealed in her speech. She always needs to say something, perhaps to reassure herself, but also because she thinks that speech is the ultimate means to keep contact with the child: if she remained silent, the child would no longer pay any attention to what is going on. In fact, when mother stops speaking to Julie, she suddenly seems ill at ease and laughs.

While her mother keeps silent, Julie (02'27" and 02'34") remains centred on her own self and makes no attempt at turning towards her mother. It is only when mother speaks again that the child returns to the interaction.

Name, nicknames, and pronouns as attempts at establishing or maintaining contact

Calling somebody by his or her name is an attempt to obtain an answer from the person and secure the person's attention. The use of the first name has an appellative function and makes it possible to call out to someone who threatens to escape or avoid interaction. Generally, one calls a person by his or her first name when he or she is far away and out of eyeshot. Calling a person by his or her first name can also be a way to establish or confirm joint attention. We have already noted the difficulties that Julie seems to have in establishing eye contact with her mother. This, of course, gives the impression that she is not paying attention to what is happening and especially not to what her mother does. We can thus suppose that it is because mother tries to establish an interaction with Julie (and because this interaction is constantly threatened) that she calls her by her first name (Extract 2).

Extract 2.   Names and nicknames: Julie

Name	Nicknames
M2: oh :: Julie	M3: oh :: ça ça fait du bien :: hein? ma puce ["that's good, eh? little one"]
M9: oh :: Julie elle nage ["oh, look at Julie, she's swimming"]	
M17: petite main à Julie? ["Julie's little hand?"]	M22: t'éclabousses avec tes pieds, chérie ["you're splashing around with your feet darling"]
	M26: ok bébé ["ok baby"]

In comparison, when mother is giving Tiphaine bath, she establishes regular and reciprocal visual contact, and this could explain why she does not need this strategy of calling the child by her first name.

Contrary to first names, emotive nicknames (such as "my little one", "baby", etc.) do not have a vocative function but a phatic function: they are used to maintain contact between partners, not to initiate it. This is why, unlike with names, they are placed at the end of the statements and not at the beginning.

With Julie, the use of these nicknames seems to correspond to two different purposes: as a way to maintain contact, and as a means to indicate to the child that a reaction is expected from her. In other words, aside from their obvious emotional value, these nicknames also reveal a communicative intention. They are numerous because the mother has no other way of making contact with Julie. With Julie, the mother is bound to use these very powerful emotional means, and she has difficulty in modulating the strength of the emotion conveyed by her speech. Her language is a constant attempt to reinforce communication and exchanges with the child.

Pronouns

We have just seen that mother mostly (though not always) calls and refers to Julie by her name or nicknames. The situation is totally different with Tiphaine. With Tiphaine, the mother mostly uses pronouns to address her and for references.

The position adopted by the mother towards her child is different when she says "you" (*tu*) and "one" (*on*) (Extracts 3, 4). When she says "you" and refers to her daughter, she is addressing her child in a direct way, in a sort of face-to-face relationship. On the other hand, when she points to the father behind the camera and uses "*on*", she establishes with her child a joint attention: their gaze has the same target, and their identities cease to be completely differentiated, at least in the representation of the mother: they share a common interest in the same person.

Generally speaking, the pronominal form "you" allows the mother to comment on an action of the child or express a judgement about her attitude. The target of the speech is directly focused on the child and is located in the here-and-now. This accounts for the fact that this pronoun is being used only with verbs in the present tense. The mother employs "you" to refer to what she is carrying out.

Extract 3.   Pronouns: Julie

Tu [you]	On [one]	Elle [she]
M5/M6: tu barbotes? ["you're having good time in the water?"]	M12: on va faire les cheveux? ["let's wash your hair, ok?"]	M8: Julie elle nage ["Look at Julie, she's swimming"]
M16: tu regardes ta main? ["you're looking at your hand?"]	M29: on va mouiller le ventre? ["now let's wash your tummy?"]	
M22: t'éclabousses? ["you're splashing around, are you?"]	M31/M32: on rince? ["let's rinse the soap off?"]	

Extract 4.   Pronouns. Tiphaine

Tu [you]	On [one]
M16: t'es grande, hein? [look how tall you are"]	M12: on filme ton bain pour la postérité ["we're filming your bath for posterity"]
M17: tu touches tout dans la baignoire ["you can touch both sides of the tub"]	
M21: t'aimes bien l'eau? ["you like the water, don't you?"]	

In everyday French, the pronoun *"on"* is generally a loose equivalent of the use of "we"—that is, two persons or more sharing the same thought. Therefore, as a rule, the use of *"on"* corresponds to the first-person-plural pronoun and refers to the dyad resulting from the association of mother and child. It refers to the common subject of the interaction the mother is carrying out with her children. Yet in some cases, it can also correspond to an indeterminate reference, comparable to "one" in English.

Interestingly enough, the values of the *"on"* pronoun does seem to be different with Julie and Tiphaine. Generally the mother uses *"on"* with Julie when she wants to explain what she is going to do next—that is, when she is about to wash her. Using this pronoun, she associates her child to the action to come, but not as a full co-participant. With reference to the future, *"on"* does not fuse mother and child into a true dyad. In that context, *"on"* is closer to the value of the first-person-singular pronoun "I", even though, of course, the mother is waiting for a participation on behalf of her daughter . In other words, in her discourse, the form *"on"* is an attempt at, a plea for, shared attention, but nothing more. If the mother had referred to her self by "I" instead of *"on"*, she would of course have excluded her child from all agency. But her "*on*", in the context of future action, does not refer to a clear mother-child community of interaction.

The various occurrences of the pronominal form "*on*" in the interactions with Tiphaine follow a different kind of logic. The mother employs the form with the intention of establishing a community of thought between the child, the father behind the camera, and herself concerning the same object of attention. There are, therefore, two differences between the uses of "'*on*" in the discourse addressed to Tiphaine and the use of "*on*" in the discourse addressed to Julie: with Tiphaine, "*on*" refers to three persons; in addition, "*on*" has become a thinking community, not an acting community, so to speak.

Now let us focus on the pronoun "*elle*" [she]. It is used in structures such as "*Julie, elle* . . ." and constitute an anaphora of the name "Julie" which establishes the topic of the statement. This type of linguistic structure is quite common in French. In oral speech, the anaphoric pronoun often follows the name. However, in the present case, Julie is facing her mother and looking at her while her mother speaks to her. By addressing her like that, mother excludes Julie from the situation of communication. She is the one the mother talks *about*, not the one she talks *to*. The discourse of the mother no longer builds a fiction of a dialogue shared with her child. Julie could not take her place as an interlocutor in what the discourse of the mother builds around her. She is the centre of interest for both her parents, but she is not assigned the position of a virtual interlocutor.

Prosody

Intensity.   The mother adopts two kinds of linguistic behaviour: with Tiphaine, most of the time she speaks with a low intensity, except when she wants to stress a statement in particular because the child has expressed a reaction that pleases the mother (Extracts 5, 6). The situation is quite different with Julie: the intensity of the statements is stronger, but the mother lowers the pitch of her voice when she tries to create joint attention (Extracts 7, 8).

Intonation.   The variations of the pitch (F_0) of intonation in the mother's discourse correspond to various communicative intentions. Mother raises F_0 to stimulate her child and maintain face-to-face interaction. It is a way to require attention. When mother reiterates the same rising melody several times in a row at the beginning of a sentence, it is because she has not received from her child any clear sign

Extract 5.   Prosody: Tiphaine

Verbal mother	Nonverbal Tiphaine
M9: oh ! qu'est-ce que c'est?($\downarrow$ +)	
	T14: looks at sponge

Extract 6.   Prosody: Tiphaine

Verbal mother	Nonverbal Tiphaine
	T23: is cambered
M14: oh :: ($\uparrow$) c'est agréa :: ble ça ($\downarrow$ +)	

of entry into the interaction and participation in it. This explains why this type of intonation is much more frequent with Julie than with Tiphaine (Extract 9). Under normal circumstances, the intonation falls at the end of a sentence if the discourse comes to an end. However, when the mother talks to Julie, her intonation always rises, as if she is afraid of losing contact. With Tiphaine, though, it varies; it can either fall or rise when there is something to be added.

The mother's variations of pitch are definitely more noticeable when she speaks to Julie than to Tiphaine. This again is because she is never sure of catching Julie's attention and participation. She then makes constant modulations to attract Julie's attention and create

Extract 7.   Prosody: Julie

Verbal mother	Verbal Julie	Nonverbal Julie
	J21: throat sounds	J21: looks at her hands
M16: tu regardes ta main? ($\uparrow$ –)		

Extract 8.   Prosody: Julie

Nonverbal mother	Verbal Mother	Nonverbal Julie
Puts her hand on Julie's belly	M29: ah :: ($\downarrow$ –) ça fait du bien ($\rightarrow$ –) / on va mouiller le ventre? ($\uparrow$ +)	J44: curls up and looks at her body

Extract 9.   Intonation: Julie and Tiphaine

pitch (F$_0$)	Julie	Tiphaine
rising	M3: ça ça fait du bien:: hein	M2: oh la la
	M9: Julie elle na::ge	M4: /wa di dõ/
	M11: /pik/	M5: /wa::/
	M15: ça fait du::bien::	M7: regarde là ["look there"]
	M25: mm mm mm	M11: la caméra? ["the camera?"]
	M30: /le bõbõ/	M12: on filme ton bain pour la postérité?
	M34: sous les (↓) bras:: ["under arms?"]	M13: oui?
	M35: les che(↓)veux ["the hair"]	M15: oh oui::
	M41: Ben il filme son bébé ["he films his baby"]	M21: t'aimes bien l'eau?
	plus all the questions	
falling	M2: Julie	M3: c'est bien:: ["it's good"]
	M3: ma puce	M9: qu'est-ce que c'est? ["what is it?"]
	M22: t'éclabousses avec tes pieds chérie	M14: c'est agréa ::ble ça
	M26: ok bébé	
	M36: un poisson ["a fish"]	
level	M18: mm	M1: qui est-ce qui va être nettoyée avec l'éponge? ["who will be cleaned with the sponge?"]
	M19: /mekwake/	M2: ça c'est chouette ça
	M27: /kwak/	M15: mm
	M29: ça fait du bien	M16: t'es grande hein?
	M33: les pieds:: ["feet"]	M17: tu touches tout / dans la baignoire
		M18: des pieds à la tête ["to feet to head"]

interaction. The constant use of rising melodies reveals this fear of absence of contact. Yet it also reveals the mother's difficulty in seeing her child as a full co-participator.

A medium pitch with almost no variations is more current in conversations between adults than in a language addressed to a child. There are few instances of that type of intonation in the discourse addressed to Tiphaine, which supports the idea that mother considers Tiphaine as a partner in communication and a co-thinker, contrary to what happens with Julie.

Lengthening.   Syllable lengthening does not have the same value in the discourse of the mother when she is addressing Julie and when she is addressing Tiphaine (Extract 10). With Tiphaine, lengthening has a positive value, supporting maternal comments on the pleasure

Extract 10.   Syllable lengthening: Julie and Tiphaine

Julie	Tiphaine
M3: ça ça fait du bien::	M3: c'est bien::
M9: Julie elle na::ge	M14: c'est agré::ble ça
M15: ça fait du:: bien::	M15: oh oui::
M33: les pieds	
M34: sous les ::	

the child is feeling in the bath, whereas with Julie it conveys an affect of appeasement when the child appears tensed and not reactive to her mother's comments on her actions and reactions. For example, when the mother puts her hand on her daughter's belly, Julie reacts negatively by bending herself and groaning. At that moment, mother seems to use the lengthening of syllables as a way to calm her daughter and gain her confidence.

Deictics and presentatives.   We have focused our analysis upon the use of "that" and of "it is". The role of the deictic "that" is different according to whether it appears at the beginning or the end of a sentence. At the end of a sentence, "that" indicates that the enunciator wants to make sure that the judgement he has issued is clearly referred by his co-speaker to the element of the situation to which it has to be referred. It is used in a way to prevent misinterpretation, but on the assumption of joint attention. However, at the beginning of a statement, "that" only directs the child's attention towards what is happening. It is meant to establish joint attention. Thus we can understand why the mother uses "that" at the beginning of her sentences with Julie (Extracts 11, 12, 13): she constantly tries to recreate shared attention, and therefore has to focus the child's attention on her object of speech with each new comment.

The expression *"c'est"* appears in the discourse addressed to Tiphaine (Extracts 14, 15, 16). It seems to be a sign of the mother's will to measure and appreciate her child's state of mind. If it appeared in an interrogative form, it would imply that the child does not pay attention to her mother. But we have already noted that Tiphaine constantly looks at her. So here, the use of *"c'est"* appears as the mark of preliminary shared attention between the two participants: it cannot be used if the speaker does not have a representation, even a vague one, of the other's thoughts.

Extract 11.   Deictics and presentatives: Julie

Verbal Mother	Verbal Julie	Nonverbal Julie
	J3: throat sounds	
		J4: moves her feet
M3: oh:: ça ça fait du bien hein? ma puce		

Extract 12.   Deictics and presentatives: Julie

Verbal mother	Verbal Julie	Nonverbal Julie
		J16: moves her feet, grimaces, and turns her gaze
	J17: throat sounds	
M15: oh ça fait du:: bien::		

Extract 13.   Deictics and presentatives: Julie

Verbal mother	Verbal Julie	Nonverbal Julie
		J42: furtive sideways gazes and movements of arms and legs
		J43: puts her hands on her belly, stops her movements, and looks at C
M29: ah :: ça fait du bien		

If our assumptions are correct, such markers as *"ça"* and *"c'est"* reveal the position of the child in the interaction in the mother's mind and the state of joint attention she considers they are in. As a result, even if the mother's judgements are the result of her subjectivity only, even though none of her children can speak, when she talks to Tiphaine what she says is not sheer monologue. Her utterances have the status of a response in a dialogue, as if she were talking to someone who could have an opinion and could answer. Her comments show her expectations towards her child and the receptive behaviour she projects into her as the interaction develops.

We have also noticed differences in the quantity of language the mother addresses to each of her children, and the ways she refers to them. Why is that so? It all stems from the fact that she probably feels that something is going wrong with Julie. Consequently, she

Extract 14.   Deictics and presentatives: Tiphaine

Verbal mother	Nonverbal Tiphaine
M1: qui est-ce qui va être nettoyée avec l'éponge?	T1: looks at M, mouth open
M2: oh la la, ça c'est chouette, ça	

Extract 15.   Deictics and presentatives: Tiphaine

Nonverbal mother	Verbal mother	Nonverbal Tiphaine
		T3: looks at (M)
Puts the sponge under T's chin	M3: oh c'est bien	

Extract 16.   Deictics and presentatives: Tiphaine

Nonverbal mother	Verbal mother	Nonverbal Tiphaine
Moves her hand under T's body		T23: is cambered
	M14: oh:: c'est agréa ::ble ça	

constantly tries to attract her attention and maintain contact with her. In that respect, the use of the child's name, especially at the end of her sentences, has no vocative function but is an effort to maintain contact. With Julie, the mother is constantly insecure. She does not feel sure about what her daughter does or feels. Her empathy falls short; she is puzzled, and this is revealed by her rising intonation. In fact, all her sentences look like questions, no matter what she actually says to her daughter. With Tiphaine, however, the mother is able to interpret what is going on, and her intonation varies. When she talks to Tiphaine, the mother speaks to a co-locutor, a potential co-thinker (anticipatory illusion): once she has expressed an opinion, she wants to be sure that Tiphaine is sharing that appreciation with her; she is seeking consensus with that imaginary interlocutor. That is the role of "ça" in "c'est chouette, ça". This form of discourse—with the pronoun "ça" at the end of the sentence—typically marks a request for assent addressed to someone with whom the contact is already established. This form never appears when the mother talks to Julie. Instead of "ça" at the end of the sentence, we find a vocative ("Julie, ma puce"), which shows the mother's efforts to keep her child's attention.

The language of any mother is marked by the universal ambition to consider the child as a true partner in communication very early. However, with Julie, it is difficult to establish contact and maintain it in order to interact. Therefore the mother's speech is full of elements with a calling function—interjections, questions, rises, and lengthenings. On the other hand, with Tiphaine, the mother exchanges glances and can maintain the contact without using speech. This enables her to make more assertive statements, and her prosody comes closer to what can be observed in adult conversation.

The general impression that arises from this comparison is that the mother's attitude depends on the child. If the child is attentive to the situation, the mother's speech will be more natural, with fewer attempts towards attracting attention. Moreover, the child's behaviour enables the mother to see her either as a co-speaker with whom she can share thoughts, or as a receiver who receives messages but gives no signs of understanding. In this respect, Tiphaine's reactions correspond to mother's expectations: she is smiling, moving, and so on. The child gives a brief feedback to each message that she receives from her mother. Julie, on the contrary, does not: she makes queer faces or shows nothing at all. Her answers are negative or non-existent, and her interest is not directed towards her mother but towards her own self.

Conclusion

The comparison between the two situations has enabled us to draw certain conclusions regarding the communication of the mother and the posture and gestures of both children.

The discourse and communication of a mother is quite revealing of the place that she gives to her child in the interaction. In our study, the mother's productions reveals that her expectations are different with each of her daughters, even though she is not aware of it.

Yet the difference is not what one would have foreseen. The mother is quite attentive to Julie's difficulties, as is clearly shown by the mass of speech she delivers and her active verbal stimulation of her child; however, she does not address her as a full partner with whom she could share affects and judgements in the face of the world. She does not want to convince her of what she thinks about objects and events, as if Julie were only her partner in the interaction; Tiphaine, on the other hand, is not only a partner in the interaction, but also a co-thinker. The mother does not expect as much of Julie, and although she is not aware of it, her discourse reveals these differences. The difference in speech and communication is not a question of quantity, but of quality.

Concerning the attitude of the children, it is clearly apparent that while plunged in water, the children are somewhat puzzled and have to cling to something to calm down and enjoy the situation. The attitude of each sister is different. Tiphaine is calm and relaxed, but she constantly keeps eye contact with her mother, as if she were stuck to her gaze. Julie, on the other hand, the girl who will turn out to be autistic, seems to cling to her own self, and her tonus is very tense. In fact, she only looks to her mother when she is coming close to her face; while her mother is bathing and moving her around in the bath, Julie does not seem able to compensate for these body movements in terms of her own eye movements. This lack of continuity in eye contact could be the outcome of a lack of intermodality and of a difficulty to convert cenethetical information concerning her own position into compensatory movements of the eyes, enabling constant eye contact regardless of the movements of the body. This, of course, could be regarded as an early instance of dissociation.

APPENDIX
Abbreviations and symbols

M	the mother
J, T	Julie, Tiphaine (the children)
C	the camera man (the father)
Mn	M's statement number
Jn/Tn	J's or T's reaction number
↑	rising pitch F_0
↓	falling pitch F_0
→	constant pitch F_0
+	increase in intensity
−	decrease in intensity
< >	sound productions, non-articulations, and comments on these productions
/ /	sound productions from the child and sound productions without sense from M
::	syllabic lengthening
/	short break
in italic	examples

CHAPTER FIVE

The PREAUT research:
early communication perturbations
that could lead to a developmental disorder
of the autistic spectrum

Graciela Cullere-Crespin

The autistic-spectrum disorders are specified by qualitative and quantitative alterations of social and communication interactions, as well as by restricted, repetitive, and stereotyped behaviours and activities. Currently, these disorders are usually diagnosed at the age of 3 years (Baird, Cass, & Slonims, 2003; Volkmar et al., 1999), though sometimes they are identified around the age of 4 years during the systematic paediatric examinations conducted in France by public health doctors in pre-primary school.

There is widespread agreement about the need for early diagnosis in order to reduce disabilities due to autistic disorders (Bryson, Rogers, & Fombonne, 2003; Bursztejn et al., 2003), and numerous publications state the favourable evolution of children with autistic-spectrum disorders when early diagnosis and intervention have taken place (Lovaas, 1987). Furthermore, even if the autistic signs are not obvious and rarely complete under the age of 3 years, all collected data—especially parents' observations—verify that such signs exist in 75–80% of the cases before the age of 2 years and in 31–55% of the cases during the first year of life (Young, Brewer, & Pattison, 2003).

Consequently, it seems very important to validate reliable markers that are easy to use within the framework of routine paediatric consultations in order to identify, during the first two years of life, signs of communication disturbances that could lead to developmental disorders of the autistic spectrum.

Historical background

In 1998, a group of psychiatrists, psychologists, and psychoanalysts, all autistic-disorders practitioners, founded PREAUT, the Association for the Prevention of Autism, in order to carry out research aiming at the validation of early communication disturbances that could be linked to an autistic-disorder risk.

The PREAUT research, called "Evaluation of a Consistent Set of Tools Identifying Early Communication Perturbations That Could Lead to a Developmental Disorder of the Autistic Spectrum", is promoted both by PREAUT (Paris), represented by its president, Jean-Louis Sarradet, and by the Programme Hospitalier de Recherche Clinique (PHRC) of the Strasbourg University Hospital (France), represented by Claude Bursztejn.

The PREAUT research is aimed at paediatricians and GPs working on the frontline who see babies, from birth and during the earliest months of life, within the framework of the Protection Maternelle et Infantile (PMI—French public health centres providing free paediatric care). Since 1999, PREAUT psychoanalysts have trained over six hundred paediatricians and GPs all over France to recognize early warning signs of the risk of an autistic evolution.

Without favouring any particular aetiology, the PREAUT hypothesis is that there must be psycho-relational situations that support cognition, making it possible, during the early months of life. These situations should be observable in the relation between a baby and his familiar others (normally his parents), well before the cognitive markers usually sought—such as *proto-declarative pointing* and *pretend play* of the CHAT scale—become observable (Baron-Cohen et al., 1996).

The PREAUT research protocol

The PREAUT signs

Several theories show evidence that, from birth, a baby shows an interest in certain specific elements of his mother's voice: the *mother-ese* phenomenon, pointed out by Fernald and Kuhl (1987) and later studied by Trevarthen and colleagues (1998), which coincides with what Lacan (1964) proposes as the *invocatory drive*. During the first year of life, two other drives are also easily detected by paediatricians: the interest the baby shows for watching and being watched (called the *scopic drive*) and that for eating and being "eaten up" for fun (*oral drive*).

According to Freud (1915c), the drive process, to complete its circuit, has to go through three phases:

1.   The first phase is *active*: the baby seeks the object of satisfaction.
2.   The second phase is considered to be *auto-erotic*: the baby takes a part of his or her own body as an object of satisfaction.
3.   The third phase turns into drive *passivation*: the baby makes him/ herself the object for a familiar other (usually the mother), and seeks the other's satisfaction.

If we put these three phases of the drive circuit into clinical terms, we can consider, as far as the oral drive is concerned, that in the first phase, *active*, the baby seeks the object of satisfaction: the breast or the bottle; in the second phase, *auto-erotic*, the baby takes a part of his own body as an object: his thumb, fingers, or the dummy.

These two phases are already well known to paediatricians and GPs, who consider them as important developmental markers. But the third phase of the oral drive circuit is less well known and may not be so well observed; it goes like this:

• The baby offers a part of his body to the mother to "taste" whether it's good (usually, his fingers, toes, or tummy);
• The mother pretends to taste, and she says, joyfully, something like: *"We could eat up a baby like that!"*
• The baby shows his joy at having caused the pleasure he reads in his mother's face (scopic drive), and in her voice (invocatory drive).

Many spontaneous family films show this type of fun-playing between mothers and normal babies during everyday feeding, nappy-changing, or bathing.

The PREAUT signs are based on the hypothesis, proposed by Marie Christine Laznik, that the baby who is at risk for autism would have a *failure of the third phase of the drive circuit*.

The following scenes are taken from a video recording of family films used by PREAUT for the training of paediatricians. The scenes show evidence of a normal baby, Fabien, who seeks to provoke his mother's joyful reaction, whereas those of a sick baby, Marco, do not.

Figure 5.1.   Fabien

Fabien, a normally developing 4-month-old, offers his fingers and toes to his mother to "taste" whether they are good to eat (Figure 5.1). The mother pretends to taste and says, joyfully, *"We could eat up a baby like that!"* (Figure 5.2). Then Fabien re-starts the interaction, offering his toes to his mother to have her "taste" them again (Figure 5.3). And finally Fabien shows his joy at having caused the pleasure he reads in his mother's face (scopic drive) and in her voice (invocatory drive) (Figure 5.4).

This third phase is necessary to allow the second one to become "auto-erotic". Babies who will become autistic can have sucking movements that are pacifying procedures, but these are not yet auto-erotic, since the erotic link to the important others (usually the parents) is lacking. Family movies show that babies who have become autistic can

Figure 5.2.   Fabien   Figure 5.3.   Fabien

Figure 5.4.   Fabien

sometimes smile and look back during "proto-conversation", but they do not look and mainly do not seek to be looked at during everyday activities such as changing, feeding, or bathing.

In the following scenes from the PREAUT video recording, Marco, age 2½ months, does not seek to provoke his parents' joyful reactions in everyday activities, but he does remain able to respond when actively stimulated by his parents in the "proto-conversation" situation, as described by Trevarthen (Trevarthen & Aitken, 2001).

Marco smiles and looks back during the proto-conversation situation (Figure 5.5). However, he neither looks nor seeks to be looked at during everyday nappy-changing or bath scenes (Figure 5.6).

Therefore, within the PREAUT research, we consider that early-warning signs should start flashing when a baby does not seek to be looked at for fun, either by his mother or the doctor, during the regular paediatric consultations at the ages of 4 and 9 months. Normal babies very easily perform the *"seeking to be looked at for fun"* sign, usually long before the age of 4 months.

Consequently, the PREAUT signs result from the combination of these two behaviours current in normally developing babies:

1. the baby does not seek to be looked at by his mother (or his significant other) while she is not stimulating him;

Figure 5.5.   Marco

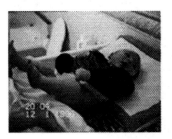 

Figure 5.6.   Marco

2.   the baby does not seek to provoke the joyful reaction of his mother (or his significant other) while she is not stimulating him.

There is a *consistency* between the PREAUT signs and the CHAT items validated as autism-risk indicators, particularly the pretend play.

Let us consider the oral-drive PREAUT sign as being the fact that the baby does not try to get his mother to "eat him all up", in a joyful mood. In this example, this means that the baby does not feel himself to be a good object of satisfaction for his mother, and therefore he does not seek to verify how satisfactory he is for her. This is the absence of drive *passivation*.

In the pretend-play item tested by the CHAT scale, children are supposed to pretend to pour something good and then to drink or eat it. Normal developing children perform this item very easily and also do something else: they give the good thing to eat or drink to the mother (or the adult who is playing with them). We can consider that, thereby, the child feels he has a very satisfactory object to give to the other and thus to verify how satisfactory he is being with him/her.

Bob is a charming 6-year-old autistic boy who, although he is able to pretend-play that he is eating, is not able to give someone else something to eat (Cullere-Crespin, 2002). His pretend play stays thus completely autistic. Following the PREAUT hypothesis, despite his capability to perform pretend play, we can consider that his drive circuit is not completed.

In summary, we consider the PREAUT research to be an evaluation of a *consistent* set of tools identifying early communication perturbations that could lead to a developmental disorder of the autistic spectrum.

The QDC and the CHAT

Several years ago, the CHAT scale (Checklist for Autism in Toddlers) was validated by S. Baron-Cohen and colleagues (1996). This scale studies three areas that have been assessed to be absent in autistic children: joint attention, proto-declarative pointing, and pretend play. At the end of the study on 16,000 children, the 10 suspected children were assessed to be autistic at the age of 42 months. The CHAT scale can therefore be considered as specific, although, as a later study carried out by the same team showed (Baird et al., 2000), not sufficiently reliable. Despite this limitation, the PREAUT team considered the CHAT scale to be an interesting tool to be tested within our protocol, with some comple-mentary items added in order to improve its reliability.

Within the framework of a multicentric study carried out by Bursz-tejn and his team at the Strasbourg University Hospital (CHRU de Strasbourg, France), 27 items identified during the routine paediatric examination as being possibly predictive of autistic disturbances have been tested on 2,350 children aged 8 to 13 months. As a result of this study, 8 of those items, which have been assessed to be present in nor-mally developing babies, were selected to constitute the QDC (Ques-tionnaire du Développement de la Communication [Communication Development Questionnaire]).

The PREAUT team decided to include both these scales along with the PREAUT signs, and therefore the full PREAUT protocol tests the complete set of these tools, as follows:

- The PREAUT signs (Laznik et al.), on babies at ages 4 months and 9 months;
- The QDC (Bursztejn et al., 2003), on babies age 12 months;
- The currently modified French version of the CHAT scale (Bursztejn et al., 2003), on babies age 24 months.

Running the research

The PREAUT research has been set up in France on a nationwide basis in cooperation with districts where the partnership between paedia-tricians and psychiatrists already exists, or where there is a desire to create one. So far, this partnership has been established with twelve French districts.[1]

Paediatrician training programme

First day:

- The importance of early interactions with the significant others in the construction of the psychic apparatus.
- Paternal and maternal functions: their relative influence on the link-ing set-up.
- The three main drives during the first year of life: oral, scopic, and invocatory.
- Positive signs of development and signs of linking disturbances within each drive.

• Prevention and intervention in early linking disturbances: a practical guide.

Second day:

• Presentation of theoretical and clinical elements of the PREAUT signs.
• The three phases of the drive circuit according to Freud; importance of the third phase or *drive passivation*.
• The relationship between gaze and voice: the "proto-conversation" situation.
• The relationship between drive and cognition.
• Presentation of the QDC (Communication Development Questionnaire).
• Presentation of the CHAT (Checklist for Autism in Toddlers) scale, as modified by the complementary items added by the Strasbourg team.

Third day:

• Presentation of methodological and logistical aspects of the PREAUT research to the medical teams joining it.
• Setting up partnership networks between public health paediatric care centres (PMI centres) and the professionals of the child-psychiatric departments. This day is jointly organized with colleagues from the local child-psychiatric departments.

Paediatricians receive a booklet for each child, composed of four duplicated forms to be sent back for data collecting. Each form corresponds to the paediatric examinations at 4 and 9 months (PREAUT signs), 12 months (QDC questionnaire), and 24 months (the CHAT). Translated versions of the original forms of these questionnaires are presented in the Appendix.

A regional research team has been built up, with child psychiatrists and psychoanalysts in each district participating in the research. Thus, the medical teams are able to refer to their nearest research member about any child identified as at-risk according to the research criteria.

For every child included in the research sample, the four questionnaires must be systematically filled in, irrespective of whether or not the child presents at-risk. Children for whom a risk has been detected according to the research criteria of any one of the examinations are oriented towards diagnosis verification through internationally recognized standardized tools (CARS: Childhood Autism Rating Scale; ADI: Autism Diagnostic Interview; ADOS: Autism Diagnostic Observation Schedule).

Several monthly teaching seminars on early interactions have been set up for the medical teams. These seminars allow them to present and discuss clinical situations as well as prevention and intervention issues. The clinical situations discussed in the seminars are published yearly in the *Cahiers de PREAUT*, along with scientific and clinical issues about autism and early intervention and care.

Feasibility study results

From January 2002 to November 2004, a feasibility study was conducted in three pilot districts (Aude, Gard, and Hauts de Seine), from which 47 free paediatric care centres (PMI centres) participated.

The feasibility study included 1,800 babies. Out of these responses, none could be said to be at risk of autism at both examinations (4 and 9 months). Only one baby presented risk criteria at 4 months, but he recovered at 5 months, and his 9-month examination was normal. About 8% of the babies seen were engaged in a linking difficulty with their mother, not specific of autism. These data correspond to current predictions of statistical incidence.

Expected results and perspectives

The operational phase started in 2005. The whole study should include 25,000 babies, which means that, in all the districts, a three-year inclusion will be necessary to meet the sample size required in view of the low statistical incidence of autistic-spectrum developmental disorders.

Apart from our interest in the evaluation of the set of tools, we are confident that using the database created by our research will lead to numerous possibilities of developing further knowledge on the autistic-spectrum disorders as well as on larger linking disturbances of early infancy.

Note

1. Aude, Bouches du Rhône, Côte d'Or, Essonne, Gard, Guadeloupe, Hauts de Seine, Loir et Cher, Loiret, Paris, and Pyrénées Orientales.

APPENDICES

The PREAUT Questionnaire

First part of the questionnaire: *4th & 9th months*

QUESTIONS TO THE DOCTOR	ANSWER	VALUE
1. Does the baby seek to look at you:		
(a) Spontaneously?	Yes	4
	No	0
(b) When you talk to him (proto-conversation)?	Yes	1
	No	0
2. Does the baby seek to be looked at by his mother (or his important other):		
(a) When she doesn't solicit him, babbling, wriggling, and intensely looking at her?	Yes	8
	No	0
(b) When she talks to him (proto-conversation)?	Yes	2
	No	0

TOTAL SCORE

If the score is over 3, you do not need to answer Questions 3 and 4.

Second part of the questionnaire: *4th & 9th months*

QUESTIONS TO THE DOCTOR	ANSWER	VALUE
3. When his mother (or his important other) is not soliciting him:		
(a) Does he look at his mother (or his important other)?	Yes	1
	No	0
(b) Does he smile at his mother (or his important other)?	Yes	2
	No	0
(c) Does the baby seek to provoke a joyful interaction with his mother (or his important other)—for instance, offering his tummy, hands, or toes to be eaten up for fun?	Yes	4
	No	0
4. While being stimulated by his mother (or his important other):		
(a) Does he look at his mother (or his important other)?	Yes	1
	No	0
(b) Does he smile at his mother (or his important other)?	Yes	2
	No	0
(c) Does the baby seek to provoke a joyful interaction with his mother (or his important other)—for instance, offering his tummy, hands or toes to be eaten up for fun?	Yes	4
	No	0

Clinical remarks:

The QDC (Communication Development Questionnaire)

Communication development examination, 9–13 months

	Parents' answer		Observed by the doctor	
	No	Yes	No	Yes
1. Can you easily obtain eye-to-eye contact with the child?	○	☐	○	☐
2. Can you easily understand what the child feels through his facial expressions?	○	☐	○	☐
3. Does the child take an object or a toy you hold out to him?	○	☐	○	☐
4. Does the child smile to his mother or his important others? ("smile—answer")	○	☐	○	☐
5. Does the child respond when you talk to him—for instance, looking, listening, smiling, or babbling?	○	☐	○	☐
6. During the paediatric examination, did you find the postural exchanges adapted? (adequate holding)			○	☐

Clinical remarks:

Checklist for Autism in Toddlers (CHAT)

The CHAT

To be used by GPs or health visitors (HVs) during the 18-month developmental check-up.

Section A: Ask Parent:

1.   Does your child enjoy being swung, bounced on your knee, etc?
      YES/NO
2.   Does your child take an interest in other children?
      YES/NO
3.   Does your child like climbing on things, such as up stairs?
      YES/NO
4.   Does your child enjoy playing peek-a-boo/hide-and-seek?
      YES/NO
5.   Does your child ever PRETEND, for example, to make a cup of tea using a toy cup and teapot, or pretend other things?
      YES/NO
6.   Does your child ever use his/her index finger to point, to ASK for something?
      YES/NO
7.   Does your child ever use his/her index finger to point, to indicate INTEREST in something?
      YES/NO
8.   Can your child play properly with small toys (e.g. cars or bricks) without just mouthing, fiddling, or dropping them?
      YES/NO

9.   Does your child ever bring objects over to you (parent) to SHOW you something?
     YES/NO

Section B: GP or HV Observation:

i.   During the appointment, has the child made eye contact with you?
      YES/NO

ii.   Get child's attention, then point across the room at an interesting object and say
      "Oh look! There's a [name of toy]!" Watch child's face. Does the child look across to
      see what you are pointing at?
      YES/NO*

iii. Get the child's attention, then give child a miniature toy cup and teapot and say
      "Can you make a cup of tea?" Does the child pretend to pour out tea, drink it, etc.?
      YES/NO**

iv.   Say to the child, "Where's the light?", or "Show me the light". Does the child point
      with his/her index finger at the light?
      YES/NO***

v.   Can the child build a tower of bricks? (If so how many?)
      (Number of bricks: _____)
      YES/NO

---

*(To record YES on this item, ensure the child has not simply looked at your hand, but has
actually looked at the object you are pointing at.)
  ** (If you can elicit an example of pretending in some other game, score a YES on this item.)
  *** (Repeat this with "Where's the teddy?" or some other unreachable object, if child does
not understand the word "light". To record YES on this item, the child must have looked up
at your face around the time of pointing.) (Baron-Cohen, Allen, & Gillberg, 1992: Copyright of
MRC/SBC 1995.)

Complementary items to be tested for in the French version:

	Parents' answer		Observed by the doctor	
	No	Yes	No	Yes
1. You can easily understand the child's feelings from his facial expression				
2. He stretches out his arms when you go to pick him up				
3. He is interested and accepts the objects or toys offered\ to him				
4. He is interested in other children or adults				
5. He responds when called by his first name				
6. He seeks help from well-known people when he gets hurt				
7. He attracts other people's attention through mimicking, sounds, or words				
8. He says "goodbye", or "no", nodding his head, or he sends kisses				
9. He does not make any repetitive movements—other than when going asleep				

Clinical remarks:

PART III

EARLY PSYCHOANALYTIC
INTERVENTION APPROACHES

CHAPTER SIX

From a distance:
early intervention as a way to attune
and find a channel for communication

Stella Acquarone

"From a distance there is harmony. . .
From a distance you look like my friend. . .
From a distance I just cannot comprehend
what all this fighting is for. . .
From a distance . . . no one is in need . . ."

Bette Midler lyrics, *From a Distance*

C ertain kinds of babies appear in my clinical practice who are too quiet or are felt as distant. I shall comment on how I came to treat these very young babies and how I came to think about them. I also review the pertinent literature influencing and stimulating my research in this field accompanied by my findings. Included is a scale I use to mark the beginning of the work and monitor progress, regression, or staying the same. It is an outline of how we reached paths of change and humanization. Presented, too, is a clinical example that illustrates aspects of our approach: it is a case worth thinking about.

Findings

Early intervention with 6-month to 3-year-old infants with autistic behaviours shows the possibility of reversing the progression of this disorder and the subsequent cognitive delays (Acquarone, 2004; Alonim, 2002a; Kobayashi et al., 2001).

Field observations from my clinical work in psychotherapy with adults, adolescents, and children made me realize that everyone in a population with autistic behaviours had had previous morbid signs of the pathology to be treated. These signs could even be taken back to the first year of life.

Beginning in the early 1980s, I organized clinical research in health centres and paediatric and child and adolescent departments in hospitals to pay attention to mothers who had concerns about their infants. I wanted to treat the "problem" at an early stage. Over the years, I have made and supervised over 3,500 early psychoanalytic interventions. Because part of this population (3%) were babies showing early autistic behaviour, or some kind of communication disorder, I developed an "early-intervention" approach to open a channel of communication to "distant" (or pre-autistic) babies.

Different strategies were tried to observe positive results. Follow-ups at 5, 10, and up to 20 years later (in two cases) showed that infants treated early with mild or severe symptomatology, including early autistic behaviours, resolved this aberrant behaviour and developed normally. Generally, these babies and their families needed no more than a total of 6 hours spaced over weeks and months. In particular cases (as in early psychosis), we increased these 6 hours up to 14 hours in total, and seven cases took 180 hours or more. In 1996, when I took a sabbatical and left babies with autistic behaviours to colleagues who practised family therapy, child psychotherapy, or child psychiatry, my colleagues did not focus on the babies' individuality or deficits and worked only with the parents' mental representations about themselves and their children, with the consequence that the same children were diagnosed as autistic at 4 years of age. The young adults I treated were free of neurotic or psychotic symptoms and developed normal and happy lives.

What accounted for the different outcomes? Over the years I have concluded that:

• signs of pathology can be found even in the first year of life;
• infants treated early may resolve problem behaviour, be understood by parents, and develop normally;
• professionals who do not focus on babies' individuality or deficits and work only with the unconscious in parents' mental representa-

tions may be deferring problems, which will later lead to further treatments needed for 3 to 5 years, five times a week, or to special-needs schools.

For "distant" babies, the underlying objective of the early intervention is *attunement*, which begins by understanding the mental representation of the mother and the specific individuality of the baby. To develop this basic objective into a pragmatic and workable clinical approach that reaches the "distant" (or pre-autistic) baby, I combined the resources of the Parent–Infant Clinic and the research and training arm of the School of Infant Mental Health to create an early-intervention "laboratory" in order to observe, explore, and understand these important interpersonal relationships. The psychoanalytic setting and method used in our approach provides an ideal laboratory:

- it provides tools such as transference and the countertransference;
- these nonverbal tools are deeply related to internal processes;
- these processes are important to discover and verbalize in the mother (father) as well as in the infant.

These tools are nonverbal and relate to the transmission of affects and feelings. It is because this hidden "communication" is so deeply related to internal processes that can make interpersonal relationships so difficult. And the psychoanalytic setting and method seems to be a better method of addressing a relational problem than intensive behaviourist treatments with different interventionists providing 40 to 45 hours per week for two or three years (Lovaas, 1987).

Background

The idea behind early intervention is simple and powerful: most of brain development occurs in the first three years, particularly the first two years of life (Schore, 1994) (see Figure 6.1). Since two-thirds of brain development occurs within the first two years, the earlier we can find and maintain attunement, the less damage there will be to the child–parent attachment and communication and the corresponding neurological system. When we first began our work with infants and parents three decades ago, we were working from clinical intuition. Today, neurobiological research seems to be validating our early findings that healthy bonds and healthy brains depend on quality

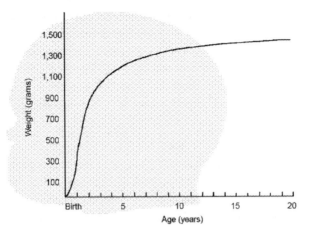

Figure 6.1.   Brain development in the first three years of life
(after Schore, 1994).

relationships with the primary caregivers (usually parents) and on the connections of neurons in the brain.

The number of cells (neurons) in the brain—about 100 billion—remains the same throughout our lives. In the first year of life, each neuron forms about 15,000 synapses (connections). By the end of the second year, the brain will have formed 1,000 trillion connections. It is all these connections that make the brain of a 2-year-old so much heavier than the newborn's—four times as much.

There is much evidence for the "use it or lose it" theory of brain development. Between the ages of 2 and 3 years, some serious pruning must begin in order for the brain to be "wired up" efficiently.

Research by Dawson, Ashman, and Carver (2000) shows that the signals of autism are from birth and, if not treated, would only increase the chances of its irreversibility.

Our approach

Our approach is based on a psychodynamic model. The core of our model is psychoanalytic. This means that all behaviour is seen to have meaning (even meaningless behaviour):

- the autistic baby engages in a variety of puzzling, challenging, or dysfunctional behaviours;
- there is a communication in these behaviours;

- these communications can be understood in humanly meaningful ways with the help of some psychodynamic thinking.

It is important that the family as a whole has to be involved in the treatment. This gives the family and the therapy team every chance for understanding the member of the family who is struggling.

To put the complex of the early intervention with babies with communication difficulties into motion, let us set the characters.

- the babies exhibiting autistic behaviours;
- the parents/family;
- the therapist.

Let us now set the stage for the early intervention.

Step 1: change your perspective

The move to understand the baby's internal world includes neonates in the arms of their parents or in special-care baby units:

- it combines observation, being with and thinking with practical suggestions;
- it encourages empathy and continuation at home with different members of the family (and not with different therapists!), and it includes all the family.

Step 2: focus on the development difficulty

Our approach aims to reclaim potential non-autistic aspects in the autistic baby by addressing the autistic baby at the level of the developmental difficulty that will make the baby delayed if not understood in time.

Step 3: look for the early signs

There are a series of early signs of alarm that can be seen in infants during the first year of life that can be helpful in early detection of autistic-spectrum disorders (ASD). This is especially important as many of the characteristics and signs that are usually used to diagnose ASD are often not appropriate or useful for infants under a year old.

We consider that if four or more of the following signs are present at around 6 months, then early, skilful intervention is imperative:

- *Primary intersubjectivity or relating to persons*
  —lack of immediate response and interest in adults' intentions
  —no attraction for mother's face
  —lack of anticipation of mother's intentions
  —interest in objects (object-relatedness)
  —lack of imitation and, furthermore, lack of provoking the adult into interaction
  —lack of babbling
  —lack of joint attention
  —gaze-avoidance
  —no orientating towards the parents
  —no smiling.
- *Deficits in the sensorial spectrum*
  —dislike of the tone/volume of voice
  —preferring whispers (auditory hypersensitivity)
  —hypersensitivity to touch or specific touches
  —visual, auditory, or speech impairment.
- *Poor motor (psychomotor) skills*
  —hypo- or hyper-tonicity
  —lack of moulding to mother or caregiver's arms
  —lack of grasping
  —stereotypic movements and noises, grimaces
  —dislike of being picked up or held (throwing themselves backward)
  —move non-stop by themselves, or extremely quiet
  —excessive or strange interest of moving tongue in the mouth.
- *Deficits in the transmission of affect*
  —extreme defences (such as denial, rejection, and isolation)
  —extreme anxiety or distress, or complete lack of them
  —fears
  —irritability.

- *Behaviour that has an effect on caregivers* (leaving them feeling desperately helpless)

  —avoids or ignores human contact

  —no desire to share what he or she sees, thinks, and feels

  —doesn't look, pay attention to, imitate, signal, or point

  —prefers objects to people, hard objects to soft ones, and handles them in repetitive and stereotypical ways

  —induces lack of interest in other people.

Step 4: consider the parents

In addition to observable "signs" in the child, it is also important to consider the parents.

- Consider the degree of difficulty the parents have in relating to their child (their flatter, slower, unaffectionate manner: Trevarthen, chapter 2) and in finding pleasure and satisfaction in joint encounters
- Parents are usually the first to feel there is something wrong with their child; in fact, they can be a good mental-health radar for realizing—from their baby's communications—the need for help or attention

Step 5: consider the siblings

Siblings are always dealing with their ambivalence about "others in parents' minds and hearts". There is rivalry as well as relief in having siblings. If there is a sibling who finds it difficult to relate and tends to be isolated, brothers and sisters are perplexed, confused, and at times guilty that their negative feelings might have really damaged the withdrawn child. Meetings and work with them about understanding their feelings and their autistic sibling is essential to help integration in the family of the pre-autistic child or withdrawn baby.

Step 6: consider the therapist(s) involved

The psychotherapist is receiving and understanding what is transferred by the baby and, therefore, is immersed in experiences that are nonverbal and, most of the time, primitive in origin and are difficult to decode. The support and discussion of early treatments with colleagues—mostly the ones involved in the same case—will validate the work, bring a new perspective, help in learning more about the patients' unconscious, and provide support for the psychotherapist's work. A particularly important function of the team is to hold and be able to bear the difficulties and negative or new feelings that arise.

Step 7: use a scale to chart difficulties

We have created a scale (modified from Massie & Rosenthal, 1984) to set down on paper the initial difficulties that are visible and then for the professional working on the case to monitor progress (see Appendix). This is then easy to pass on to or share with other professionals.

Step 8: keep in mind the different theories

Despite more than ten years of intensive research, experts still argue about the causes of autism. A book by Dzikowski (1993) on the current theories of the causes of autism lists over 100 different theories and approaches. The present debate includes a wide range of questions, such as whether this developmental disorder of early childhood is caused by brain dysfunction, genetic deficits, food allergies, vaccination damage, cognitive deficits such as lack of "theory of mind", environmental factors, a combination of some of these, and many more.

Alvarez, in her book, *Live Company* (1992), summarizes the different views held by two opposing camps, the organicists and the psychodynamicists:

Organicists	*Psychodynamicists*
Organicists seek explanations in some organic defect or deficit whereas . . .	. . . psychodynamicists study the mental mechanisms of autism, regardless of its biological components.
Organicists now dominate the debate, finding psychoanalytic hypothesis impossible to prove, even though . . .	. . . psychodyamicists find it much less problematic to embrace the findings of the organicists.
Part of the problem is language . . .	. . . psychoanalytic object-relations discourse is difficult for the uninitiated.

The differences of approach formulated by organicists and psychodynamicists are not just in style and substance, but stem from wholly different mindsets. The psychodynamic approach views human beings as having an internal world.

The debate continues between the two sides over the origins of autism: if the psychodynamicists act early to prevent autism, the organicists may later try to say that the autistic diagnosis was wrong.

When professionals do stop arguing over origins and consequences, yet another debate starts: this one about what to do after the early signs are seen. Here the debate is between psychological research and psychoanalytic findings:

- Some psychological research describes the psychological condition of autism as a class of manoeuvre humans can make using their minds for protection or defensive purposes (see in particular Murray, 1992; Murray & Trevarthen, 1985; Stern, 1977, 1985). Many of these studies focus on the richness and specific attributes of normal babies compared to communication components "missing" in the autistic baby. These studies state as fact that the autistic child is unable to identify with another person and that this "fact" cannot be changed or explored, only behaviour-managed.

- Psychoanalytic authors on autism go some way towards explaining what motivates the puzzling autistic behaviours (e.g. Alvarez, 1992; Bion, 1967b; Meltzer, Bremner, Hoxter, Weddell, & Wittenberg, 1975: Ogden, 1992; Spensley, 1995; Stern, 1985; Tustin, 1981). Psychoanalytic thinking dares to probe further into this phenomenon, asking not only "What does it feel like to *be with* him?" but also "What does it feel like to *be* him?"

As a process of communication, psychoanalysis is able to shed some light on the underlying mental processes of the "distant" baby who does not respond, and the following are the models:

- *Mind full of "living objects"*

  Anne Alvarez describes the underlying model of psychoanalysis as of "a mind as an inner world full of living objects, memories, and thoughts lit up by meaning. A mind is a vast landscape of thought-about feelings and felt-about thoughts which are constantly in interaction with each other" (Alvarez, 1992). We could then think about the nature and "communicativeness" of the autistic baby's *internal* world and objects: the pre-autistic baby may have an *internal* object that is itself not interested and does not *want* to communicate; the baby's deficits may have to be found within the baby's self and mind, where it might be treatable and redeemable, rather than in a permanent biological damage to the baby's brains.

- *Trauma-based psychoanalytic mental model*

Other psychoanalytic thinking is that autism of certain children appears to be a response to post-natal and early-infancy traumas. As babies they seem to have suffered from an "infantile post-traumatic stress disorder" (Alvarez & Reid, 1999), or "reactive autism" as it is sometimes called when talking about babies that develop autistic behaviours in orphanages, like those in Romania. Early trauma for the baby could also be a traumatic event in the parents' life, which Rascovsky (1971) and Maiello (2001) extend back to pre-natal life. Maiello mentions that the trauma might have left the mother numb and unresponsive; the baby then might take itself as the cause and feel guilty of a damage it did not do but felt responsible for.

- *Protective-based psychoanalytic mental model*

Research has shown convincingly that avoidant and autistic-like responses can occur in normal babies as a protective response to certain situations of overstimulation (Brazelton, 1992, p. 249). Such a trauma may, in a baby or young child, go entirely unnoticed, as it may have been a minor event from an adult point of view or a series of small events around a particular child's birth and early history.

- *Integration-based psychoanalytic approach*

There are other theories that stress the sensorial capacities of the infant. For example Mahler (1968) pointed out that these babies seem to receive many sensations from the inside of the body and from the environment through senses separately, and the autistic child cannot integrate such sensory impressions into a meaningful whole or into coherently perceived objects. Emphasis in the sensorial spectrum is shared in a different way by Meltzer et al. (1975) who speak about the abnormally acute perceptual sensitivity and emotional sensibility. He explains "dismantling" as a process in which the child suspends attention to the whole function of an object and allows each of the senses to wander to the most attractive parts of the object at any one moment, but then has difficulty in integrating the experiences. The consequence is a scattering of the awareness and therefore a dismantling of the self—a difficulty in finding sense, and lacking continuity, in the experience. The child is left dominated by primitive emotions, some of which may be painful. Frances Tustin (1981) also gives importance to the predominance of disorderly sensations in the life of the autistic child, and one aspect mentioned is the concept of the fear of falling from mother's arms.

- *Deficit-based psychoanalytic mental model and approach*

French and Lacanian psychoanalysts are exploring an approach based on another model of early-age development:

—they stress the importance in therapy of using specific words referring to the body, food, emotions, and so on; introducing a link between a baby's first mental representations and the somatic areas
or zones that are charged with psychic energy (autistic children
have severe difficulties in forming this mental representation;

—this process addresses a "deficit" in the third phase of the drive-
development process (as outlined by Cullere-Crespin in chapter 5
and by Laznik in chapter 8).

- *Perception-based psychoanalytic approach*

After reviewing the infant research literature, Hobson (2002) mentions the fact that some babies are built differently and are not so
socially attuned nor so hungry for social engagement. He poses the
question, "do individuals with autism see beneath the skin, and ap-
prehend the feeling that lies behind expressions of emotions in other
people?" This different way of perceiving leads us into unexplored
areas that need to be addressed individually.

- *The second-skin model*

The second-skin model focuses on the conditions for meaningful
relationships between mother and baby (object relations) to actually start to happen (Bick, 1968). We have to explore each individual
case, *helping the conditions* for the perceptions of "the distant baby"
to get integrated in a mind. These conditions follow the basic needs
of emotional attunement: it might be in holding the baby in a particularly important way; or it might be that the eyes are felt as persecutory or empty (coloured by personal strange emotions such as
uncontainable anxiety, fear of void or emptiness, and others that are
placed outside them, in the outside world).

For the mother to be able to be received in her reclamation, the
baby needs to be discovered and known *in its own ways of perceiving*—including how it feels, what its make up is, and how it's body
language is a mechanism of interpersonal engagement.

How do we go about this? Through our observational skills, giving time and allowing our personal reactions (countertransference)

to take shape and talk for the baby. We are then producing or reproducing a kind of specialized maternal reverie. It will be then that
slowly the facial gestures might be discovered as interesting, or feeling at ease and secure when held might develop, or wanting to emit
signals to reach people outside, to look, smell, touch the other, to feel
curiosity, to be able to anticipate, to be able to find reciprocating and
interesting engagement with the caregiver, to create emotions in the
other, to play games and have fun and joy in companionship.

Case presentation
Rio

1st session:
Assessment in the family

Rio, age 6 months, was referred by a health visitor because the mother
was becoming depressed as a consequence of her baby's lack of interest in her and persons around (Figure 6.2); he was contented by
himself, not wanting to be held, and crawling around in circles always
going away from parents. He liked only hard objects, which were held
for a long time. He preferred to be looking out of a window or looking down if held, and he liked doors and the spinning of the washing
machine. The family needed help to attune and find a channel for
communication.

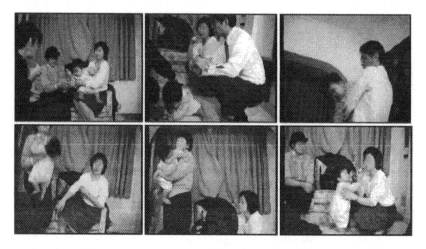

Figure 6.2.   Assessment *(faces have been blurred).*

Conclusions of assessment

The baby comes with worried parents. Mother feels dispirited in the face of rejection. She holds the baby loose and slippery on her lap. She sings, jokes, and speaks softly, confused at the lack of affectionate response.

The baby doesn't want to be held, doesn't want proximity, doesn't look at mother's face or eyes, doesn't cuddle, doesn't signal, doesn't show interest; his attention is to objects, not people; he shows no affects and seems very happy moving around.

The father, who works a lot and doesn't see the baby much, held and played with the baby for a minute, and baby seemed to look at him, but when father stumbled, the baby started looking down and did not want to look any more. The same thing happened with the grandmother (mother's mother).

Objectives: infant–parent psychotherapy

Rio seemed to have no relationship with mother's eyes, cuddles, arms, or voice. In fact, he seemed depleted of an internal world integrated with benevolent parental figures interested in having fun and entertainment with him. Therefore, an aim was to explore his individuality with the mother alone in order to discover channels of communication.

It was important to emulate attunement and attachment in order to provide a base for meaningful relationships and development of affects: how to find each other's eyes, hands, voice, cuddles, and fun.

Rio had become lost in his own whirlwind of emotions, without finding his mother—her feeding breasts, her voice, her arms—as a container and transformer of his experiences. He showed just his own movement, his uncontained anxiety disturbing any possibility of getting attached lovingly, and wanting to get rid of it. People were frightening as nothing would calm him, and mother became sad.

I had two working hypotheses:

1. *Go back to mother and baby alone.* In my presence I would allow the mother to be the baby herself, as well as the mother of her baby, and try to recover the maternal reverie and be immersed there. I would help her to bear the transferences of the baby to her.

2. *Explore the baby's behaviour and likings from a distance and feel what kind of affects appear in the relationship.* We all sat down on the floor

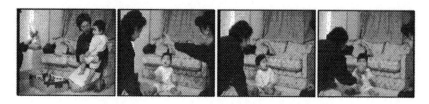

Figure 6.3.   Mother–infant psychotherapy.

and tried one activity at a time. Perhaps the baby did not like mother's holding, and this had lowered mother's self-esteem; the holding probably then became looser and created or perpetuated a fear of falling or being dropped (in the mother's mind).

In the sequence shown in Figure 6.3, the general body avoidance to the mother is noticeable. However, he immediately calmed down and slowly engaged with me with the sponge ball; with the mother, though, he looked away after an initial brief contact. In that triangular situation of exploration in the baby (Figure 6.4), we discovered that he was interested in the mother's singing (with the train)—another type of affectionate holding through sound rather than the arms. It appeared significant as a new positive start of relating to each other, helping to integrate experiences and finding human sense in the world (Figure 6.5).

Figure 6.4.   Repairing the relationship.

Figure 6.5.   Singing becomes the new link between baby and parents throughout the treatment.

Once the relationship started to grow and common ground was found and understood, mother could share with the therapist her childhood and adult negative experiences, reactivated by the initial rejection from baby. She had been the only baby and a girl of a married couple in a culture where baby boys are very much expected and cherished because it is their role to look after the elderly parents. Deep down, the mother held a feeling of having to apologize because she was always disappointing the other. Interestingly, she did not feel that way with the baby, but the internal father and grandfather figures appear as a ghost in the distant baby. She could not get it right with the males in the family, and the mother was not strong enough internally to stand confident in this.

It is interesting because being held in the uterus and sounds are the two most primitive prenatal experiences, so one modality can help the other; the result is the development of shared expression of affects.

Treatment process

The sequence in Figure 6.6 shows Rio's 6-year-old brother at the meeting. I asked the mother to bring him to a session to see how they play and how he communicates with his baby brother and mother (he was being seen separately by another child psychotherapist as part of the overall treatment of Rio).

Another sequence (Figure 6.7) shows the whole family playing or learning to play differently. In meetings, the baby showed behaviour conducive to relating to others when:

Figure 6.6.   Treatment process from Sessions 5–8.

Figure 6.7.   Treatment process from Sessions 9–13.

Figure 6.8.   End of the treatment process: Session 14.

- it was distal, and only he would seek proximity;
- there was some singing in it (father learned to sing as well);
- there was a calm face-to-face encounter;
- the child took the lead, and after a while I made very small variations;
- only one stimulus was offered or stayed with for a time, letting him explore it fully;
- we (mother and I) waited and searched for what baby liked and/or reciprocated;
- we created rhythms, following baby's mood;
- we discovered turn-taking possibilities and took turns in the communication once he started trusting the person in front of him;
- I respected baby's rests and only initiated activity when looked at, for him and mother to feel held in the process.

Gradually, the baby trusted the parents' arms and could cuddle (Figure 6.8). The parents felt involved with the baby and were able to communicate with care and curiosity rather than fear. The baby developed both a calmer attitude and the ability to look at the person with whom he would play or interchange signs or sounds understandable by both parties. Rio's parents learned a lot about his personality and about their handling of him. By the age of 15 years, although he tended to be shy, he had two friends and did well in school and in music.

Case summary

Rio was 6 months old and avoiding personal contact with his mother, father, and others. The whole process took about thirty sessions. The first two were assessment with the family, including grandmother. The scattering of the attention and constant movement did not allow for him to be calm with anybody. Three sessions of infant psychotherapy with the mother helped to find the conditions that Rio needed for the mother to be perceived (Alvarez, 1992) and for the mind to find structure so that experiences could be integrated (Meltzer, 1975). Once the baby's particular sensitivities and communication needs were known, the mother started talking about herself and how she was feeling. The rejection by the baby had reactivated past experiences of rejection in her childhood (Sinason, 1986).

Worries about the elder son appeared, and he was brought to two meetings to help the mother and the brothers to relate.

The father came to three meetings—two at the beginning to understand the process—and he learned about what was helpful to the child. At the end he came feeling happy that he had recovered his wife and son. The triangle was effective: father, mother, and son could relate in different combinations and tolerate the relationship to others, and their relationship with each other became closer and more intimate. Rio could become "possessive" and let go. He could come close to mother's internal occupants (Rhode, 2004)—the relationships with her own parents (Acquarone, 2004)—and not feel to be causing further damage by making mother retreat into her infantile grievances.

I have presented this case to show a process whereby the baby used "distance" to achieve a sense of peace and harmony since he felt insecure. He was always putting distance between himself, his parents, and others who insisted on close proximity and play with him. Careful observation of the video showed an interesting aspect of his habit: whenever he was insecurely held or felt intruded by instructions, he would run away or pull back, creating a space suspended in time. The different psychoanalytic approaches discussed in this chapter provided a frame of reference to explore. Rio and his family helped to create the conditions by which Rio could perceive his mother (and father), feeling soothed by her rather than persecuted (through singing and, later on, dancing). In this way Rio could internalize the mother and start the process of symbol formation, from a then secure base. Mother then could help the transformation of his raw feelings (Bion, 1962), the dismantling of his mind (Meltzer, 1975)

Meeting his terror of falling was also his terror of falling from mother's consciousness when she was relating to father. The proximity—to be close to, to imitate, to incorporate, to reciprocate—started to develop, as is seen in the photographs (Figure 6.6) where mother picks up the telephone and Rio also does, establishing a relationship including interest, eyes, hands, and sounds.

While all cases are different, there are, however, some general remarks that can be thought about and discussed, such as:

• *What was the primary component that did not allow Rio to look at the mother and made him unable to relate to persons?*

As discussed previously, in Rio's case, his fragility was shown in his fear of falling—concretely and symbolically. He could not feel secure in his mother's arms, and fear of encountering her eyes made him uneasy, needing to move away.

The mother, for her part, learned to talk more and to respect his individual needs—in particular, space—trying to find him where he was without imposing herself, since that was increasing the baby's panic and pushing him further away. It was very interesting to discover that mother needed to speak about her feeling a failure as a mother, which reactivated her feelings of inadequacy as a daughter. Since the husband brought them to therapy, there was a nice healthy triangulation, helping a separation of proper attachment in this case, in the request for help and his later willingness to be included in the therapy. The choice the mother made of husband, her companion, was complementary to her childhood resolution of oedipal conflicts; however, the difficulty in understanding her baby boy created a split in her mind which separated her from her husband by reactivation of the negative experiences from the past. The working together in the short treatment brought her back from her sadness to the joy and fun in the relationship with the child, who then became able to relate with both his parents and with the other known adults around. In this way, the husband felt reunited to his wife in the new liveliness felt with the "recovered" baby. The cradle for emotions to develop better was created.

Conclusion

Any after-the-fact observer could say that perhaps to intervene early is an alarmist approach and could only frighten parents. However, our approach offers not just an awareness but a concrete sharing of concerns and treatment (if necessary), along with a set of parameters to keep in mind that specifically address difficulties in the communication spectrum.

Think of the early-intervention approach this way: immunizations are given for many childhood infectious illnesses, and alerts about the signs of meningitis are displayed in surgeries—so why not do the same with signs of communication difficulties?

Early intervention is a new field specifically focused on babies who are experiencing difficulties in relating to their parents and siblings. As a discipline, early intervention can be learned. The work is with the baby and family in different arrangements. The aim is to help the integration of experiences, working with their individual sensibilities, inner phantasies about the world and other human beings, and staying with the experience as long as necessary to be able to feel one's way in, understand it, and be specific when helping these parents to reach and promote emotional and mental growth at such an important stage in brain development, in order to avoid the diagnosis of autism.

APPENDIX

The following four pages contain the Early Signs of Alarm scale (modified from Massie & Rosenthal, 1984), which we have developed for observing the quality of mother–infant observations. The first two pages record separately for infant and for mother the initial difficulties that are visible. The next two pages are for subsequent follow-ups, to allow progress to be monitored at regular intervals. This information can then be passed on or shared with other professionals

In the scale for observing the infant it is important whether the attention is more towards objects rather than persons; if in doubt, it should be possible to check whether what is interesting to the infant is the object that the adult is holding or whether it is the adult. This is why we differentiate in the scale, using "O" for object.

In the complete scale—for infant and for mother (caregiver, or significant "other")—we observe carefully whether the relationship is important and how deficits in the sensorial spectrum and motor spectrum are intimately linked to this. The two extremes are signalling "risk" if there are three or more tics. We have to remember that all sorts of behaviours can appear at different stages in development and states in the child. For this purpose we recommend administering the scale when the baby is well rested, physically healthy, and not hungry. If there are concerns, it is important to continue observing once a week for a month to verify content.

EARLY SIGNS OF ALARM
OBSERVATION OF THE QUALITY OF MOTHER / INFANT INTERACTIONS
Stella Acquarone. PhD
School of Infant Mental Health

INFANT

Name: **d.o.b.**

Date of observation:

Please write "O" if the interaction is with an object rather than a person

INTERPERSONAL	Never	Rarely	Freq >2 times	Always	Observer reactions
GAZING –The eye-to-eye contact within a relationship and the maintenance of this contact					
BABBLING –The making of vocal sounds for the benefit of the partner in the parent-infant relationship					
SIGNALLING –The facial expressions –Noises or gestures that seek to produce an affectionate response from the partner					
IMITATION –Moving mouth, tongue, etc. in imitation of mother's (or another) –The repetition of a sound or a movement heard or seen by the infant					
PROVOKING –Inciting the person into interacting					
JOINT ATTENTION –Looking in the same direction –Smiling or vocalising about people or objects (specify)					
POINTING –Indicating with index finger to a person about an object of interest					
FEEDING –Infant's attitude during the intake of food, including anticipatory behaviour (e.g. head-turning, moving arms, sucking reflex)					
SENSORIAL					
TOUCHING –Skin-to-skin contact initiated by infant for play or affection					
RESPONSE –Response to sounds –Response to name					
MOTOR					
HOLDING –The posturing of the infant when he is supported in the arms of the mother (e.g. comfortable, floppy, rigid, restless) –General muscle tone (at 5+ months) when sitting or crawling –Stereotypic movement of arms, eyes, etc.					
AFFECT					
EXPRESSIVENESS –The body or facial expression of emotional states (e.g. sad, worried, anxious, bland, happy, or others) specify					
COMFORTING –Infant's ability to find relief from distress by him/herself (e.g. thumb sucking, touching hands)					

Frequency of this observation in 1 hour

ANY OTHER OBSERVATIONS NOT LISTED ABOVE

EARLY SIGNS OF ALARM
OBSERVATION OF THE QUALITY OF MOTHER / INFANT INTERACTIONS

Stella Acquarone. PhD
School of Infant Mental Health

MOTHER (or caregiver)
Affecting the baby or being affected by the baby

Name: **d.o.b.**

Date of observation:

Please write "O" if the interaction is with an object rather than a person

	Never	Rarely	Freq >2 times	Always	Observer reactions
GAZING – The eye-to-eye contact with the baby and the maintenance of this contact.					
BABBLING –The making of vocal sounds for the benefit of the parent-infant relationship					
SIGNALLING – Facial expressions, noises, or gestures seeking to produce an affectionate response from the infant					
TOUCHING –Skin-to-skin contact initiated by parent for play or affection					
COMFORTING –Mother's ability to find relief for the baby's distress					
HOLDING –The posturing of the mother when the infant is supported in her arms or any other way (e.g. secure and tender, rough, balanced precariously)					
FEEDING –Mother's attitude towards infant's hunger and need to feed: a. Does she anticipate behaviour and have meal or breast easily available? b. Does she pay attention, talk with the baby, and enjoy feeding? c. Does she interrupt with any excuse (i.e. talks to others and looks away)? d. Is she fearful, full of anguish, or has she any delusions? e. Is she apathetic?					
GAMES –Playful encounters, including songs and teasing					
AFFECT –Expression of emotional state (e.g. sad, worried, anxious, bland, happy, others) *specify*					
UNDERSTANDING OF EMOTIONS –in themselves –in the baby					
PAST –Psychiatric illness –Other difficulties					

Frequency of this observation in 1 hour

ANY OTHER OBSERVATIONS NOT LISTED ABOVE

EARLY SIGNS OF ALARM
OBSERVATION OF THE QUALITY OF MOTHER / INFANT INTERACTIONS

Stella Acquarone. PhD
School of Infant Mental Health

FOLLOW-UP OF INFANT

Name: **d.o.b.**

Date of observation:

Please write "O" if the interaction is with an object rather than a person

INTERPERSONAL	Never	Rarely	Freq >2 times	Always	Observer reactions
GAZING					
BABBLING					
SIGNALLING					
IMITATION					
PROVOKING					
JOINT ATTENTION					
POINTING					
FEEDING					
SENSORIAL					
TOUCHING					
RESPONSE					
MOTOR					
HOLDING					
AFFECT					
EXPRESSIVENESS					
COMFORTING					

Frequency of this observation in 1 hour

ANY OTHER OBSERVATIONS NOT LISTED ABOVE

EARLY SIGNS OF ALARM
OBSERVATION OF THE QUALITY OF MOTHER / INFANT INTERACTIONS
Stella Acquarone. PhD
School of Infant Mental Health

FOLLOW-UP OF MOTHER (or caregiver)
Affecting the baby or being affected by the baby

Name: d.o.b.

Date of observation:

Please write "O" if the interaction is with an object rather than a person

	Never	Rarely	Freq >2 times	Always	Observer reactions
			Frequency of this observation in 1 hour		
GAZING					
BABBLING					
SIGNALLING					
TOUCHING					
COMFORTING					
HOLDING					
FEEDING					
GAMES					
AFFECT					
UNDERSTANDING OF EMOTIONS					
PAST					

ANY OTHER OBSERVATIONS NOT LISTED ABOVE

CHAPTER SEVEN

Infants at risk—early signs of autism—diagnosis and treatment

Hanna A. Alonim

In the late 1980s, when the age for diagnosing autism was lowered to 3 years, this was considered an early diagnosis. In the late 1990s, when the diagnostic age was lowered to 2 years, this was considered not early enough.

Over the past eighteen years of interviewing parents of children diagnosed on the autism spectrum, the same words have been heard time and again: "My child had a completely normal development until the age of 1 year, and then I began to notice regression . . ."

The crucial question is, then, what happens during those months of transition between the first year of life and the second that causes regressive processes in cases such as these?

Basing our knowledge on a theory such as that established by Mahler (1968), who approaches the process of a baby's emotional development based on three stages—the autistic stage, the symbiotic stage, and the separation–individuation stage—a number of hypotheses may be constructed to explain this thin line dividing the first and the second year of a child's life, and even these may subsequently be refuted.

Over the last decade, research has been carried out into the first year of life with children treated at the Mifne Center, which incorporates a programme using therapy for young children with autism and their families.

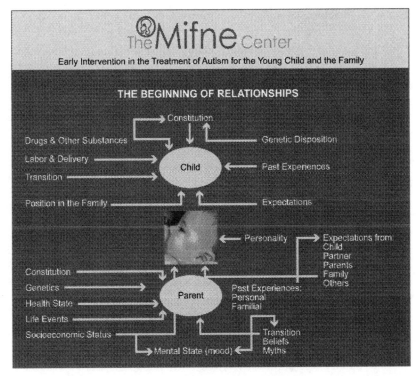

Figure 7.1.   A family set-up in general. (Devised by the Mifne Center.)

The most comprehensive and reliable data are provided by parents. The mother says, "I remember, when he was 10 months old, he used to look at me and smile", while the father retorts, "I don't remember he did anything like that". On the other hand, a mother occasionally admits, "From the beginning I felt something was wrong with my baby, but everyone told me I was being a hysterical mother . . .".

Deep inside, mothers know what scientists discover—that relationships between babies and mothers are mutual. Figure 7.1. shows the family constellation into which the child is born, as well as the reciprocity between the two systems, of parent and child, which are influenced by broader ones.

Method

The initial attachment process between a baby and his parents (Bowlby, 1969), especially with his mother, whether she is aware of it or not, confronts the mother with her own early childhood experiences and with those initial and most significant objects in her own world.

To understand the baby's characteristics, the inner world of his parents must first be understood (Winnicott, 1956).

An increasing number of families arrived at the clinic for their initial interview equipped with extensive documentation about their baby from the moment of birth. This material is fascinating if scrutinized carefully. The symptoms observed in some of the babies were minor, implying that the majority of parents would probably not notice any irregularity. When watching the videotapes of these babies from an analytic aspect, however, it is possible to collect data indicating warning signs, or what have come to be called "red flags."

One of the most interesting pieces of documentation came from a family who runs a circus. The parents sent a lengthy video showing pictures taken from the time of the birth of their son until he was 3 years old. They mentioned in their accompanying letter, "As you can see, our son was a normal child until that awful thing happened . . .". The "awful thing" that happened was this:

> Following a performance by elephants in the circus, the music stops and a little boy with golden curls gets up on the stage, dressed in a suit and bow tie. He is brought over to centre stage, and the audience starts clapping madly. Apparently this is the child's very first performance. The child suddenly becomes paralysed, immobile, until his father eventually has to carry him off of the stage. In an acute way, the child shuts off and becomes introverted, and during the rest of the video he does not utter a sound.

> An episode like this can definitely be traumatic to any child. And yet, when examining more carefully the earlier stages of his life, when he is still a baby, it is possible to see that, for example, his father overexerts himself every time he wants to attract his attention, and it takes the baby some time to turn his head towards him. It is also apparent that the baby enjoys concentrating on one object for longer than normal.

> The parents, who each had children from previous marriages, were unaware that anything was wrong. However, this child, who is a teenager today, is severely autistic.

On rare occasions, parents insist that they can pinpoint a traumatic episode that triggered their child's regression—a car accident, abandonment, abuse, and the like. In the majority of cases, evidence is non-existent, despite the claim by various international forums in recent years regarding the detrimental effects of MMR.

It is important to note that in ultra-orthodox Jewish circles, where most of the people do not vaccinate their children on principle, there are no fewer cases of autism, and some families even have more than one autistic child.

In November 2003, the US National Institute of Mental Health published a statement: "Don't wait for a late diagnosis; start treatment when children are already a year and a half, when you notice the red flags . . .".

According to the Mifne perception, red flags should already be pinpointed during the first year of life.

Diagnosis

When approaching diagnosis during the first year of life, we should be cautious and use the term "attachment disorder", which may develop into a syndrome diagnosed on the autism spectrum (Massie & Campbell, 1983).

There is no comparison between the effect of intensive treatment on an 8-month-old baby and that on an infant aged 18 months. The developmental process of the brain during the first year is the most dynamic in our entire lives. The baby is exposed to stimuli that have a decisive effect on cell growth. This is a stage that never returns.

The eight early signs—the red flags—in preverbal infants during their first year of life, as identified at the Mifne Center, relate to an ongoing disorder in attachment development during the first year of life.

Red flags

1. *Excessive passivity*

Excessive passivity in babies is categorized as lack of crying, having an overt tendency to immobility, and failing to achieve the crucial stepping stone of initial interest in their surroundings, as can already be seen from 2½ to 3 months (Stern, 1985). According to Stern, babies discover and show social motivation from the age of 2 months.

We often hear it said: "My child is an angel. He never cries." "We didn't know there was a child in the house—from the start I slept through the night." In a number of cases of girls like these, the parents mentioned that because their first child was a boy and very active, they simply thought girls were different.

2. *Excessive activity*

As with constant crying that has not had a medical diagnosis, excessive activity represents a lack of physical calmness, which is a symptom at the opposite pole to Sign 1.

It is interesting to note that some children who were obviously passive became hyperactive during their second year of life. A study by Wolke, Rizzo, and Woods (2002) indicates that babies who cry incessantly are more likely to become hyperactive.

> An 8-month-old baby was examined in the diagnostic unit at the Sourasky Medical Center in Tel Aviv. The baby was born prematurely; his head-holding was still unstable, he was agitated and cried constantly when he was awake, it was very difficult to calm him down, but when he was carried to-and-fro he quietened down somewhat. All the tests came out negative, although a metabolic disorder was suspected. The baby appeared to be in a state of total irregularity, lacking a sense of self, his entire body transmitting the message "I don't want to be here . . .". When asked how she was coping with this situation, the young mother replied, "Even before I became pregnant, I knew I'd have a disturbed child . . .".

3. *Refusal or resistance to feeding or nursing*

A high percentage of children treated at the Mifne Center who were diagnosed on the autism spectrum had already shown an inability to adapt or regulate their eating habits during their first days of life, or at least during the first months.

It is interesting to monitor those children whose sense of smell is so delicate and who tend to smell every object, especially foods, and to hear from the mother what took place from the very beginning. Some mothers report that their baby screwed up his face in a way that expressed disgust at the smell of the breast. What is the reason for this aversion, and what could be the cause of this lack of attuning?

> One mother, whose baby refused to nurse from her, requested the assistance of her friend who was feeding her baby at the same time. She was shocked and upset when her baby did not refuse to nurse from her friend. A baby of only 3 weeks is already able to distinguish between one nipple and another. The experiential model that

should have developed both in the baby and in his mother became a negative intersubjective experience.

4. *Lack of reaction to a voice or presence of a parent*

With a baby who does not turn his head, and neither smiles nor babbles, in reaction to the voice or presence of a parent, the first detail that must be tested thoroughly is the child's hearing. In most Western countries, gone are the days when babies with attachment disorder were diagnosed as hearing-impaired and treated with hearing aids.

Some of the first children treated at the Mifne Center had also been treated within the Israeli education system for hearing-impaired children because they were considered hearing-impaired after having been diagnosed with a BERA (brainstem evoked-response audiometry) test.

It was interesting to note that the test, which is supposed to be objective, offered a clinical picture of a decrease of about 50 decibels, which was later discovered to be inaccurate. At least two of the children could easily hear sounds of less than 50 decibels if they were interested in what they were hearing; it was subsequently found that their hearing was oversensitive.

In her doctoral research about infants who underwent a cochlear implant, Dikla Kerem (2003), who works with hearing-impaired children, notes that infants are liable to feel flooded during the first year with the implant. She has seen children intentionally removing the outer part of the instrument to cut themselves off from the noisy world and return to the familiar and "secure silence".

Does audio sensitivity, then, cause gradual dissociation? According to Francis Tustin (1981), a psychoanalyst and important researcher in the field of autism, it most certainly does. A baby who responds to the presence of a parent, but not to the sound of his or her voice, will be assumed to have a hearing impairment, whereas a baby who responds to a voice but does not react to a presence will be assumed to be indifferent or as having developed a fear of the adult in question. Babies who suffer from fear or indifference to their surroundings do not usually begin to babble in the early stages. Babbling is a function of bonding, in the same way as language is a function of contact.

5. *Aversion to parental touch (or any other person)*

Brainwave tests show that the brain already responds to touch during the seventh month of pregnancy, which supports the assumption that the baby is capable of responding to attempts like these even when still in the womb. Sensitivity to touch begins in the facial area and gradually moves to all parts of the body. In reference to the previous category, it is interesting to note that Tomatis (1977) developed an auditory method that relates to the skin as a continuation of the ear—the tactile part as one large ear! What was considered for years as a lack of sensitivity is now considered as oversensitivity.

According to Tomatis's theory, then, just as the ear does not want or is afraid to hear, thus the body does not want or is afraid to sense.

Tustin, as well as Bion (1957), maintain that "flooding" takes place, and in their clinical studies of psychotic children, they found that an unbearable awareness of physical separation from the mother took place too suddenly and too abruptly for these babies. As a result, they experienced a disastrous sense of injury and physical damage, which may explain the aversion to touch.

6. *Lack of direct eye contact (eye contact exists with objects)*

Making eye contact is not easy. There are people who find it hard to look a person in the eye. More than any other part of the face, the eye is the most sensitive, the most revealing, the most self-conscious. The word "pupil" comes from the Latin word *"pupa"*, meaning doll. Stern maintains that interaction with another person contributes to the development of positive emotional experiences, whereas a response to stationary objects contributes to what Piaget defines as sensorimotor development.

In her book *Mother-Infant Attachment and Psychoanalysis: The Eyes of Shame*, Mary Ayers (2003) offers a fascinating theory about the eyes of shame. She tries to understand what the baby sees when he looks into his mother's eyes. She suggests that shame is a characteristic that originates from environmental failure, that it is already deeply rooted in the early developmental stage that began with the meeting of the infant's eyes with those of his mother, and that this has a decisive emotional effect on the rest of his life. The following example illustrates this point.

> A mother of a 7-month-old baby boy arrived for a meeting. She claimed that because this was her fourth child and she had a great deal of experience, she sensed her child was not making eye contact with her. The woman, aged 40, was somehow familiar to me.

Having told me that this child was unplanned, and that she was very much involved in bringing up her 2½-year-old daughter, I then remembered where I had seen her. Some months previously, on a flight from the north to the centre of Israel, she had been sitting beside me with her little daughter, playing with her during the entire flight in such a warm, clever, and containing way. As I watched them, fascinated, I thought how lucky this little girl was to have such an intelligent and mature mother, and what a wonderful role model she made. When I related my experience to her, she smiled. This incident is important to illustrate this aspect of her excellent qualities as a mother.

We were three experienced therapists who saw the baby at that meeting. He made immediate eye contact and smiled at each one of us. He followed our movements and was very inquisitive for a baby of his age. His mother behaved very warmly towards him, cuddling him. When she tried to turn his head towards hers, he immediately looked aside and began to take an interest in the objects on the floor. During the 90-minute-long meeting, she did not manage to get her baby to make eye contact, and yet, shortly after she left the room, he began to cry; he may have been hungry. She immediately nursed him. During the course of our subsequent conversation, she told us that her second son had died five years previously, aged 4 years. She had become extremely anxious and had already been aware of her anxiety during the pregnancy.

She vividly described how her first gaze into his eyes was full of fear, and she added, her voice full of pain, "I was also ashamed because I didn't want him . . .".

7. Delayed motor development

Delayed motor development is often characterized by hypotonia, and all developmental stages are delayed. Some children also have high, stiff muscle tone. Yet this parameter ought not to represent a significant criterion, because some children who are later diagnosed with autism do indeed show especially quick motor development.

It is important to note that many children with developmental disorders are built well physically, yet they tend to have illnesses connected with breathing and metabolic difficulties.

8. *Rapid growth of the circumference of the head
    in relation to the initial point*

Prior to magnetic resonance imaging (MRI), the developmental brain basis of autism was virtually unknown; however, in recent years, MRI has revealed a distinctive pattern of growth abnormalities in cerebral structures.

Brain behaviour evidence is consistent with the more general hypothesis that autism involves widely distributed aberrant functional organization in cerebella, cerebral, and limbic regions, and these defects appear to underlie multiple cognitive-behavioural deficits. One functional MRI (fMRI) study found that autistic patients have robust brain activation to the mother's face in the posterior cingulate, a region thought to play an important role in normal human social emotional experience.

In his research, Courchesne (2003) compared 48 young children diagnosed with autism with a control group of normal children (Figure 7.2). In the group of autistic children, the circumference of the head was smaller at birth, but during a year of growth, the circumference grew rapidly in comparison to the other group. The research indicates the existence of the phenomenon but is unable to show the reason for it. (Increased head growth can also point to other problems

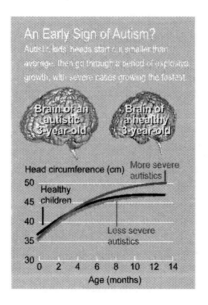

Figure 7.2

that are unconnected with autism, such as hydrocephalus or Weaver syndrome.)

An interesting definition is offered by Margaret Bauman, of Harvard Medical School:

> Normal brain development is not a monologue but a dialogue, in which the brain generates neural circuits and the child's experiences determine which ones survive. The first year of life is a critical period for this experience-guided growth. The brain's circuitry would expand haphazardly as cell growth outpaced experience, creating a chronic sensory overload, which could possibly explain sensory oversensitivity in such children. [Bauman, 2005]

* * *

The above eight signs form the basis of the Early Signs of Pre-Autism Scale for Infants (ESPASI) (see Appendix). The diagnosis unit for the early detection of infants at risk for an attachment disorder was established by the Mifne Center at the Sourasky Medical Centre in Tel-Aviv. Infants found to be high risk following their assessment at the unit, based on the ESPASI, are referred to the Mifne Center for treatment.

The Mifne Method

The Mifne (Turning Point) Center was established in 1987 by Hanna Alonim. This model of early intervention for autistic children in Israel was the first to recognize the importance of individual therapy, intensive treatment, and parental participation. The approach is based on Bowlby's (1969) attachment theory, and it incorporates psychodynamic concepts introduced by Tustin (1981) and the systemic approach to family therapy of Minuchin (1978).

The Mifne Treatment Model (Alonim, 2004) is a sequential family programme for young children and infants with a diagnosis of the autism spectrum and includes three stages:

1. Intensive system therapy for the child and nuclear family, in residence at the Center.

2. Follow-up therapy at the family home.

3. Integration of the child into a mainstream nursery.

The basic concept underlying the therapeutic model views the family as an organic unit.

The nuclear family takes an active part in the intensive therapy, which begins with a residential segment lasting two weeks (for infants) or three weeks (for children under the age of 5 years), all day, seven days a week. This is followed by an aftercare programme when the family returns home.

The initial short-term therapy aims to give the family the opportunity to reflect upon themselves and their child, to gain a better understanding of their challenge. It identifies the parents—and, in a broader sense, the nuclear family—as the focal point for treatment. Special attention is given to the siblings in the family, who are included in the programme.

A retrospective evaluation of the programme undertaken by the Schneider Medical Center (Apter, Farbstein, Spiegel, & Vograft, 2001) revealed that children showed improvement in almost all items on two scales: the Childhood Autism Rating Scale (CARS) and the Social Behaviour Rating Scale (SBRS). Total scores on both scales confirmed significant improvement after a three-week period and after six months.

Follow-up data show that 73% percent of the children treated at the Center have been integrated into mainstream schools.

Intervention

The individual sessions with the child are based on Reciprocal Play Therapy (RPT) developed at the Center, which helps the child to discover the pleasure of human contact and communication. The goal of RPT is to engage the child by easing him into the experience of social interaction as a source of pleasure, by encouraging him to feel the comfort of unconditional acceptance, to enable the growth of trust, and to stimulate the child's motivation to engage in social interaction.

The three stages of RPT proceed as follows:

1. Tempted Play (TP): The therapist tempts the child with a favourite object that the child can reach for and may start to pay attention to the therapist working with him, who may then offer him another favourite item. This is the seed from which trust in the provider of pleasure grows.

2. Sensory Play (SP): Gradually the therapist will sensitively touch, hug, massage, or carry the child and try to comfort him. Sometimes this leads to the first smile or cry.

3. Cognitive Play (CP): This focuses on the development of basic

skills such as looking for a toy, putting a block into a box, and so on.

This is a cumulative process, in that it is enhanced by, and incorporates, the elements of the previous stages. In addition to the process in the therapy room, which is sparingly equipped, hydrotherapy is included to strengthen gross motor skills and improve spatial orientation.

Parents view therapeutic sessions through a one-way mirror. They also have separate sessions together with their child and are helped to become skilled observers of his behaviour patterns.

Parents

The parents are considered as the primary figures who fulfil the family ideology. The term "family ideology" incorporates the entire range of expectations; basic assumptions and beliefs; culture and family tradition; and the roles of the family members and the means to carry them out. Family ideology is significant in consolidating the family structures and characteristics from within, on the one hand, and in delimiting them externally, on the other. When attempting to understand family ideology, we make use of terminology taken from the intergenerational approach (Boszormenyi-Nagy, 1965) and the systems approach (Minuchin, 1978).

The concepts may be generally described as follows: Two people—two worlds—bond in order to experience together "what is common" to both of them and, while so doing, they attempt to bridge the gaps that exist between them. During the consolidation of a family unit, the members must surmount various obstacles (the need for independence, the sense of loss of freedom, acceptance of responsibility, etc.). The intention is that the common aspects forming during the consolidation process between the couple be transferred to the next generation. A significant part of this experience is the bringing-up of children.

A child who is different confronts the parents with a difficulty. Lack of feedback from the baby might cause the parents to feel a sense of failure in the main mission they have taken upon themselves, both individually and as a couple. The couple mobilizes the joint means taken from their family ideology, in order to cope with the difficulty. When these means are perceived as ineffective, the parents undergo a gradual process of regression. This regression is expressed by searching for individual means to cope. It leads to the widening of the personal gaps between the parents and causes the natural family-formation process to come to halt. Regression increases the adherence to individual mechanisms based in the personal biography (defence and coping mechanisms) and may reduce the functional ability of the family.

A family in a state of insufficiency is dealing with a struggle to survive. This struggle, which leads to a secondary consolidation—the focal point being the special baby—leads simultaneously to an internal-individual ingathering of its components. In many cases, families adopt a style of ambiguity, which on the one hand affects the family communication system and on the other causes confusion. Confusion might increase the emotional detachment of the infant. The family finds itself in a vicious cycle and seeks help.

The therapeutic environment, based on principles of a bio-psychosocial model, attempts to encourage the gradual evolution of the child and each family member towards individual and mutual growth.

The family programme is designed to help the parents understand the basic principles of the treatment, which serves to improve their awareness of their life and needs. The work with the parents aims to enable them to broaden their ability to achieve insight into themselves, to understand their own behaviour both as an outcome of the way they perceive themselves as individuals and as part of a role dictated by their family ideology.

The Mifne method uses a variety of techniques such as clinical meetings, verbal and nonverbal communication, individual and joint couple meetings, family sessions, feedback, and team consultation with the parents. One of the strategies applied is Bollas's (1987) concept of the "unthought known": what you do is based on what you know, but are not always aware of.

This clarity contributes to the development of the family's ability to listen to each other, their attempt to understand one other and to create a supportive, encouraging environment, all this in order to help their child thrive.

Case study

Ada was 3 months old when her parents noticed that she was unresponsive. Ada had been seen by different paediatricians and professionals. Each of them was aware that Ada was not developing well; she never cried (Sign 1), there was no babbling (Sign 4), she had no facial expression, made no eye contact (Sign 6), and her motor development was very poor (Sign 7). Some of the paediatricians said that the mother was hysterical, and others said they should wait another six months and see what happens.

When Ada was 5 months old, her parents approached the Mifne clinic for treatment.

Ada was the youngest child ever treated at the Mifne Center. She underwent two weeks of intensive sensory and emotional therapy.

Ada was treated during all her waking hours, with the family taking an active part in the therapy and receiving an enormous amount of guidance.

Family background

Vera (age 28), Simon (32), and their daughters Bonnie (5 years) and Ada (5 months) were treated intensively at the Mifne Center for a period of two weeks.

Vera—the mother

Vera is the second child in a family of five (three girls and two boys). Her father was a Holocaust survivor from Romania; her mother is Hungarian. Having lost his first wife and five children in the Holocaust, the father made the decision to bring five more children into the world and to name them after the five who perished. Vera is one of them. Her parents immigrated to Israel after World War II. Their difficult relationship had an effect on Vera, who maintained that having a father who was a Holocaust survivor made a significant difference to the atmosphere she absorbed in her parents' home (the father spoke about "the Holocaust" but never related to anything pertaining to his personal experiences). Her father's illness and death (from a brain tumour) was an extremely painful period for her, and she was intensely affected by his loss. She devoted much of her time to taking care of him while pregnant with her elder daughter Bonnie and during the first year of her life. At the same time, she had underlying guilt feelings and a sense of helplessness because of what she considered was her limited ability to help him and offer him emotional support. Her negative relationship with her mother was fraught with tension.

Simon—the father

Simon's father, Romanian in origin, was brought up in Israel. His mother was born in a kibbutz. He is the middle of three sons.

The couple met in the town where Vera was living, and they had been living there ever since their marriage of seven years' standing. They gave the impression of having a positive relationship; they were open with one another and had a great deal of common understanding, with a certain measure of devotion and mutual dependence. Simon had the tendency to protect Vera from her acute concerns and anxieties.

They made a joint decision to come to the Mifne Center to get help with the problems resulting from Ada's condition, and they were prepared to be full-time partners in the work with her, as well as in the family treatment.

The couple reported that the first pregnancy had been relatively easy, although her father's condition during this period took up much of Vera's time and was a cause of extreme concern to her. In addition to this was the worry about Vera's state of health, as she herself was suffering from thrombocytopenia.

The second pregnancy was fraught with ambivalence and considerable tension between the couple. Vera maintained that she badly wanted another child, contrary to medical advice. At the same time, she felt that "a time-bomb was ticking" during the course of the pregnancy. She had the feeling that she would die during the delivery, leaving Simon a widower.

Vera's anxieties were varied and expressed themselves in different areas. Apart from the issues mentioned previously, they were coloured with a sense of a damaged self-image and self-imposed guilt as the person ostensibly responsible for Ada's condition. She assumed that the anxiety from which she had suffered during the pregnancy affected both its course and Ada's foetal development. She found herself unable to picture the baby to whom she would be giving birth. Her maternal concept was in direct opposition to how she perceived her own mother: she (Vera) would be a devoted mother, aware of her children's needs, happy at the prospect of their arrival, frank and honest with them, and full of love. As a result, she expected that if she were to behave in this manner, Ada would react accordingly.

She started to blame herself both for her child's condition—especially when she became aware that Ada was spurning any contact with her—and for her own subsequent frustration. She therefore came to the conclusion that she was either a failure or not a good-enough mother, or, alternatively, that Ada had an incurable defect.

Vera wavered between the two options. By means of the first ("I am not a good mother"), Vera interpreted Ada's reactions to her with an underlying degree of self-destruction—that is, Ada is unable to communicate with a mother who transmits to her negative messages such as "a mother suffering from depression", "a mother who is constantly pressurizing", "a tense mother", "a mother lacking in self-confidence". The second possibility ("Ada has a defect") indicated that Ada might be "a retarded child", a child with a "physical defect", a child with autistic traits.

Although the second possibility released her somewhat from part of the responsibility for the actual situation, it still left her with guilt feelings for her part in creating the problem. Wavering between the two possibilities removed the secure base from which she could choose the correct behaviour to use both towards herself and towards Ada. The fear of approaching Ada who "rejected" her, and mainly because of the tension present in every situation involving contact with her, was also indicated in the way she physically held her. Her anxieties occasionally reached a point where they became somatic ("pressure and pain in the upper chest"), with evidence of great stress.

Simon had an important role to play in the family in general, and between Ada and Vera in particular. He perceived Vera's anxieties intuitively. His role was to be a calming influence and a mediator. Sometimes he protected Vera with loving intentions, thus "releasing" her, as it were, from coping with those difficult situations that could be challenging and could ultimately lead to positive and liberating experiences as far as the bond between her and Ada is concerned.

It was interesting to note that, all this notwithstanding, Bonnie was developing nicely. She was not a source of tension, and the bond between her and her parents appeared satisfactory.

Emphasis was placed on cultivating behaviour patterns between Ada and the parents during the course of the "Mifne" treatment. As previously described, Vera and Simon were given guidance how to develop basic habits that would build up the relationship between them and Ada. This was done by consistently observing their behaviour, offering pointers for change, and giving feedback. They were encouraged to talk about their feelings during the exercises, to examine them, to focus on success, and to make their own choice for change. During the course of a week, a significant amount of progress was achieved in the capability for mutual bonding between Ada and her parents, and there was a noticeable improvement between her and Vera. At the point when they managed to break the "vicious" circle of "closing up, frustration, anxiety, self-blame, blaming others—and closing up again", an emotional relaxation was noticeable (a mellowing of body language), and there were many moments of pleasure. Vera's relative progress enabled Simon to give her more space, which increased her ability to face her maternal challenges. Nonetheless, his role as supporter and the person who was helping her overcome her anxieties remained significant, and it will probably continue as such until Vera manages to receive support from other sources, such as individual therapy.

Ada

Ada was brought to the therapeutic centre when she was 5 months old. She used to be an "easy baby . . .". She had no eye contact, she was unresponsive to any voice, she did not turn her head. She neither smiled nor cried. Her motor development was very poor. Ada was treated at the Center for two weeks, twelve hours a day, including her rest periods. The parents were shown how they could communicate physically with their baby. The therapists used massage, movement, and hydrotherapy for the development of her body experience. On the second day, as the therapist was trying to roll her over, Ada cried for the first time. On the third day she began showing some interest and looked directly at the therapist. During the first five days of treatment, the mother gradually relaxed and opened up to various stimuli that brought pleasure to both her and her baby. Ada began to react to facial stimuli and discovered her mother's face. On the seventh day, after many attempts, Ada was willing to be spoon-fed and began to babble for the first time. Two days later, as a therapist was attracting her attention in the mirror, the mother entered the room and the baby became completely focused on her.

The parents were offered the following recommendations:

1. Vera should be allowed to confront her anxieties and process them by means of supportive individual therapy. Vera needs to have her fears justified, as long as they are bound up with the reality of her state of motherhood and Ada's condition. This way she will be able to face them and succeed in coping with aspects of acute anxiety.
2. Simon should participate in the therapeutic process as much as necessary to clarify his role and the part he plays in coping with Vera's anxieties, in order to process his own fears and lighten the heavy load on his shoulders.
3. Bonnie's place within the family should be firmly established, in order to ensure the continuation of her normal development.
4. Time should be made for consistent and ongoing practice, as this will be beneficial for the development of additional communication skills. These should be of mutual benefit (positive reinforcement) for the entire family.
5. As the family lives far from the Center, they may phone any time for consultation. One of the Mifne therapists should see Ada every three months.

Results

Ada was treated at home for a period of a year by her parents and by one therapist.

At 2 years of age (Alonim, 2002b), she began to attend kindergarten with her peer group.

At 5 years of age, Ada was functioning well above her peer group in all spheres of development, and she was very attached to her parents and sister.

Discussion

The question is often asked: what would have happened to Ada had she not undergone that very early treatment. This question, naturally, cannot be answered. While reviewing previous videotapes of a hundred children over the last decade who were diagnosed with the autism spectrum at the age of 2 or 3 years, there were some indications pointing to early signs of attachment disorders, which gradually developed into the autism spectrum. This is why the term "pre-autism" is used. As a baby progresses towards the end of his first year, he develops more skills in all areas of functioning—motor, cognitive, and social. This is a crucial period of time, emphasizing the gap between the normal and the abnormal development process. This might be one explanation for the minor indications during the first year of life. And thus, when parents do notice that something is wrong with their baby, they lose valuable time, either owing to their own difficulty in recognizing that there is a problem, or because of the lengthy procedures that many professionals take to follow up the baby's development. It is also interesting to note that babies whose parents came to the clinic of their own initiative, and underwent a therapeutic process, achieved better results than parents who were influenced by a third party, such as grandparents or paediatricians. Much thought has been given to "how not to cause panic among parents". Yet, at the same time, the level of awareness must be increased.

In the videotapes taken regularly by parents, only very few children had not shown any early signs during their first year of life. It is important to note that there were some videotapes that were taken with large time gaps between. These cases should be studied further.

Conclusion

Following the treatment of infants who showed early signs of pre-autism, and the rapid changes they underwent, it is clear that we must reach the stage where the early signs that could develop into autism are recognizable. The basic assumption leads to the conclusion that if babies were diagnosed and treated from early infancy, the development of autism might well be prevented in many cases. There is a reasonable basis to assume that this awareness can save many children in the future from being labelled with a developmental disorder on the autism spectrum.

The Mifne Center established a pioneer project in collaboration with the Child Psychiatry Unit of the Sourasky Medical Center in Tel-Aviv headed by Nehemia Kaysar. The unit provides a novel service for the early detection and diagnosis of attachment disorders in infants from 3 to 12 months of age, with the aim of promoting awareness of the importance of early diagnosis and treatment.

A year after the diagnosis unit was established (2004), they saw about one infant weekly. During the second year, this rose to about two infants each week. The number of infants brought for diagnosis is steadily increasing. Those who show clear signs according to the ESPASI (developed by Alonim, the Mifne Center) are referred for intensive treatment. All the infants seen at the unit enter the follow-up process until the age of 3 years.

APPENDIX

Early Signs of Pre-Autism Scale for Infants (ESPASI)

The scale is appropriate for infants aged up to 12 months.

The observer should complete the scale immediately following **at least two clinical observation meetings** (one hour each, on different days and at different times of the day) **+ a videotape taken at home.**

The same questionnaire should be completed by the parents.

Each item is rated on a scale from 0 to 5:

   0 = **The sign does not exist** (during observations)
   1 = **Doubt if the sign exists** (the observer is unsure)
   2 = **The sign does not appear consistently** (not in every meeting)
   3 = **The sign rarely appears** (once or twice in a meeting)
   4 = **The sign appears quite often** (a few times during a meeting)
   5 = **The sign is very obvious** (appears consistently).

Early Signs

1. **Excessive Passivity** (lack of crying, immobility, lack of interest in surroundings)

2. **Excessive Activity** (lack of physical calmness, incessant crying)

3. **Refusal or Resistance to Feeding or Nursing** (breastfeeding/others)

4. **Lack of Reaction to Voice or Presence of a Parent** (doesn't turn his head, doesn't smile, doesn't babble)

5. **Aversion to Parental Touch** (or any other person)

6. **Lack of Direct Eye Contact** (eye contact exists with objects)

7. **Delayed Motor Development** (followed by hypotonic/high stiff muscle tone)

8. **Rapid Growth of the Circumference of the Head** (in relation to the initial point).

At least two characteristics of the eight signs must exist, over a period of at least three weeks.

All the relevant medical tests must be carried out before testing for suspected Early Signs of Pre-Autism.

1. **Excessive Passivity**
   0   1   2   3   4   5

2. **Excessive Activity**
   0   1   2   3   4   5

3. **Refusal or Resistance to Feeding or Nursing**
   0   1   2   3   4   5

4. **Lack of Reaction to a Voice/Presence of a Parent**
   0   1   2   3   4   5

5. **Aversion to Parental Touch**
   0   1   2   3   4   5

6. **Lack of Direct Eye Contact**
   0   1   2   3   4   5

7. **Delayed Motor Development**
   0   1   2   3   4   5

8. **Rapid Growth of the Circumference of the Head**
   0   1   2   3   4   5
   Initial size: _____   Present size:_____

Total Score: _____

Evaluation of Rating:

  0–6   No attachment problem exists
  7–12   Recommend follow-up of the baby in 3 months' time
  13–18 Recommend consistent guidance for parents
  19–24 Recommend immediate weekly treatment
  25–40 Should be referred for urgent intensive treatment.

Baby's name: _____ Date of Birth: _____

Address: _____ Phone: _____

Observer's name: _____Date of Test: _____Place: _____

Signature

Joint mother–baby treatment with a baby of 3½ months who shows early warning signs of autism

Marie Christine Laznik

Marine and her mother go to a mother–baby encounter group at their neighbourhood PMI.[1] The group is led by some members of their team, and they are worried by this baby, who does not exchange looks with his mother and whose gaze becomes more difficult for the team to catch each time. They ask the PMI psychologist to come and observe the baby. The psychologist is also very worried, even though she is able to catch the baby's gaze. Marine has hypertonia of the upper torso, and she arches herself backward in way that evokes opisthotonos. The psychologist, who has psychoanalytic training, sent her to me the next day.

We thought that this baby was showing warning signs of a risk of developing autism, so I arranged to see the mother as soon as possible—the day after New Year's Day. It is still very rare for us to be able to receive children like Marine into psychoanalytic consultation. Even if the mother is depressed, it is not clinical depression and still less psychosis. Thus the alerting symptom comes from the baby, but it is not one of the symptoms that parents usually complain about, such as sleep or feeding disorders. Since Marine is only 3 months old, separation problems are not yet an issue. She is one of those babies whom we usually see only much later. I congratulate the clinical psychologist on the foresight and determination she has shown in enabling this family to get an appointment right away.

The mother telephoned the very day she was given my number. It is Christmas Eve, and I give her an appointment for 2 January.

First session (2 January 2002)

Marine arrives in a baby carrier on her mother's stomach. She is arching herself backward, in what looks like opisthotonos, and her gaze seems to be trying to fix on the ceiling. I see the look of worry in the eyes of our centre's secretary.

In the office, the mother tells me that she cannot catch her daughter's eye, though her husband can. She tells me of the enormous difficulties she has had with her baby's intense abdominal pains. She had spoken about this with the paediatrician, who minimized it by explaining that it was frequent in babies and that with time it would go away.

But she tells me that Marine cries for a long time and in a very intense way. The mother is overwhelmed by her baby's crying and cannot soothe her—indeed, she is in distress at her daughter's screaming. Later, when we know each other better and this is all in the past, she will tell me that she once thought of throwing herself and her baby out the window. For her, this is not a mere figure of speech, but an admission of real distress.

In this first session, as soon as mother holds Marine on her lap facing her in order to catch her gaze, the baby throws herself backward. She is very hypertonic in the chest, as her mother points out to me. The parents, worried by this, have already consulted an osteopath. I am able to catch Marine's gaze, as long as I put her in a baby-chair in front of me.

I tell Marine what her mother has just explained to me. My sentences are simple, and I think that Marine is clinging mainly to the intonation of my voice. She calms down, very slowly. I introduce her mother, at whom she looks while making little movements with her arms. I immediately interpret these as, "Mummy, I want to go into your arms." Her mother cannot interpret these movements as being addressed to herself. She tells me several times: "She doesn't ask for me, she doesn't call me."

I tell her, on behalf of Marine, that at 3½ months we don't know how to make movements any better than that, and the mother, touched, takes Marine into her arms. I am struck by what happens. This hypertonic baby relaxes in her mother's arms, as if she were letting herself go, and while I am quietly telling her how well she is there in her mother's arms, she falls asleep.

The mother then tells me how lost she feels, with her husband at work all day. She has her parents, but she can't expect much from them. In any case, her mother has told her that babies are tiring for her. Marine's mother was nearly 40 when she had her, and this is her first baby. When she told her parents she was pregnant, they asked her why she had not had a baby sooner.

They often complained to her, their only child, about not having any grandchildren. Now that she finally had a partner who wanted to have a baby with her, it was too late for her parents: it would be tiring for them. Regarding this, she associates to the fact that the only thing her mother could tell her about her own birth was how tiring, how exhausting, it was for her. That had been very difficult. Marine's mother had no other memories of what her mother might have said about her early childhood.

I listen without saying anything to the version she gives me of her early childhood. I only emphasize the terrible difficulty she is having with her daughter's pain, and I ask her to insist that her paediatrician prescribe treatment for these pains. I tell her that the doctor at our centre, who would see her with me the next time, would support her in this if necessary.

I shall not go into her discourse on her incompetence as a mother. I know that a baby who is screaming in pain, whatever the aetiology of the pain, gives affirmation to the fantasy of maternal powerlessness.[2]

This allowed me to acknowledge the pain, and the necessity of soothing it, without giving an interpretation that might add to the mother's feeling of guilt.

After half an hour,[3] Marine is awakened by her colic. This will be the first and last time I witness such a scene. Marine writhes and shaken with spasms, while her mother is in complete distress. We take care of Marine together. I speak to her for a long time about her pains, picking up the rhythm and the intensity of her own suffering. Though I manage to catch her attention and thus calm her, the mother cannot catch her gaze again, and Marine leaves with her eyes gazing at the ceiling and her upper body bent far back.

Second session

It is two weeks before I am able to see them again. In the waiting-room, it is Marine who seeks out my gaze. Our child psychiatrist is also present at this session.

The parents have changed paediatricians. The new doctor has given them medicine for Marine's pain, and her crises of suffering have stopped. According to the mother, from the first day after our initial session things had got better, and she managed to catch her daughter's gaze a little. But for the last few days, her daughter's gaze was starting to wander again, so it was time to come back and see Madame Laznik.[4]

I say again to Marine, who is in a baby-chair in front of me, what her mother has just told me. Marine gazes at me and gives me big smiles. Marine's mother says that she can now catch her daughter's gaze, and that she gives her little smiles, but that she only gives big smiles like that to her father. With her father she even voices little sounds.

Marine, who has just turned 4 months, is sucking on her hands, which are getting away from her. Very attentively, her mother tries to help her bring her little hands near her mouth. Suddenly, Marine starts sucking her mother's finger, with evident pleasure.

I speak for Marine: "Mmm! Mummy's finger is so good! It's delicious!"

Marine sucks her mother's finger even more avidly.

The mother says, "But if she likes that so much, we'll have to give her a liquorice stick!"

I speak again for Marine: "But Mummy, it's your finger I like! Mummy's finger is so good!"

The mother: "Oh, yes, it's true; you're still too young for liquorice sticks!"

I turn back to the mother to remark how much Marine loves her Mummy's finger, which is as good as a piece of sugar.

Then the mother tells me, in a confidential voice, "I will confess to you—I also find Marine's little finger as good a piece of sugar."

In the same confidential tone, I ask the mother: "And the little foot?"

The mother, whose daughter is still sucking her finger, admits with a chuckle of pleasure: "And even the little belly sometimes!"

The voice of the mother admitting to her pleasure captivates Marine, who looks at her and starts vocalizing with all her might: "Guo, . . . te, . . . re te."

The mother, very moved, tells her, "But I'd need an interpreter to explain everything you telling me!"

Such a sentence—which we do not at all expect to hear from the mother of an infant—shows the extent of her distress as a mother and how depressed she has been in her maternal function. She cannot allow herself to interpret by herself what her daughter said in this "proto-conversation".

I then tell Marine[5] that her mother was so unhappy to see her suffering with her tummy-aches—she felt so powerless to relieve her—that she lost all confidence in her capacity for being a Mummy. Marine looks at me and then at her mother, who acquiesces with a smile. Her little girl responds to her smile.

The mother weeps: "You know, Marine, these are tears of joy that Mummy is crying", she says to her daughter.

I see Marine and her mother three times a month. The mother says that Marine is always "available" in the days following the session, but after about ten days, her gaze starts to turn back towards the ceiling.

In the sessions, Marine can hold my gaze for a long time, especially if I am speaking to her, but she drops her mother's gaze much more quickly. I tell her that in Mummy's eyes she must read troubles that she doesn't want to see there.

Marine has established a protocol for the sessions that she will keep to for several months. She begins by being with us, mainly clinging to my gaze; then we talk about Mommy's worries. Her mother rocks her; in her mother's arms, she lets go of her hypertonia and often goes to sleep to the sound of my voice, which is frequently low and monotone. While her daughter sleeps, the mother talks about herself.

She is not married to Marine's father, who had already had two previous unions. He has two children, in their twenties, from a first marriage. They come to see Marine, and they get along well with her mother. But he also has a little boy, who is now 10 years old, from another union. The father goes to see him every week, but the child is unaware of the existence of either Marine or her mother. This situation hurts Marine's mother very much, especially as it repeats what is happening at work.

Marine's father and mother had met in a government ministry, where both are officials. The father has never wanted anyone to know about their affair, claiming that his supervisor would not stand for it.

The situation was so painful for Marine's mother that she finally went to work in another service. She could never brag about her beautiful daughter in front of her former colleagues and has to take a special route in order not to run into them now, when she is out with Marine in her pushchair. This clandestine situation is very painful for the mother, who feels unrecognized. When Marine wakes up, I tell her that Mummy has explained to me that Daddy was hiding her the way the President of the Republic had hidden his daughter, Mazarine.[6]

These are very long sessions, lasting more than one hour.

Some time later, Marine is placed in day care, and the mother goes back to work. The day-care centre never know what worries we has gone through. However, the staff do point out that Marine has "her ways". There are ladies whom she never answers, as though they did not exist, though there are others—especially one, Marie—to whom Marine attaches herself in a special way.

At another session, while Marine sleeps, the mother tells me the history of her own mother, who came from a farming family living on the high plateau of Larzac. The farm is so out of the way that, during the war, they never saw a German pass by there. Her grandmother (Marine's great-grandmother) had been married to the owner of that very isolated farm. He fathered three daughters with her, one after the other. It seems that she would have liked a different sort of life, and that her babies were not an enormous source of joy for her.

Of course, this gloomy version of the family history is not the only thing that Marine's mother can summon up from her childhood. But her childhood memories of her maternal grandmother's home are never very happy.

But when she evokes the parents of her father, her face lights up. During one session, she tells me that on her paternal grandparents' farm, during the war, they often saw Germans going by. Her grandfather liked to tell how he had tricked the Germans; Madame laughs with pleasure at this memory. Marine turns around, astonished to hear her mother laugh, looks at her, and laughs in turn.

When Marine was 10 months old, the mother told me that while playing with her daughter, she pretended to drink from the baby-bottle. Faced with such playful audacity on the part of her mother, Marine was first astonished, then began to laugh. But that had happened only after the establishment of a more personal therapeutic work for the mother, a month previously. This work was made possible in the following way:

Madame arrives at a session and declares: "*Marine*—she is very well."

She puts her little girl down on the floor. Marine is 9 months old; she is crawling and shows an interest in me, but also in objects. I say, "Marine is very well indeed. What about you?"

The mother hides her face in her hands and starts to cry. She had never let herself go like that before. Marine goes towards her mother and holds out her arms. She snuggles up to her mother very nicely, while I name what she is doing. The mother tries to smile at her through her tears. At this moment, to our great surprise, Marine points up to show her Mummy a very beautiful and colourful mobile hanging from the ceiling of my office.

Each time that Marine cried, her mother would show her the beautiful mobile to console her. We understand at the same time that Marine, identified with her mother, is trying to console her. The mother is very moved. Even if we both admire Marine's capacities for identification (and her cognitive capacities), the mother says that Marine is really too young to have to console her mother already. It's better for her to come talk with Madame Laznik, she says.

Our sessions seem to have enabled Madame to take on the preparations for the celebration of Marine's baptism, which went very well. Now she speaks of her family's big reunion, which will take place in the Larzac and where Marine will be presented.

What has struck me in the last session of June is that Marine now seeks out her mother with her gaze every time she is going to perform an action or even enter into contact with me. It seems to me that a bond has been established between them, but I decide to continue to see them after the vacation. For the mother, the work is perhaps just beginning.

Comments

I was very touched to see how the introduction of the third phase of the drive circuit was able to bring about a completely different dynamic between this baby and her mother.

In the second session, which took place in the presence of the child psychiatrist, Marine sucked her mother's finger. I introduce the idea that this maternal finger is good to suck, that it is a source of joy for Marine. After a depressive phase where the mother proposed a liquorice stick instead of her finger, the mother accepted envisioning herself as a good object for her daughter to suck.

In Freud's terms, she has accepted making herself the object of the third phase of her daughter's oral drive. Freud calls this phase *passive*; he says that, here, the "*Ich*" makes itself the object for another subject

(Freud, 1915c). Her drive passivation consists in letting herself be sucked. We are not in the register of need here, because we are dealing with a finger, and thus with sucking for pleasure alone.[7]

Not only is she the oral object of this third phase of her daughter's drive circuit, she is also a source of pleasure for her ("the finger is so good"). At the same time, the mother can admit that her baby is also a delicious object to suck—her little hand, her little foot, her little belly. This recognition of her baby as a source of joy—of great pleasure—for the mother probably induces a modification in the prosody of the maternal voice. The baby is called by this voice and enters into a real "proto-conversation".

The mother must still be supported in order to be able to respond; she has lost too much confidence in herself to allow herself to find, all alone, the significance of what her daughter says.

Our work as an analyst with a baby and her mother greatly resembles what we do in psychoanalytic psychodrama: role-playing in order to get across some possibilities for representations that are not necessarily addressed to the mother's conscious, vigilant ego.

Marine: relapse at 15 months

Prosody with babies at risk for autism: treatment and research

After the summer vacation, I found an adorable little girl of 13 months who was now walking and who addressed her mother, the receptionist, and myself in an invigorating-sounding dialogue. She seemed utterly happy. Since the daughter seemed to be doing so well, the mother asked if she could continue coming to talk about herself, and I agreed. She used her individual sessions to work on her relationships with her own body and with her husband. But at the end of the first session, she remarked that Marine was somewhat withdrawn. At the next session she made this comment more insistently. One month later, she suddenly revealed that she and her husband were worried about Marine, who had become completely withdrawn and was wandering around incessantly. She asked me to see Marine again.

When I received her, I was confronted with a little girl drifting everywhere, who didn't make eye contact for the first 30 minutes, even if she followed what I was doing. The next session was hardly any easier. Although Marine did not look like a 15-month-old baby who was on her way to becoming autistic, which had never been treated as her refusal to communicate had not prevented her from following intellectually what was happening, I had to acknowledge that she had had a serious relapse.

After the All Saints' Day holiday, the father accompanies the mother to her individual session. He has never come before this, despite my invitations. He says he is very worried about his daughter, who has spent the weekend alone in a corner, stacking video-cassette boxes. He asks me whether I have ever thought that his daughter might be autistic. I reply that this illness is diagnosed as such only at 3 years of age, and that we are doing what is necessary to prevent such a diagnosis from ever having to be made. This is an answer that, while not negating his intuition, leaves the door wide open for hope, especially insofar as our work with Marine between 3 and 12 months had initially allowed us to suppose that Marine had completely recovered. With children over the age of 2 years, when the positive autistic spectrum is starting to develop, I do not hesitate to confirm the diagnosis. In passing, it should be noted that parents do understand their children's problems once they dare to talk about them.

During the two years that followed Marine's relapse, we filmed practically all her sessions.[8] Here are some excerpts from the third session, which took place a few hours after that interview with both parents.

Upon arriving, the mother says in a tone of forced cheerfulness, "On the way here we looked a lot at the ceiling of the Metro, of the elevator." I answer in the same tone, "A way of proving to Mummy that she's right to take the trouble to bring her to see Mrs. Laznik." This cheerfulness is a way of facing up to the total absence of contact with Marine. The latter is seated at a little play-table, tirelessly putting big felt-tip pens into a pot in front of her, then removing them again. Marine, who has a slight fever, has refused her snack at the day-care centre. The mother starts to give her some yogurt; this will be the only time that she feeds her daughter during the session. Marine allows her dummy to be removed without once taking her eyes off the pens, not even for an instant. Still gazing at them, she opens her mouth for a spoonful of yogurt, with her mother complaining that she can't catch Marine's eye. "I try sometimes, but I can't manage it. She turns away." When I speak to Marine, she doesn't respond to me either. It is as if my voice were just a noise like any other. The successive spoonfuls go into Marine's mouth; she lets herself be fed without taking her attention or her gaze away from the felt-tip pens. A pencil falls off the table. Marine whimpers as she tries to reach it. I hand it back to her saying, "Here, Marine." She takes it without even glancing at me. I comment for her, "No, I don't look at Mrs. Laznik." The mother, with whom we did much work during the first year of Marine's life, answers for Marine: "I've found my little chair, I'm all settled in—and that's that." This kind of speech "turn", which had amused her so much as a baby, now falls flat. The mother, continuing to feed Marine, misses, and the yogurt winds up on Marine's face. Marine does not react in any way.

It has been ten minutes since the session began, and the session seems to be turning out like the two preceding ones, without any bond between Marine and us. I tell myself that it can't go on like this: the child is in danger. This withdrawal, which has been going on for almost two months, can only be harmful to her psychic apparatus.

Dialogue with Monica Zilbovicius

René Diatkine and Jean Bergès[9] both used to say that there must be a "psychosomatic" of autism, that the non-use of the organ must injure the organ.

Two months after this session, I was to hear Monica Zilbovicius, at the Congress on Autism, in Bonneval (Belgium), presenting research that, in my opinion, offers concrete support for this hypothesis. She and her colleagues compared 21 primary autistic children with a control group of 12 children (Boddaert et al., 2004). They note a significant reduction, in the autistic children, of the concentration of grey matter in the superior temporal sulcus (STS), which is responsible for listening to voices. These results seem compatible with the hypothesis of a hypo-perfusion of these different zones in autistic children.

This led to a discussion of the innate or acquired character of such a difference, and Zilbovicius admitted that no one could be sure that this difference was not acquired. Last year, the mainstream press got hold of another of her studies, this time on adult autistic subjects (Gervais et al., 2004). This study, carried out using fMRI, showed that in normal adults, the STS is the zone specifically devoted to the treatment of vocal signals, while the fusiform face area (FFA) is devoted to the recognition of faces: recognition of the human voice and recognition of faces constitute two of the main axes of social interaction. The study compared five autistic male adults with a control group of eight adult males. The results showed that, in autistic subjects, there was practically no activation of the STS: in these subjects, cortical activation for voices was identical to that for noises in general, the latter being treated as in normal subjects.

I cannot help but agree that this research is interesting—though I nevertheless find it remarkable that it is seldom pointed out that this a study involving adults. This way of presenting things enables the mainstream media to report that the cause of autism has been found, whereas—as the research now stands—there is no way to tell whether we are dealing with a consequence or a cause.

This is fascinating research, leaving aside its aspect of unproven aetiological explanation. What is certain is that at 4 years of age, and perhaps earlier, the non-use of this organ will leave the STS out of play, perhaps permanently.

This is what Zilbovicius herself has to say on this subject:

> We have shown that, in autistic subjects, the perception of the human voice does not lead to the activation of a very specific area of the brain that deals with the human voice. . . . They treat the human voice like any other sound, that of a car or a bell, for example. All of this happens in the course of development. The human being is born with a particular attraction to human stimuli, and so we specialize, we become experts in the human voice and face. There is probably something innate in autists: they are not born with this attraction. So they do not become experts and their brain does not develop in the same way. [Zilbovicius, 2004]

These hypotheses corroborate other MRI studies on imagery dealing with the perception of faces: these suggest that this kind of perception is not associated with an activation of regions involved in attributing emotional value to a stimulus. The hypothesis would be that the absence of emotional activation in the course of development would lead to a lack of expertise in dealing with faces and, as a consequence, a lack of development of the gyrus fusiform, which is responsible for the recognition of faces. This model, known as Schultz's model (Schultz et al., 2003; cited in Mottron, 2004, p. 97), when coupled with Zilbovicius's proposals, provides a scientific basis for Bergès's and Diatkine's hypothesis concerning the irrefutable effects of the psyche on the soma in the case of autism.

This leads Zilbovicius to recommend early intervention with children (starting at 4 years of age[10]) to make them want to listen to voices and—other studies lead us to add—to look at faces. Up to this point I can only concur with her and state that psychoanalytic practice is able to instil this desire. This is what I try to show in this chapter.

On the other hand, I am worried when she talks about "multimedia methods". We have known for some time that certain autistics are fascinated by audio and video cassettes. This still does not lead them to become interested in flesh-and-blood human beings, and thus it does not seem to correspond to her aims. Having suggested the use of re-educative methods combined with antidepressants, she adds: "This is not the fault of the parents, it's the fault of . . . bad luck. The parents are very important actors in the re-education of these children and in their integration into society." Indeed, I too think that the parents should be partners in the child's psychotherapeutic treatment.

It seems to me that we can also agree about this aetiology of *being unlucky*—where no explanation, whether genetic or biological, is offered. Long ago, my viewing of home movies showing children who later became autistic taught me that, from the very beginning, starting at birth, they do not go towards the other. This does not rule out the possibility that complex factors, still unknown to us, could have played some part during pregnancy. Geneviève Haag speaks of a prenatal root for sound problems—a very important factor, in her view (Haag, n.d.).

My experience with Marine and her relapse have taught me that there must be additional factors in play, beyond the one demonstrated by Zilbovicius. Even after having discovered her attraction for the human voice and face when she was a baby, Marine was capable of withdrawing again. I have often asked myself about the causes of this relapse. There was, of course, the fact that I had accepted to stop seeing her, agreeing to the mother's request all the more willingly in that the seven-week interruption occasioned by the summer vacation did not seem to have affected Marine. Later I learnt that Marine went back to the day-care centre only after my return and that it was particularly difficult for her, since the two childcare workers she had become accustomed to were no longer there. I also learnt that the mother's return to work had been marked by the replacement of her immediate supervisor and by her feeling of having been passed over. By November the mother was depressed, and it is difficult to determine who dragged whom into the downward spiral. In any case, I should emphasize that in this child there is a factor of greater sensitivity towards changes in her environment than in other children. When faced with such fragility in a child, we might even ask whether it is really appropriate to see the mother in psychoanalytic psychotherapy. We know that at the beginning of this kind of personal process, the subject is often lost in his or her own thoughts. Could this have been interpreted by the child as a loss of the bond with her mother?

What I can affirm, in any case, is that faced with this set of difficulties, Marine, like a little submarine, had battened down her hatches and dived under. In this session, all her attention, visual and auditory, was concentrated on the big felt-tip pens that she kept putting in and taking out of the pot; she was visibly attentive to the little noise they made and to their colours. Might we think of the will of a proto-subject not to hear the human voice? Could there be a factor of hypersensitivity in these babies, leading them to avoid the human voice as soon as it shows the least sign of depression—as though it could not help but provoke an intolerable depressive-type response in the baby? Zilbovicius's idea of using antidepressants on these children implies that she hypothesizes metabolic processes of this kind. Although I have great reservations about giving this type of substance to children, I must admit that when Marine's mother was on antidepressants, their interpersonal relationship improved. But this could only happen fifteen months later, when Marine had, for the most part, recovered. At first there was no question of speaking to the mother (whom I was seeing every week) about treatment for her depression, for to do so would have seemed equivalent to making her take undue responsibility in this situation, especially when Marine's state of withdrawal would have made any parent depressed. Later, when her daughter started to have a real relationship with her, she was able to talk to me about her depressive core, which was present long before the birth of her daughter. But it was, above all, her desire that her daughter's entry into school would go as smoothly as possible that made her decide to start taking "a little something" before the summer vacation. I am not saying that the mother's somewhat depressive structure could be the cause of her daughter's pathology—if that were the case, a large part of humankind would be autistic. It seems, rather, that this element brought out something analogous in the child and that was intolerable for her. Isn't this where Zilbovicius dreams of intervening?

Return to the clinical material

While opening her mouth for the spoonfuls of yogurt, Marine attentively watches the camera in front of her.

The mother, speaking for the child, says: "On the other hand, I find this camera stuff intriguing."[11]

Despite the harmonious, empathetic side of our session, Marine remains stonily unresponsive, as if our voices were just background noise. She pays no more attention to them than to the sounds of cars coming from the street. It is obvious that clinical work with such children confirms Zilbovicius's discoveries: our voices are, in fact, treated like external noises.

Marine was not going to become an "expert in human voices and faces" this way, to use Zilbovicius's expression, and her brain was "at risk of not developing in the usual way". The first results in cerebral imaging have highlighted the difficulty of coupling a voice and a visual image in autism. Laurent Mottron (2004, p. 97) has done a survey of studies on troubles of intermodal perception, citing the work of Boucher, Lewis, and Collins (1998).

It is therefore more urgent than ever to try to give back to little infants like Marine, under the age of 2 years, the desire to hear the human voice and to look at the faces of those who are close to them. And this is just what happened in the second part of this session, which was a genuine psychic resuscitation.

> I pretend to eat the next spoonful of yogurt: "Now Mrs Laznik is going to eat some. Mmm! Mmm! Mmm! Vanilla is good!" This fragment, showing my surprise and pleasure at the odour of vanilla, provokes—starting with the first "Mmm!"—a smiling gaze from Marine, as though she were sharing my pleasure. But this vanishes by the end of the sentence.

> The mother, too, tries to catch her daughter's gaze. To do this, she also pretends to eat yogurt, saying: "May I have a little? Am I allowed to have a little of this yogurt? I wonder if there's a little strawberry in it . . .", she adds, pretending to taste.

> Marine shows no sign of having perceived her mother's play. Trying not to lose her composure, the mother gives her another spoonful of yogurt. Marine is perfectly able to anticipate the arrival of the spoon by opening her mouth, but nothing in her is suggestive of shared pleasure.

> I decide to pretend to eat again. "Mrs Laznik's turn! I want some too! Mmm! That's good." At my first "Mmm!" of surprise and pleasure, Marine looks me in the eye again, with a big smile, as though sharing my pleasure. But this lasts for no more than two seconds.

My transference tells me that this latest success has caused the mother distress—I can do what she can't. I decide to turn the game around. Taking the yogurt and the spoon, I say: "Now Mrs Laznik is going to give some to Mummy."

"Ah! We've changed distributors!" exclaims the mother. Thanks to our old bond, this unusual situation—involving a 40-year-old woman, who probably hasn't been spoon-fed for decades—elicits an exclamation of surprise and amusement from the mother. Marine looks at both of us, laughing and rhythmically bringing her arms together, as though she was about to clap her hands. I comment: "I only get that when we're clowning around."

This child can clearly distinguish between the register of alimentary need and that of oral drive, necessarily interwoven with the scopic and invocatory drives, casting doubt on Freud's theory that the bond with the other comes to rely on the satisfaction of alimentary need (Laznik, 2000b). It is not yogurt that will feed her desire to be seen and listened to: it is a particular prosody in our voices, marked by alternating peaks of surprise and pleasure. These peaks are characteristic of what has long been called *motherese* and which, more recently, has been called *parent-ese*, since fathers are as gifted at producing it as mothers. We have known for a long time (Fernald & Simon, 1984) that the prosody emerging from it can be found in speech between adults only in exceptional situations where surprise and pleasure merge. Reissland (2002) has proved that surprise produces in the voice of the baby's parent a heightened peak of energy, whereas pleasure produces a very low peak. I have observed that when these two peaks are produced in succession, it gives the choppy-hills aspect proper to the prosody of parentese. But before treating the analysis of our voices, let us return to the end of the session.

I give the yogurt back to the mother, who says: "A little more?" Trying to catch her daughter's eye, she pulls the spoon away when the mouth opens, asking: "Where's the mouth?" Marine, unmovable, continues to manipulate the felt-tip pens, opening her mouth when the spoon approaches.

When she has swallowed her spoonful, I ask: "Was it good? It was good?" But she is like a stone. The contact has been broken.

I continue: "What about me? What about me? What about me?" I get a brief glance from her. But the next time I try, the trick doesn't work any more.

I am worried, fearing that she will withdraw for a long time. Knowing what I do about the "siren voice" that a prosody expressing "bewilderment and enlightenment" can have, even on babies who later became autistic, I try to create within myself an internal image that could put me into this kind of state. I take the pot of yogurt and smell its odour; I am invaded by vanilla. Then I imagine a beautiful park with a big vanilla plant. The park has a tropical atmosphere; my imaginary vanilla plant looks like a big bush with shiny leaves, covered with beautiful white flowers. I've never seen a vanilla plant, and I don't know what one looks like. No matter—in infinitely less time than it takes to describe it, I am propelled into a magic world of surprise and pleasure.

I hear myself say to Marine, as I hold a spoonful of yogurt up to her nose for her to smell, *"Look at the smell!"* There is plenty of enthusiasm in what I say and the prosodic peaks of my voice must convey it, for the little girl looks at me with a smile. As for the apparent absurdity of my utterance, it is surely due to a condensation of my desire to make her smell both the joy of the scent and the beauty of the flowers. I would even offer the hypothesis that the drive, when it takes the other into its mouth, produces co-modality.

Twenty minutes later, Marine herself, using her tea set, will offer me a dish and a spoon, pretending to feed me in turn. But before analysing the value of this scene, it is worth while to point out that it took place just after another one: Marine wants to push a little chair around the room. At this time, she used to move the furniture all around, to the despair of her parents, who rightly saw it as a withdrawing action on her part. This also happened during the preceding sessions, but now, instead of throwing the doll that was on the chair to the floor, Marine places it on my lap. I decide to sing it a lullaby: "Cuddle, cuddly, cudd-a-ly, cudd-a-ly, cuddle, cuddly, cuddly for dolly." The rhythm is slow, but marked by repetitions, and the vowels are especially accentuated and lengthened. Marine doesn't take her eyes off me during the song, but she stops paying attention the minute the singing is over. However, she herself picks up the chant a few sessions later, while rocking the tiny, two-centimetre-long baby in its tiny cradle. There is certainly much to reflect upon regarding the power of such rhythms in the treatment of this kind of child.

But let us return to the point in the session where she feeds me. I am filled with great hope at that moment: she has just succeeded in spontaneously answering one of the key questions of the CHAT,[12] a question normally given to children older than she is: her *capacity for pretending* is established! My inner joy at such success on a cognitive test rests on the fact that I have long believed that the question "Is the child, using a toy tea-set, able to offer a cup coffee or tea to his or her mother?" goes well beyond the *capacity for pretending*. Its bedrock is none other than the completion of the third phase of the drive circuit. When a child plays at offering something good to the mother, he is outside the register of the satisfaction of need. In addition, this particular object is good for the mother but not for the child, who is at an age where neither coffee nor tea would be liked. The bedrock of the child's capacity to provide a positive response to this question from the CHAT thus depends on the child's capacity for wishing to make himself the bearer of the object that answers the mother's oral drive. Whereas the infant offers his little foot or hand to his mother so that she can enjoy pretending to eat them, the older child offers, to the drive enjoyment of the other, not a piece of its own body but, rather, a sublimated object.

> When Marine spoon-feeds me, I pretend to eat a delicious imaginary object. Marine follows attentively the signs of pleasures on my face and in my voice. Her father comes with her to the next session. She plays restaurant again, feeding us by turns, delighted to be giving us so much pleasure.

Marine confirms my current hypothesis about the establishment of the psychic apparatus: her pleasure in functioning is a tributary of the pleasure she causes in the other. This formulation is not without analogy to that which prevails for older people, and which we owe to Lacan: the desire of the subject is the desire of the other.

But in Marine's case these happy moments are still just tiny islands emerging from a sea of indifference. Even the session from which I have just recounted several excerpts is spotted with this indifference, which prompted Pierre Ferrari, a well-known researcher in autism in France, to say, as he watched a video of it: "Do you think we can come through for her?" This question, asked with tenderness, gives a glimpse of his legitimate worry. At the time I didn't know how to answer it either; I only know that at 15 months she was much more difficult to mobilize than at 3 months. Only a year later was I able to say that she seemed to have recovered. It is not possible to remind paediatricians too much of how important it is to send these children to us in the first months of their lives!

The entire work of the psychic reanimation carried out in the session rests on interdisciplinary work that I have undertaken in parallel.

Research: prosody in interactions between babies who became autistic and their parents

The research discussed here is derived from our studies on the early signs of autism.[13] It is a multidisciplinary, multi-focused research in conjunction with Filippo Muratori and Sandra Maestro,[14] who study the early signs of autism using home movies (see chapter 3), and with Erika Parlato, a psycholinguist.[15] Trevarthen and Fernald have demonstrated, in all their research in linguistics with newborns, that from birth the baby shows an interest for certain elements of his mother's voice. I have linked these research studies with the hypotheses about the "invocatory drive" advanced by Jacques Lacan. Let us not forget that Lacan added the gaze and the voice to the list of drive objects described by Freud: breast, penis, faeces. My interest in this subject came to me when I noticed some strange phenomena in home movies showing babies who were later to become autistic. Babies who, during the daily activities of changing, bathing, and feeding, did not look at the parent who was taking care of them were suddenly able not only to look but to answer, entering into a veritable "proto-conversation."

One striking example is found in the film of little Marco (see chapter 5). This baby, then aged 2½ months, who can remain perfectly indifferent to the human world around him, suddenly shows himself capable of looking at his mother and answering her by gurgling when she hums him a song. Their sustained interaction goes on for nearly three minutes. When this fragment of the movie was shown by Maestro and Muratori without any explanation of the context, it provoked lively reactions from colleagues all over the world: how can one accept the very idea of such a baby becoming autistic? Does it mean that it is impossible to make a prediction at this age? But in practically all the rest of this home movie, the baby's state of withdrawal is easily detectable. How do we account for such disparity in this baby's relational modes? This is one aporia that got me working. Without ignoring the triggering factor of the mother's song, a study of the prosody of the two parents, both present in this scene, shows that the father's voice presents the prosodic characteristics of the motherese described by psycholinguists. Even if this paternal voice cannot be heard well on the movie's soundtrack, it was able to sustain the pursuit of the visual and vocal bond between mother and child. So we decided to compare the voice of Marco's mother, when she is speaking to her child, with the voice of a mother speaking to her normal baby in a comparable situation: when the baby's diaper was being changed.

Figure 8.1 shows the spectrogram of the two voices. In spectral analyses, the horizontal axis represents time and the vertical axis represents frequency. The degree of darkness of the streaks indicates the level of energy.

1. The voice of Marco's mother does not present the characteristics of motherese. The comparison of the two spectrograms is striking, even for those who are not specialists in acoustic analysis: Marco's mother has a very monotone voice, whereas Fabien's mother's voice has more intonation. Nevertheless, there are two reasons why we cannot derive an aetiological hypothesis from this remarkable difference. First, at the time of the earliest research into the prosody of motherese, Fernald (Fernald & Simon, 1984) demonstrated that

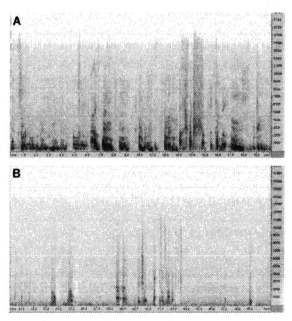

Figure 8.1.   Spectral analysis of the voice of the mother of a normal child (Fabien's mother: A) compared with the voice of the mother of an autistic child (Marco's mother: B).

a mother is incapable of producing this kind of prosody when her baby is not with her. Even if she knows that her baby is going to hear the recording afterwards and she tries her best, her prosody is not the same in front of a microphone as it is in front of the baby. We can therefore think that a baby who does not react much will eventually foster the "in-front-of-a-microphone" prosody in his mother. So there is no possibility of fabricating fake motherese. Second, recent work by Burnham at the University of Sydney (Burnham, Kitamura, & Vollmer-Conna, 2002), on the prosody of motherese with normal babies, shows that the baby's reactions amplify the contours of prosody curves in the mother's voice. For many parents, then, this prosody is the result and the reflection of their relationship to the baby.

Fabien (whose development we know to have been normal) and his mother present in this scene a fine example of what psycholinguists call "speech turns". The mother speaks for the baby, in the first person, then answers him as though he were the one who had spoken. In the following dialogue, the baby actively supports her with his gaze and his voice:

"I'm feeling better, Mummy! I'm feeling better!"

(The baby, looking at his mother: "Wah.")

"Yes, of course, yes, of course, it's better!"

(The baby, still looking at his mother: "Aah.")

The mother picks up the baby's "Aah", adding: "Ah, yes! Ah, yes! Are you gargling?"

(The baby, looking at her: "Gah goo ghee.")

"Ah, yes, I'm gargling, I'm making noises with my throat, I'm making noises." . . . "You make noises with your throat!"

(The baby, smiling at her: "Ga goo.")

The prosody of the mother's voice communicates the surprise and joy this situation makes her feel. The mother is speaking motherese. According to Dupoux and Mehler (1990), motherese is the dialect of all mothers all over the world when they talk to their babies: the voice is a tone higher and the intonation is exaggerated.

Figure 8.2 is the spectral analysis of a small fragment of the mother's speech, the "Ah, yes! Ah, yes!" that she says to her son. This

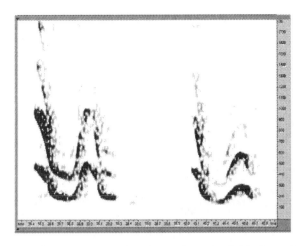

Fig. 2.   The melody of "motherese" in the mother of a child whose development
is typical.

image shows clearly how motherese is manifested by modifications of the voice and the prosody, by melodic forms that are soft, long, sweeping. The effect of the prosody's rhythm is amplified over several repetitions. We also see clear breaks between the two sound fragments. These breaks are an essential part of motherese.

Even though baby Fabien was obviously collaborating here, I asked myself the following question: what would happen if, in spite of everything, an adult managed to produce motherese prosody when faced with a baby who would later become autistic? Would the baby respond?

Pedro is another baby from the sample of Pisan home movies. He enables us to put this question to the test, and to discover that its answer is affirmative. Pedro is a baby who never looks at his mother or responds to any of her appeals. He sometimes responds to his father when the latter deploys a lot of energy, even resorting to strong-arm tactics to get Pedro's attention. A friend of the mother, who came to spend a holiday on their farm, couldn't once enter into contact with him.

We have analysed the mother's voice during a poignant scene where she calls out to him with increasing desperation in the face of his indifference.

"Pedro? Pedro? Pedro?" She approaches, as the baby looks, ostentatiously, the other way. The tone of the mother's voice becomes

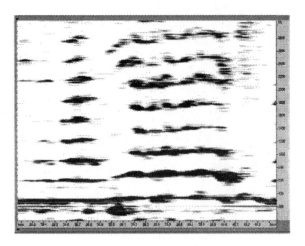

Figure 8.3.   Melody of the mother of Pedro, an autistic baby.

ever more pleading: "Look at me! Look at me! Look at me!" She presses her face to the baby's tummy and cries out her distress, "My baby! My baby! My baby!"

Figure 8.3 shows the spectral analysis of this last fragment of maternal speech. Despite the force of the mother's despair as she cries out to her baby—which led the father to intervene, by coming to take the baby in his arms and thus putting an end to the scene—we see that there is no prosodic peak. Her voice remains flat. We may also note the absence of breaks between the sound segments.

Nevertheless, in this long home movie, there is one extraordinary little scene. This baby, who practically never responds, entered into a visual and tonal dialogue—an inter-modal dialogue—with his uncle, who happened to stop by. This scene took place when the baby was about 6 months old. It occurred in the barnyard where the father and the uncle, who live in separate houses, were working together on their farm, which produces organic cow's milk. This detail is important because the men's workload is very heavy in the spring, when they must not only take care of the animals and the milking, but also plant the forage they use to feed the animals. It is not difficult to imagine that the uncle has little opportunity to become aware of his nephew's communication problems, since he probably does not meet with him very often.

Two minutes before the uncle intervenes, the mother once again attempts to enter into contact with baby. Her voice indicates that she is doing this out of a sense of duty; she doesn't much believe in it, but she tries anyway. Not only does the baby not enter into contact with her, he also flops down on his side in the little cloth bed his mother had set up in the garden for him.

The uncle starts by extending his hand to the baby, eliciting no response from him. But as soon as the uncle's voice is heard, it wrests the baby out of his state of prostration; Pedro, smiling, begins gazing at and vocalizing to his uncle, like a completely normal baby. The change in the baby is sudden and astonishing.

When we compare the spectrograms of the voice of the mother and the voice of the uncle (Figure 8.4), the difference is striking. The uncle's voice, unlike the mother's, does present the prosodic characteristics of parentese (Fernald & Kuhl, 1987).

Figure 8.5 is another presentation of a little fragment of the discourse that the uncle addresses to his nephew, as he plays with the baby's dummy and asks him which of them it belongs to—himself or the baby? The uncle seems to be in ecstasy over the dummy, as he

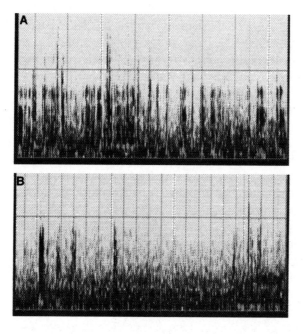

Figure 8.4. Comparison of Pedro's uncle's voice (A) and Pedro's mother's voice (B).

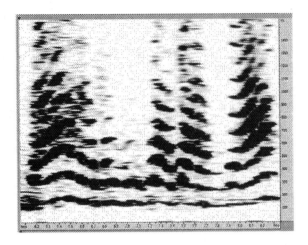

Figure 8.5.   Fragments of the uncle's voice, addressed to the nephew.

asks playfully "De chi è? De chi è questo, ein?" ["Whose is it? Whose is it, eh?"]

Here we can see the outlines of the contours of the prosodic curves, as well as the empty spaces between the blocks of sound. This baby shows us that the presence of prosodic peaks proper to "parentese" in the voice of the adult who is speaking to him can induce a response even in babies who later turn out to be autistic. This means that even if the baby does not spark this type of relation with his other, he is equipped to receive it. But we should proceed with caution, for even if Pedro cannot help but respond to the siren voice of his uncle speaking parentese in this scene, he does not re-initiate the conversation. Nowhere in this home movie do we see him provoking his interlocutor. This concept of "provocation", implying a dimension proper to the appeal to the other, has been developed by Emese Nagy, a researcher in developmental theory (Nagy & Molnar, 2004). His concept brings clinical support to the research of Laznik (2000a) (see also chapter 5) concerning the third phase of the drive circuit, the phase when the baby *makes himself heard*—for example, by another person. There is one exception in the film: when Pedro was around 15 months old, his mother became completely silent. She settles for simply filming Pedro as he tries, in vain, to enter into verbal contact with the farm dog, offering it pieces of Lego and a long speech. The dog goes away, perfectly indifferent, and the mother is now unable to pick up for her own use the "discourse" that the child has addressed to the dog. If there is an "invocatory drive" in this child, it could only be addressed to a dog that made nothing of it.

Alfredo is another of the Pisa babies who later became autistic. When his parents speak to him, they sometimes produce prosodic peaks. Nevertheless, throughout the first three months of his life, Alfredo seems to avoid perceptions from his parents or even from his grandparents when they come to visit. Here we could also speak of an apparently voluntary avoidance, of the kind that Selma Fraiberg (1982) describes. If we do a micro-analysis of a scene between the baby and his mother when the baby was aged 1 month and 20 days, we hear the modification in the maternal voice, which grows weary as all its sweet and tender attempts fail. Even little caresses around his mouth cannot win her the attention of her son. The father, who is filming them, asks her to try again. She makes another attempt, with the father's support. In vain. A freeze-frame at the end of this scene allows us to perceive a slight crease of bitterness forming at the corner of the mother's mouth, surely unbeknownst to herself. The parents, faced with this absence of response from their baby or, indeed, with his active refusals[16] (he ostentatiously turns in the opposite direction to where his mother is), mutually sustain each other and seem to remain confident.

We have closely analysed the scene in which, for the first time, the baby looks at one of his parents: his father. The baby is then 3 months old. The movies are made mainly during the weekend when the father is there.

> This time, the father is holding the baby in his lap while the mother films. As is usual with them, they keep up a repartee as a way of facing this blatantly absent baby. They are heartened by their repartee, and at one point the beginning of parentese appears. The baby answers it with a smile that is not addressed to anyone; the parents are so pleasantly surprised by this that it gives rise to a new prosodic peak in the father's voice. The baby looks at him and smiles. This event is welcomed by a concert of surprise and joy in the parental prosody, which enables the baby to keep looking and smiling. The father, his voice choked with joy repeats, "He's looking at me, he's looking at me." But he accepts it very well when the baby wants to break the contact; he is in harmony with his son.

> Ten minutes later, the mother takes her baby in her arms and starts talking to him. Her voice is still imprinted with her surprise and joy at the event that has occurred, as can be seen in the prosodic curves (Figure 8.6).

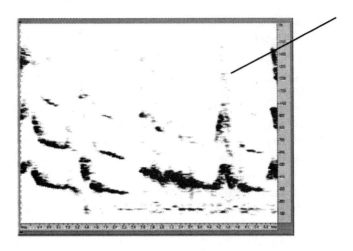

Figure 8.6.   Peak preceding the moment when the baby starts to cry.

Indeed, in one of his first articles on the prosody of "motherese",
Fernald pointed out that this particular form of mother's prosody is
virtually never found in the language of one adult speaking to another adult, except in extremely rare conditions where great surprise
is combined with great pleasure (Fernald & Simon, 1984). Fernald did
not draw any conclusions from this, but I have been extremely interested by these two terms, surprise and pleasure. They encompass the
notions of bewilderment and enlightenment that Freud (1905c) found
so interesting in the role of the third person in jokes. I have revisited
them elsewhere in reference to my psychoanalytic treatments of autistic children (Laznik, 1995b).

> Alfredo's mother speaks to him in a voice that has this prosody;
> he cannot help but look at her, at the precise moment when she
> produces an especially significant peak (Figure 8.6). But as soon as
> the baby sees his mother's face, he starts to cry.

What hypotheses can we make here? Is there already a problem with
intermodality? With moving from the *heard* to the *seen*? But with his
father, ten minutes earlier, the baby did not present this problem.
Could he have seen something so unpleasant? Perhaps the features of
the mother's face? Worries about an unresponsive baby are perhaps
erased more slowly from the face than from the voice. Let us not forget
the slight crease of bitterness that was starting to show at the corner
of her mouth.

Three days later, the mother manages to enter into a long exchange with her baby. They are lying together on the parental bed, and the baby has to make an effort to turn towards the mother's face, which is partially hidden by the mattress he is resting on. It is possible that the mother's very relaxed position contributed to the quality of her prosody, but one could also imagine that the mother's position prevented too close a reading of the discreet worry lines on her face. As soon as the baby responds by looking at her, the mother's outburst of surprise and joy improves her prosody even more. She says lots of nice words to him, declares her love to him in every possible way, and laughs joyfully at her son's responses. But though she can echo some of her vocalizations, she does not allow herself to speak in the first-person singular. She does not attribute to him phrases supposed to be addressed to herself, the mother.

Because of this, it may be necessary here to speak of a pseudo proto-conversation. That dimension of madness which consists of speaking in place of the other—in the sense of mothers' necessary madness—is perhaps only possible when a mother feels sure of her maternal capacities. An unresponsive baby must put a great strain on its mother.

Two little fragments of maternal speech are presented in Figure 8.7, in which we see how prosodic peaks, repetitions, and empty spaces between phases of speech are all quickly constructed as soon as the baby responds.

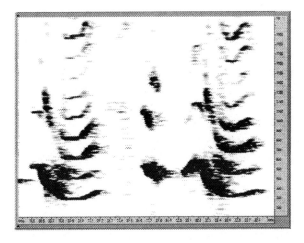

Figure 8.7.   Fragments from the mother's dialogue with Alfredo.

Perceptual acoustic analysis, carried out by Parlato and compared by her with work on motherese published in Italian, indicates that throughout this scene the mother's speech presents energy variations and a prolongation of vowels characteristic of motherese. But it is important to know that while the sequences in the film where the baby does respond to his mother coincide, in 100% of the cases, with those where the mother produces motherese, the baby does not respond every time the mother produces it.

Above all, though, nowhere in the movies available to us does Alfredo show any sign of a third phase of the drive circuit. Not only does he not try to be heard, but even when stimulated by his mother, he does not try to make himself the object of her drive.

> One instructive scene occurs when Alfredo is on the changing table, and his mother playfully stimulates her son. She shows him how appetizing his little foot is, even inviting him to taste it, which the baby does, not without pleasure. But it never occurs to him to offer this little foot to his mother's mouth, as close as it is.

This is not a baby who likes to get nibbled by the other. He does not seem to be interested in what could give pleasure to this other. Trevarthen likes to say that babies are born with "a motif for the motif of the other". But this is not the case for the babies in these home movies.

Back to Marine:
interweaving treatment and research

As a psychoanalyst, research is of interest to me insofar as its hypotheses can make me imaginative in difficult clinical situations, such as those involving babies at risk for autism. It is obvious that Pedro's laughing for his uncle is in my mind when I undertake to resuscitate the relationship with Marine. Also, when she stops responding to my play, it makes me think that I have lost the freshness of real surprise with her, so I try to refresh myself with representations that occur to me, such as the vanilla plant. But will this show up in the voice analysis?

The hypotheses I could formulate about the material of this session were:

1. If the first time I mimic my surprise and my joy at the yogurt, the child looks at me, this must indicate that my voice has the prosodic characteristics of parentese.

2. If the mother has no success when she plays, it must be because her voice is flat, which is noticeable when one listens to the tape, but about which one can never be sure.

3. If the little girl becomes so enthusiastic when I pretend to feed her mother, laughing at us both and making rudimentary applauding gestures, it is because our two voices must then have these same prosodic peaks.

4. If she looks at me during my two scenes of play-acting, there must be elements of parentese in my prosody.

5. On the other hand, if, during the following attempt, she did not deign to look at me, could I not imagine that repeating the same scene had diminished my ability to let myself be surprised? The absence of surprise must have eroded my prosodic peaks.

6. If she followed me again in my invitation to look at the fragrant vanilla bush, it was because my surprise and pleasure were genuine.

The recordings of Marine's sessions were given to the psycholinguist Erika Parlato, and her laboratory analyses of the spectrum of vocal prosodies confirmed these hypotheses. During my fourth repetition of the scene, Marine no longer responded because there was no more parentese prosody. This shows that there is no such thing as fake parentese. So it would be absurd to suggest that anyone could imitate parentese in his or her speech—it results from a subjective state of surprise and pleasure. It can't be forced. But in the last scene, the one with the flowering bush, Erika Parlato said that she observed—at the moment when I say "*Look at the smell*"—a rounding of intonation, a prolonged use of vowels, along with a heightened intensity, which is characteristic of parentese prosody.

Psycholinguistic research and psychoanalysis

How can these acoustic analyses prove of interest to the analyst? In my view, they confirm that there is an element of bewitchment in the voice of the "Other",[17] which, like the voice of the Sirens, cannot be received without provoking an irresistible attraction in the listener.[18] The Greeks had been aware of this from the time of Homer, who speaks explicitly of it in the *Odyssey*. This probably corroborates the alienating dimension of the constitution of the subject, as long as we do not forget the dimension of separation, which plays in the other direction.

But what is fascinating is that this specific prosody only works when the coordinates of the other's pleasure are present. We can think that, from the moment of the baby's birth, the pleasure and surprise provoked in the mother by the sight of the baby will enable her to produce a prosody of motherese right away.[19] We have seen that these two elements produced well-differentiated peaks in this prosody (Reissland, Shepherd, & Cowie, 2002).

Also, on the strictly clinical level, Roland Gori (2002, p. 65) has emphasized the importance of a state of distress, just before the blossoming of passionate love. I think that this state of lack, of inner emptiness, is always necessary if the massive libidinal investment of a new being is to become possible. The most striking example is that of "the baby blues"—the moment when the loss of usual points of reference, and the extreme fragility in which women find themselves after the birth of a child, can enable them to fall in love with their infant and to invest the infant in the place of the Ideal. If this process is usual, it is nonetheless dangerous: some women can prolong this state into postpartum depression.

But when everything happens normally, the infant shows a drive appetite for this kind of prosody: he literally feeds off it (Laznik, 2000b).

Lastly, in the metapsychological register, it should be noted that surprise and pleasure hark back to what Freud (1905c) was able to formulate concerning the *third person*. This is the person who, faced with a truncated, mispronounced word, can—after a moment of surprise and amazement—let himself be invaded by the pleasure that suddenly illuminates him, the pleasure of the *joke* that he hears in what the first person has unwittingly proffered, which bewildered and delights the one who hears. The prosody of motherese is, I think, the perceptible translation of this state in the mother: she marvels, even as she is upset, bewildered. In the case of the infant, we can think that, in the first days, this is played out in the register of the gaze. What makes one marvel is not only what one can see in the infant, but also the infant's own gaze. But very quickly, sonic, gestural, and mimetic responses coming from the baby will come to support the mother's prosody. This is why I insist that the prosody is a function of the drive interplay between a future subject and the one who at the same time becomes his Other.

This prosody produces a trace in the memory of the infant, which will be re-activated with each new excitation. It can then be re-lived by him, primarily in a hallucinatory way. In the moments when the baby daydreams while sucking his thumb, these traces of the coordinates of the primordial Other's pleasure make me certain that Eros is present and that we are really faced with an auto-eroticism. If we remove the Eros, then we find ourselves faced with autism—with all the consequence that this brings, among which is a lack of motivation for *becoming an expert in the human voice and face*, as Zilbovicius says.

Notes

1. Protection Maternelle et Infantile. This PMI is run by the Red Cross.

2. I was very interested in a communication, from an association of parents of autistics in France, that shows that in babies who later became autistic, the incidence of serious gastro-oesophageal problems is ten times that of the normal population. It is possible that these troubles are themselves psychosomatic in origin. But when faced with pain, we have to break the vicious cycle.

3. For several months, I will keep this mother and baby a very long time. There is a first "session" with the two of them, then Marine will fall asleep, allowing the mother to talk with me until Marine wakes up, on her own, and we can say good-bye.

4. The mother repeats this at the beginning of each session for three months.

5. It is obvious that the content of what I say to the baby is addressed to the mother. The child is surely more sensitive to the prosodic aspect of what I say.

6. This comparison with the secret daughter of François Mitterrand (who at that time was the French President), known to all people, makes the mother laugh and takes the tension out of the situation.

7. All this can be understood only in light of the distinction between need and drive, a distinction that was introduced by Jacques Lacan and is followed by practically every psychoanalyst in France. This distinction was never made in Anglo-Saxon psychoanalytic literature.

8. This idea originated with Charles Melman and proved to be very useful for the work of deciphering the situation through micro-analysis. The first film-maker was Anouk de Bordas, a colleague who began her studies in psychology after a long analysis. I believe it is indispensable for the "film-maker" or "scribe" of a session with an autistic child to have a background in psychoanalysis. In terms of the transference, it would be difficult for me to feel that someone was judging what I was trying to establish in order to make contact with the child. The following year, the film-maker was Catherine Thomas, who has the same sort of background. Both of them were essential to the work, and I thank them very much.

9. Both had been students of J. Ajouriaguerra.

10. The same age is given in another research paper that Zilbovicius presented at the conference in Belgium. Personally, I think that one must intervene at a much earlier age.

11. In all films showing babies who later became autistic, we notice this interest in the camera. In the past, when the camera had to be placed in front of a human face, it was possible to have some doubt as to which object was being invested by

the baby's gaze. But now that cameras are used from farther away, it is clearly the machine, not the face of the cameraman, that is being watched.

12. This is a cognitive questionnaire designed by Baron-Cohen; it allows us to pinpoint, as early as 18 months of age, children who will be autistic at 3 years. In our research at PREAUT, on the early sign of autism, we use a slightly modified French variant of the CHAT (see chapter 5).

13. Under the aegis of the Association PréAut.

14. Fondation Stella Maris, Pisa Medicine Faculty.

15. Brazil. This work produced an earlier joint publication.

16. The idea that there is, from the moment of birth, a prototype subject capable of wilfully refusing is rather rare in psychoanalysis. The French psychoanalyst Françoise Dolto may be the only one to have made this hypothesis, without, in my opinion, supporting it enough. Current research on infants' competencies tend to support this idea. Trevarthen (2003) asserts that there is an innate intersubjectivity in the newborn and thinks that the latter can conceive of himself as separate from the adult who cares for him.

17. I am indebted to Hervé Bentata (2001) for this idea.

18. We are here in the presence of the Other that constitutes the unconscious.

19. This has been shown by Fernald & Simon (1984) to be the case with normal mothers of normal babies.

CHAPTER NINE

Changing destinies:
the theory and practice
of reaching emotionally withdrawn infants

Stella Acquarone

The pre-autistic baby may well feel in regard to persons that, as Jean-Paul Sartre declared in his play *No Exit* (1955), "Hell is other people". To some babies with genetic tendencies, developmental processes and environmental factors make relating to others, accommodating to others, and having to compete with others a nightmare to be avoided, to the point that they retreat into private worlds. They become difficult to reach, withdrawn, too quiet, or uninterested in relationships, struggling to regulate and protect themselves or regressing to earlier behaviours.

The aim of this chapter is to present and discuss some of the detailed intricacies involved in the ongoing treatment of babies who withdraw completely from any level of personal human interaction. Early intervention is the technique used to observe the emotional aspects at work among babies who behave as if "hell is other people", in order to actually change their destinies, positioning the attachment problem that an emotionally withdrawn infant develops.

History

The Parent–Infant Clinic

The Parent–Infant Clinic has been attending to infants and their parents and siblings since 1990, following the awareness that early interventions in the first year of life should be made available to all young families, regardless of catchment area. The awareness of how effective early intervention could be was the natural consequence of clinical research work undertaken since 1980 in health centres and paediatric wards in different boroughs in London and in a women's prison that accepts mothers and their babies. The research showed that attending to parents' concerns over the sleeping, feeding, crying, communication, and other difficulties their babies may be displaying made for a better relationship, allowing their infants to develop a secure attachment and an ability to integrate experiences. In one health centre, I was in a position to personally follow the sixty referrals coming each year for treatment. As a result of our early-intervention approach, I observed that an average of only three out of sixty would later be seen at the child and adolescent departments for other difficulties.

Our approach has been explained in chapter 6 and is derived from psychoanalysis.

Early intervention with early autistic behaviours

Today we give babies check-ups to screen for physical difficulties and developmental difficulties. We should be screening for a third: emotional and relational difficulties. Changing destinies is an early intervention of this third kind.

In order to reach emotionally withdrawn infants and have any chance of "changing destinies", we must intervene early, and a successful early intervention depends in large part on our ability to "read" and interpret relationships. Three working fundamentals underlie the early intervention:

1. Relationships are said to be the important fact of existence between human beings. Without relationships there is little chance of survival for individuals or species (Darwin, 1872). A person needs the other to exist, to share, to enrich, and to give meanings to their lives. The mirroring aspect of the mother or caregiver developed by Winnicott (1967), Rhode (2005), and others, in which infants see the reflection of themselves as being seen and admired by the mother, is the exact opposite in emotionally withdrawn infants, where the other can be felt as hell. In Sartre's view, through the look of other people we are transformed into objects and made part of a torturous inner world.

2. Relationships make up a dynamic system. The relationship is a dynamic system where interactive forces from other generations, fatal or unforeseen circumstances, family events, and trigger responses promote or discourage the development of integration

3. Each member of the relationship has an internal world full of mental representations which can be known (conscious) or unknown (unconscious). All of us hold memories of relationships with important others—starting with mother and father—and these mental representations are loaded with emotional meanings.

Keeping in mind the underlying fundamentals of this specific early intervention, there are two necessary conditions needed to make it work. First, the therapist or caregiver must accept that babies have innate capacities and need to relate actively to other human beings with passion and in joy, sympathy, fun, and exploration (Panksepp, 2001; Trevarthen 1998a). However, circumstances related to the parents' difficulties and/or to the baby's make-up could jeopardize this. Second, the therapist or caregiver must proceed in the belief that each baby has potential awaiting to be discovered, along with strong emotions ready to be picked up by another empathic person, usually the mother.

How does it work?

All treatment plans are matched to the needs of the baby and parents and the siblings: one session may be all that is required, though it might be ten or as many as two hundred sessions . The sessions are clustered or spaced out as the therapist (or therapy team) thinks best. We always include the parents and siblings in the treatment plan. They suffer too, and they feel relief and learn from seeing and feeling the struggle of the therapist in getting to know the baby. All treatments include home visits by a therapist who monitors the process, finds out how sessions are experienced, information gained is being integrated into daily life, and how the home situation has changed.

The process is to contain, explore, communicate, unblock. Without training and patience, the process can prove impossible. Premature assessments, premature expectations, and premature pushing will only lead to complications. The psychotherapist must first be prepared to contain the deep annoyance or anger usually encountered. These reactions are typically related to either a narcissistic injury about having to urgently treat their baby for a potential life-disabling difficulty, or to a release of their deep fear of damage. Keep in mind that our early-intervention approach assumes that all gestures, behaviours, and movements have meaning—even those that seem meaningless. The baby with autistic behaviour engages in puzzling, challenging, or dysfunctional behaviours or simply does not engage at all—which is also a behaviour.

The concepts of projective identification, countertransference, and empathy make it possible to think more creatively about the feelings of utter helplessness and despair that the non-responsiveness or continuous irritation may produce in parents or carers.

What is hard to realize but starkly apparent is that pre-autistic babies have difficulty in integrating experience. Our early-intervention process focuses on reclaiming potential non-autistic aspects in autistic babies by addressing babies at their level of developmental difficulty that make them delayed if not understood in time. The therapist's role is to encourage those aspects that are healthy and engage the baby; to slow down or stop those that are anti-developmental; and to examine maternal and paternal internal representations of the baby's past and present in order to create a relationship and secure attachment.

The exploration process, therefore, is to discover in the baby and in the parents:

- how they use their senses, their posture—the parents' motor response to hold and the baby's response in being held;
- the individual capacities;
- the causes and forms of defensiveness;
- the causes of extreme anxiety or distress;
- the quality of relationship with the parent;
- the mental representations in the parent that are an obstacle to understanding the child;
- the development of a relationship with the therapist and the parent.

Background thinking

In a paper I wrote in 1992 about excessive crying, I mentioned Stern (1985) and Stern-Bruschweiler and Stern (1989) in their conceptualization of mother–child interactions and how psychoanalytic ideas greatly help to understand relationships and the internal model of behaviour transmitted not only from the parent to child, but also from the child to parent. Murray and Trevarthen (1985) also show how the behaviour is a two-way street, each influencing the other. Psychoanalytic ideas show the deeper link to the behaviour seen between parents and baby and how it becomes imprinted in their brains and greatly influences future behaviours.

The following conceptualization about types of relationships between parents and infants is brief but of interest: care-giving, scare-giving, no-care giving, and vulnerable infants (Acquarone, 2004).

Care-giving parents: This is, within normal development, influencing the baby's development, personality, or make up, and vice versa. Promotes brain growth by neurons getting connected and being able to integrate positive and negative experiences. Parents and babies become predictable. They become well attached (secure).

Scare-giving parents: This is a situation when the parent(s) drink, take drugs, or are abusive or violent to the other day after day. This behaviour has an impact on babies, and their needs of growing safely and being able to trust a person are not formed. Instead, they behave in an erratic and frightened way. They develop an anxious attachment.

Little or no care-giving parents: This is a subgroup of the previous category; it is passive rather than active aggression. The only caregiver may be extremely depressed, does not take medication, and could be without a healthy partner-relationship. Under these circumstances, delayed development may occur. Psychological and physiological needs are not met. As Murray, Cooper, Wilson, and Romaniuk (2003) describe, "development is delayed". Their attachment is insecure.

Care-giving parents—vulnerable infant: Having care-giving parents is not enough with some babies who are difficult to understand or meet their needs. This behaviour in the babies could be due to unknown sensibilities, deficits, or emotions that do not help the integration of experience. Parents are unable to attach to the baby, because the baby does not show interest, pulls back, or even runs away. The attachment is unmatched (this lack of attachment can cause a sense of loss in the parents and can motivate them to retune the relationship).

The baby may feel overwhelmed, rejected, or pain when connected, and so the distraught relationship starts, devoid of common signs of having fun, attuned reciprocity, or imitation of other people or of the mother (Trevarthen, St Clair, and Danon-Boileau show this well in chapter 2).

We can differentiate this from *regulatory disorders*—problems of an infant who is not able to regulate its body sensations, experiences, and needs but is attached to the parents, by looking and having interest in them —and from *pseudo-attachment from parents,* which manifests as an unconscious accommodation to this kind of baby and is based on unconditional love and denial.

Brief theoretical background

Mother–father and each baby: The Eternal Triangle

The classic triangular positioning of mother–father–baby is central to the development of emotions. Despite the psychodynamic complexity of infant–parent–family relationships, many babies, if not most, develop normally. But in the case of autistically inclined babies, emotional development is delayed, hijacked, or blocked in some way, and essential infant–parent communication and interaction never proceeds.

The Oedipus complex— psychodynamic "tensegrity"

Ultimately, the "tensegrity"—the tension and integrity—that holds the Eternal Triangle together is deeply psychodynamic. While many psychoanalytic authors explain the Eternal Triangle relationship in depth—particularly the infant–mother–father relationship and attachment—Sigmund Freud (1900a, 1912–13) was the first to isolate, understand, and explain the essential role exercised by the parent of the opposite sex in the developing child. He showed that rivalry from the "other" parent and siblings was an important dynamic. The child's unilateral love for the parent of the opposite sex fills the child with an unconscious wish to replace the parent of the same sex. The constellation of the emotions evoked in this dynamic is called the Oedipus complex, and dealing with this fundamental complex is crucial if the child is to tolerate the parental couple together. Melanie Klein (1945), in her writings about Dick, showed the connection between the Oedipus complex and the development of symbol formation, which requires the child putting together father and mother. Bion (1957) draws on the maternal function to translate the needs of the infant and to satisfy them. Winnicott (1958) presents the maternal reverie and the importance of the transitional space

Infant-needs attunement

While Klein, Bion, and Winnicott, each champion their own respective corner of the infant–mother–father triangle, Rhode (2005) champions her idea of "attunement" as a way to understand the mind of the baby with regards to imitation, mirroring, and identification. She says that *attunement* "is the right balance between the child and the mother's internal occupant (referring to the oedipal constellation) which allows primal or primary identification—that is, imitation of the developmental kind—to take place". She goes on to explain that the capacity of the child to look at the mother and be able to imitate requires a need in the child to find a *relationship* with its existence.

Infant imitation provoking the adult into communication

Imitation, according to Trevarthen (2005b), "involves apprehension not just of the same forms of movements, but of the intrinsic motive that generates the form of imitation ... and also expectation for its perceptual validation from the other person's reply." The videos of Van Rees and Leeuw (1987) show that premature babies have the capacity not only to imitate but also to provoke adults into communication to satisfy needs or to be entertained. These qualities are seen only faintly in babies who are distancing themselves from human interaction. Trevarthen observes that "the withdrawal of a shy child into a private fantasy world may have much to teach us about the pathology of symbolic thought in autism and schizophrenia".

Infant/relation to oneself

In his 1973 book *Awakenings*, Oliver Sacks describes "awakening" as a change of awareness of one's total relation to oneself and the world (p. 240). When autistic behaviours imprison babies and children, the slow process can be similar to the patients he describes who change internally in their perceptions as a consequence of taking a drug. When he talks about the fascinating world of Temple Grandin, he feels like an "anthropologist on Mars" (Sacks, 1995), where the only thing that made sense to Temple was if she thought in images and attention using only one sense at a time.

Infant/interest in oneself

Bolognini wrote a paper in which he investigates the notion that we must maintain a minimum necessary narcissism to take care of ourselves (Bolognini, 2005). He describes patients who, because they did not have the minimum necessary interest in themselves, did not have precious experiences, and did not have the necessary sense of self to introject and occupy their internal world and relate positively in the world.

Infant/avoiding contact in a fast-moving world

John Ratey (2001) observed that "autistic children often shun many kinds of physical contact". It is thought that sensory information from the outside world comes to them too fast for their brain to process, and they are simply overwhelmed by the stimuli around them. Typically, they will "shut down" or get away from the stimuli. This is compounded by their inability to pay attention because the sensory information they receive comes in fragments or pieces. Healthy babies, for example, shift their gaze within a fraction of a second from the eyes to the nose to the mouth of the mother. But an autistic baby can take up to 5 or 6 seconds just to process the nose. Because of the delay, the baby cannot take in the whole face at once, just parts; missing a social cue such a smile or a frown is therefore easy. Babies with autistic tendencies receive partial information, which is confusing. They cannot prioritize the multitude of sensory signals pouring into the brain. To cope, autistic children respond by exhibiting behaviours whose ultimate goal is to shut off the massive and confusing sensory overload—anything to block the stimuli.

Different from Ratey's concept of the mind is the concept of the developing mind put forward by Bion (1967a). Bion envisions a mind that is extended and relational, where maternal reverie functions in receiving, containing, elaborating, modifying, and returning—in a transformed state—the baby's projections and projective identifications. In Bion's mentalization, this process transforms beta (sensory) elements into alpha (elaborated) elements and is crucial in building a child's mental apparatus, allowing mothers (and analysts) to attune themselves to the sensory and proto-thoughts of children (and patients) and helping them progress.

The work is to help the attunement between the mother and the baby by creating the conditions *for object relations to actually start to*

happen, as Bick (1968) puts it. These conditions follow the basic need
of finding what is jeopardizing integration—it might be the holding of
the baby; or it might be in feelings or states that are transmitted by the
eyes of the mother or the baby and are felt as persecutory or empty to
the other person (coloured by uncontainable anxiety, fear of void or
emptiness, and so forth). *It will be much easier to help this attunement at
6 months than at 3, 4, or 5+ years old. At 6 months, there is still the brain
growth yet to come.*

The early signs of alarm

The list of clinical criteria for the early detection of the general spectrum of relational and communication disorders, including autism,
can be gleaned from research (see Baranek, 2002; Dawson, Ashman, &
Carver, 2000; DiLalla, 1990; Greenspan & Wieder, 1999; Hobson, 2002 ;
Kobayashi et al., 2001; Maestro, Muratori, & Cavallaro, 2005; Maestro
et al., 2002; Massie & Rosenthal, 1984; Trevarthen, 1979; Trevarthen &
Aitken, 2001; Trevarthen & Hubley, 1978; Volkmar & Cohen, 1985) and
the clinical work of Acquarone (chapter 6) and Alonim (chapter 7).

The areas are:

1. Deficit in relating to mother/father or other human beings.
2. Poor motor (psychomotor) skills.
3. Deficits in the sensorial spectrum.
4. Deficits in the transmission of affect.
5. Difficulty the parents have in relating to their child.

A vignette: Rolo

Rolo was referred to us by a health visitor. The 15-day-old baby displayed lethargic behaviour and refused to interact with his parents
and other siblings. The completed Early Signs of Alarm chart (Figure
9.1) revealed an alarming pattern.

He had parents who cared and who were questioning the health
visitor early on. The father and mother were perplexed and worried.
They felt guilty that perhaps they had done something wrong, and
they started to cry soon after they came. They had other children,
two older girls aged 4 and 2 years old, whose behaviour was more
animated and engaging.

EARLY SIGNS OF ALARM

OBSERVATION OF THE QUALITY OF MOTHER / INFANT INTERACTIONS

Stella Acquarone. PhD
School of Infant Mental Health

INFANT

Name: **ROLO**　　　　　　　　　　　　d.o.b. **6 months**

Date of observation:

Please write "O" if the interaction is with an object rather than a person

Frequency of this observation in 1 hour

INTERPERSONAL	Never	Rarely	Freq >2 times	Always	Observer reactions
GAZING –The eye-to-eye contact within a relationship and the maintenance of this contact	✓				
BABBLING –The making of vocal sounds for the benefit of the partner in the parent-infant relationship	✓				
SIGNALLING –The facial expressions –Noises or gestures that seek to produce an affectionate response from the partner	✓				
IMITATION –Moving mouth, tongue, etc. in imitation of mother's (or another) –The repetition of a sound or a movement heard or seen by the infant	✓				
PROVOKING –Inciting the person into interacting	✓				
JOINT ATTENTION –Looking in the same direction –Smiling or vocalising about people or objects (specify)	✓				
POINTING –Indicating with index finger to a person about an object of interest	✓				
FEEDING –Infant's attitude during the intake of food, including anticipatory behaviour (e.g. head-turning, moving arms, sucking reflex)		✓			
SENSORIAL					
TOUCHING –Skin-to-skin contact initiated by infant for play or affection	✓				
RESPONSE –Response to sounds –Response to name	✓				
MOTOR					
HOLDING –The posturing of the infant when he is supported in the arms of the mother (e.g. comfortable, floppy, rigid, restless) –General muscle tone (at 5+ months) when sitting or crawling –Stereotypic movement of arms, eyes, etc.	✓				
AFFECT					
EXPRESSIVENESS –The body or facial expression of emotional states (e.g. sad, worried, anxious, bland, happy, or others) specify	✓				
COMFORTING –Infant's ability to find relief from distress by him/herself (e.g. thumb sucking, touching hands)				Lethargy	

ANY OTHER OBSERVATIONS NOT LISTED ABOVE

Great anxiety awakened

Figure 9.1

180

Stella Acquarone. PhD
School of Infant Mental Health

MOTHER (or caregiver)
affecting the baby or being affected by the baby

Name: **ROLO**   d.o.b. **6 months**

Date of observation:

Please write "O" if the interaction is with an object rather than a person

	Never	Rarely	Freq >2 times	Always	Observer reactions
GAZING – The eye-to-eye contact with the baby and the maintenance of this contact.			✓		
BABBLING –The making of vocal sounds for the benefit of the parent-infant relationship			✓		
SIGNALLING – Facial expressions, noises or gestures seeking to produce an affectionate response from the infant			✓		
TOUCHING –Skin-to-skin contact initiated by parent for play or affection			✓		
COMFORTING –Mother's ability to find relief for the baby's distress			✓		
HOLDING –The posturing of the mother when the infant is supported in her arms or any other way (e.g. secure and tender, rough, balanced precariously)			✓		
FEEDING –Mother's attitude towards infant's hunger and need to feed: a. Does she anticipate behaviour and have meal or breast easily available? b. Does she pay attention, talk with the baby and enjoy feeding? c. Does she interrupt with any excuse (i.e. talks to others and looks away)? d. Is she fearful, full of anguish or has she any delusions? e. Is she apathetic?			✓		
GAMES –Playful encounters, including songs and teasing		✓			
AFFECT –Expression of emotional state (e.g. sad, worried, anxious, bland, happy, others) *specify*			✓		
UNDERSTANDING OF EMOTIONS –in themselves –in the baby			✓		
PAST –Psychiatric illness –Other difficulties			none		

ANY OTHER OBSERVATIONS NOT LISTED ABOVE

Both parents very worried as the baby is not behaving like the others, is not responding and is not ill

Figure 9.1 (*continued*)

181

Stella Acquarone. PhD
School of Infant Mental Health

FOLLOW-UP OF INFANT

Name: d.o.b.

Date of observation:

Please write "O" if the interaction is with an object rather than a person

INTERPERSONAL	Never	Rarely	Freq >2 times	Always	Observer reactions
GAZING –The eye-to-eye contact within a relationship and the maintenance of this contact	✓				
BABBLING –The making of vocal sounds for the benefit of the partner in the parent-infant relationship	✓				
SIGNALLING –The facial expressions –Noises or gestures that seek to produce an affectionate response from the partner	✓				
IMITATION –Moving mouth, tongue, etc. in imitation of mother's (or another) –The repetition of a sound or a movement heard or seen by the infant	✓				
PROVOKING –Inciting the person into interacting	✓				
JOINT ATTENTION –Looking in the same direction –Smiling or vocalising about people or objects *(specify)*	✓				
POINTING –Indicating with index finger to a person about an object of interest	✓				
FEEDING –Infant's attitude during the intake of food, including anticipatory behaviour (e.g. head-turning, moving arms, sucking reflex)	✓				
SENSORIAL					
TOUCHING –Skin-to-skin contact initiated by infant for play or affection	✓				
RESPONSE –Response to sounds –Response to name	✓				
MOTOR					
HOLDING –The posturing of the infant when he is supported in the arms of the mother (e.g. comfortable, floppy, rigid, restless) –General muscle tone (at 5+ months) when sitting or crawling –Stereotypic movement of arms, eyes, etc.	✓				
AFFECT					
EXPRESSIVENESS –The body or facial expression of emotional states (e.g. sad, worried, anxious, bland, happy, or others) *specify*	✓				
COMFORTING –Infant's ability to find relief from distress by him/herself (e.g. thumb sucking, touching hands)	✓				

(column group header spanning Never/Rarely/Freq/Always/Observer reactions: "Frequency of this observation in 1 hour")

ANY OTHER OBSERVATIONS NOT LISTED ABOVE
Observer felt very uneasy about how unperturbed the baby was and that nothing would make him interested in crying or asking for something, even when the mother tried not to feed him to see whether he would awake to cry. In that instance, Rolo cried but continued half sleeping, half awake. He would suck and continue in the same state.

Figure 9.1 (*continued*)

OBSERVATION OF THE QUALITY OF MOTHER / INFANT INTERACTIONS

Stella Acquarone. PhD
School of Infant Mental Health

FOLLOW-UP OF MOTHER (or caregiver)
affecting the baby or being affected by the baby

Name: **d.o.b.**

Date of observation:

Please write "O" if the interaction is with an object rather than a person

	Never	Rarely	Freq >2 times	Always	Observer reactions
GAZING – The eye-to-eye contact with the baby and the maintenance of this contact.			✓		
BABBLING –The making of vocal sounds for the benefit of the parent-infant relationship			✓		
SIGNALLING – Facial expressions, noises or gestures seeking to produce an affectionate response from the infant			✓		
TOUCHING –Skin-to-skin contact initiated by parent for play or affection			✓		
COMFORTING –Mother's ability to find relief for the baby's distress			✓		
HOLDING –The posturing of the mother when the infant is supported in her arms or any other way (e.g. secure and tender, rough, balanced precariously)			✓		
FEEDING –Mother's attitude towards infant's hunger and need to feed: a. Does she anticipate behaviour and have meal or breast easily available? b. Does she pay attention, talk with the baby and enjoy feeding? c. Does she interrupt with any excuse (i.e. talks to others and looks away)? d. Is she fearful, full of anguish or has she any delusions? e. Is she apathetic?			✓		
GAMES –Playful encounters, including songs and teasing			tried		
AFFECT –Expression of emotional state (e.g. sad, worried, anxious, bland, happy, others) *specify*			despair		
UNDERSTANDING OF EMOTIONS –in themselves –in the baby			her own		
PAST –Psychiatric illness –Other difficulties			despair		

ANY OTHER OBSERVATIONS NOT LISTED ABOVE

Sense of urgency, fear of death or delay. Asking what to do since her own mothering style was not affecting the baby positively.

Figure 9.1 (*continued*)

Mother says she was so happy to have a baby boy, but very soon after birth—about fifteen days—the baby went into a kind of lethargy. All sorts of paediatric examinations followed, but no physical cause was found. Mother started being frightened of what she might have done that could have caused her son to enter this strange condition. Father reassured mother that everything was all right and was probably just a hiccup in the development and that it was going to pass.

When Rolo was a month old, the health visitor invited me to see for myself, so I went to their home. The baby was between us, and we tried to reach him, not visually, since most of the time his eyes were closed, but using other senses. We talked to him, about our understanding that he was not interested in parents, siblings, or us. He looked as if he was sleeping but not fully: his body was floppy. His reactivity was low. Rolo showed no holding, his posture when supported in the arms of his mother was floppy, he made no eye contact, no babbling, or signalling of facial expressions, no touching, he initiated no skin-to-skin contact, nor did he display any signs of self-comforting, feeding, or imitation; his facial expression was blank.

In the second observation there are faint signs of eye contact, babbling, signalling of facial expressions, but these were limited.

Where do we start? What theory do we follow? Do we wait?

Added to this complexity, the baby's mother had two other children to look after, and her worry was overwhelming her. It was evident that something had gone wrong in those first fifteen days. One possible approach was to work with the mother's mental representations and also to try to find the child's individual capacities for proper attunement.

It was decided to observe mother–family–baby interaction (or lack of it) for an hour a week. Our interest was in seeing the family functioning as a whole. These observations went on for three and a half months (fourteen home observations), and when Rolo was 5 months old the sessions took place once a week in his home.

For three and a half months, we observed lively 2- and 4-year-olds and a mother taking care of them while trying to relate to an uninterested baby who would feed with poor body holding, hardly opening his eyes, under-reacting to noises, music, or voice. The father would change the baby in an overstimulating way and try to hold his hands and sing.

Session 1

While mother and father spoke about their anguish about the baby and recalled their first feelings and experiences—children were playing around—the baby did not respond and did not look. His body was floppy. Other senses were explored: in the mother's arms and in the father's arms; different positions; different touches, vocalizations, scents, perfumes, tiger balm. The parents started to sing religious songs (and I had the impression it was a way of calming themselves down through praying), and they also sang nursery rhymes. Lastly, I held the baby. I needed to feel the body and the muscles, his reactions to my efforts: but there was no response. I shared with the parents how difficult it was to reach the baby. I started feeling overwhelmed by the TV and the girls running around and playing and the telephone ringing; I took this as a sign coming from my countertransference. I asked them to turn the TV off, and I mentioned to the parents that perhaps the baby was finding it difficult to take in the activity of the household. They laughed and said that he was very happy at the beginning. When asked about how they knew this (since babies don't smile so early), I *felt* it was their happiness probably projected into the baby. The parents said that Rolo would look at them and maintain an alert state, gazing around.

Session 2

I had forgotten to read my email for three days, as if I had lost count of the time, and I realized that I might have empathized with an unresponsive baby lost in time—he did not seem to feel day, night, days passing by. We continued in the following session with me holding the baby, and we continued trying different approaches—now talking slowly, very softly, and touching his little arms and legs, talking about how much time, patience, and perhaps quietness he liked, how difficult it was for him to deal with sisters, mother, father, the external noises like the TV, telephones, how difficult it was to take in so much. The sisters were running around and laughing and at times screaming playfully. The space felt crowded. The noise of the TV and the people coming and going did not allow for a relaxed environment, but it was lively, and I remembered that all the studies about cot death indicate that it is better for babies to be in the middle of the home activity. I took this fear of death and realized that he might be in a continuous sleep that seems as if he is dead, and perhaps in that way he might be left alone. Also, I remembered that one way for the brain to respond to fear is to freeze—if there is no movement, the predator might not see the prey. Both thoughts indicated to me that there was a need to reduce the external noise and activity and then see what happened. I communicated these thoughts, and she said she is desperate because she fears Rolo's brain is dead. Could he have changed—a virus, perhaps?

Session 3

The next session was without the girls and the TV. Just him, us, and a different family set up—quieter all around, with the baby as the only focus of attention. And then he started holding my finger softly, his body tensing a bit and slightly moving, and at the end he almost seemed as if he was moving his eyelids. We talked softly about it and about hope. We talked about the parental realization that this was difficult to achieve in normal home life. I had a clear realization that the ambience of the room and ourselves was like a womb, dark, quiet voices, the adults feeling the secrecy of the experience, and I mentioned the need for this baby to start again.

I said that the discovery of what might help Rolo to come out of his far-away state [shutting-down state?] is a first stage. Treatment would consist of a period in which we explored in different ways what would help, and we proceeded with the family helping the baby to attach, letting the siblings know about that and helping the process of adaptation to a normal household. This baby might need total attention and a quiet, dark room for now, with soft talking. This was quite impossible to achieve with two active little girls around, but initially we could find where he was and bring him out slowly and steadily, so as to help him to trust the external reality and be able to incorporate and integrate his experiences in a less complicated way.

Session 4

In the next session, Rolo did open his eyes—and very softly we continued in a soft light and in a calm way. Without looking at him, we continued through a sort of communication at a body and voice level.

Session 5

Rolo again looked while mother held him. We talked softly about mother's nervousness about success. Mother held his little finger and talked about becoming aware of his difficulty in taking in the family, that she was sorry. I mentioned then that it was all right for her to have feelings of guilt and that discovering his difficulties meant recovering him from being lost. We thought together about providing this environment for a few sessions until we could see that he was able to tolerate the others one by one. We talked about the family's enrichment through incorporating a different member, Rolo, since he was now awake and interacting like the other children.

Sessions 6–7

Rolo opened his eyes more and more, and we talked about how mother could hold in her new excitement and keep a low, steady profile—it was important not to overwhelm the baby and to keep the mother's mood even, talking about hope, fear of damage, fear of not having enough time. We wanted to see and feel together new behaviours and feelings from the baby and be able to talk and weave in family life without jeopardizing anyone, talking to the girls about the achievements. We incorporated the two sisters, telling to them about a fragile baby who needed special care from them, and mother. It was a matter of everyone and everything changing to his needs for a while. The 2-year-old had difficulty following our thinking, and I acted out with a baby doll, for her to hold and imitate us. We needed her to cooperate rather than to compete.

Sessions 8–12

This treatment of baby with mother, siblings, and baby dolls continued for a month (five sessions), talking very quietly in turn with the girls and the mother about their feelings. The girls felt that the boy had extra parts in his body and extra attention from mother and them, talking about their fears of wanting the brother but not wanting the change. What was so interesting was that all the talking was in a whisper: not once in our sessions did their anger and wish for the boy to go away make them scream or talk loudly. I thought that, in a way, they were feeling part of the re-creation (womb) that Rolo needed. Now, rather than being a disruption, it was nice to see them and the mother (and father, if present) being around Rolo and speaking softly about deep feelings and how the environment that Rolo needed was, at some other level, enriching them all.

Mother spoke about her intense fear of being a bad mother. Her own mother was not around at the time of Rolo's birth, and she wanted to have a boy so much, from the first pregnancy, even before, having seen her nephew when she was 14 years old. She was from a family of girls. She wanted to be better than her mum and have "a boy", though perhaps she was also worried about not knowing how to treat boys.

Session 13

The baby, now 15 months old, had his eyes open, looking around, following the person talking to him, smiling occasionally, moving his body when changed, kicking with legs, moving arms, and grasping. Transmission of affects was still weak.

Sessions 14–16

Held in arms, he had started eating solids and accepted them. The mother mentioned how difficult it was for her to handle the individual needs of the girls. They liked to see a bit of TV for an hour a day, and the parents arranged for the girls to watch television in the lounge while the parents were with Rolo in their bedroom or kitchen. I sympathized with the mother's difficult task when she was alone and mentioned to her that we would slowly begin incorporating the division of her attention between Rolo and the girls. Rolo seemed to enter into panic and shutting into himself again, but I talked to him and mother about moving slowly towards it and perhaps being careful about maintaining contact with her hand on his tummy or holding him and helping to share the sisters. The siblings were starting to feel the attention on him, and jealousy had to be allowed for and attended to. Using a baby and a teddy, I talked to them about being different from expected, about them having to bear more attention being paid to the baby, and about mummies. I talked to Rolo about anger, distress, fear of not being held as he needed and wanted—and about his sisters whom he had heard while in his mother's womb. Affects then started moving in—he never cried, yet now he started to cry to show anxiety, to complain. The girls heard me and commented very sweetly.

Rolo started looking at his hand, and Romina (the 4-year-old) offered a little finger and talked about herself, saying that she loved him and sometimes hated him and she wanted him to grow up, and then she started singing:

Row, row, row your boat [*very softly*]
Gently down the stream
Merrily, merrily, merrily, merrily
Life is but a dream.

I smiled and said that she was trying to tell Rolo herself that they all had to go gently to feel merry and that life could be felt as a dream instead of a nightmare. Romina told us that she did not like me at the beginning and had been waiting for me to go away and to find everyday life easier. But now she liked me and didn't want me to go. It seemed that Rolo was becoming more mindful about looking, calling for attention, wanting playful encounters with Romina and mother. His possessiveness was worked out for several sessions, through little games with his hands and songs and games like "peek-a-boo!" The direction of his feelings out to people was evident, and we all continued with investing in his body posturing and moving from the kind of baby that the whole family had expected to the real Rolo. They were coming to terms about this particular little person, Rolo, about his needs and what he was capable of.

Discussion

There is conflict when a baby has special needs that are not evident to the family. And to find and bring out the individuality of the vulnerable infant seems tedious and unrewarding, because everybody feels affected and there is constant complaining and worry.

It is possible to wait and see what happens, to wait to see whether the baby eventually comes back and relates or grows out of the lethargic state. But how long to wait? The brain is forming connections, developing circuits according to experience, and overstimulation out of despair from parents about an unrewarding baby could push the child further into oblivion. This is that why after three months of being in a lethargy, I decided to start to know the baby with the mother, mirroring his possible states, likings, and difficulties and *to talk* about it, changing the environment to best keep up the interaction.

It took extra effort to work with Rolo's little sisters, but including them as a part of the process was critical; rather than being left out, there was a possibility of them relating to the baby. To bring them round, the girls needed metaphors with fragile flowers (orchids) and small animals that needed extra time and care. Conflicts with the girls included helping them to mourn the kind of baby/doll they were expecting at the beginning but didn't get, adapting instead to the real baby Rolo, a kind of delicate flower, who needed extra patience and care and the right environment for him to be able to relate and better develop emotionally. Towards the end and during the follow-ups, the girls seemed to understand and displayed a very careful and cautious approach, stimulating slowly, being careful of the hypersensitivity and sensitive hearing. They became switched on to Rolo's liking or preferring to communicate with one person, and not too many things, at the same time.

It is interesting for me to read now about the agreement from psychoanalysts and researchers regarding sensory stimulation in such cases—the shutting down and "stuckness" in any further develop-ment that Meltzer and Mahler (confirmed by Trevarthen and Ratey) explained, and the idea of going upstream in finding the "mysterious sensibilities", as Alvarez calls them. I use these concepts to go slowly and one sense at the time.

The conversations and trials with the mother and father alone—lowering the light, sound, voice, attention, and activity of mother and seeing whether one could recreate a kind of symbolic placenta/womb—brought good results. I was speaking with the mother about a possible frightening world of bits and pieces floating around, over-whelming him, and about sharing the unknown other galaxy. And then, after three months of re-tracking him and the family, he showed that he could see the mother and her internal occupants, that he could hear the voice again. He liked to be touched, to imitate and enjoy life around him. And even though at the beginning he had to be treated very gently, later he could cope with more. But he always kept his acoustic, visual, and emotional hyper-sensibility, with the exception that he and the family could talk about it, could eventually talk to teachers in school. Everyone was aware of the way he was processing what he was hearing and of how he integrated experiences and learned from them instead of being frightened of them, and they were able to come up with strategies to best get him started and integrated.

Conclusion

This early intervention shows the tenacity needed to continue trying to find channels of communication that enable the relationship rather than closing it up. This baby started fully aware of all the different members of the family around, but from fifteen days on he seemed to stop being engaged and resorted to closing up by constant sleep or lethargy. His waking life seemed too much, he seemed to be tired of coping; there seemed to be no fun in being engaged, and it was felt as unbearable and frightening. *To find waking life interesting again, it was necessary to restore or to find the conditions for experiences to be felt as slow or specific.* The problem was how to get cooperation from the siblings and to help the parents in a busy household start imagining how Rolo felt, without depriving the family of a normal home. The parents were at the point of stopping the intervention. They couldn't decide how much attention should be given to one as against the other two. And yet everyone sensed, as Oliver Sacks so well expressed in the foreword of his book *Awakenings*, "Other worlds, other lives, even though so different from our own, have the power of arousing the sympathetic imagination, of awakening an intense and often creative resonance in others".

I once had the mother of a 9-month-old baby patient with cerebral palsy—who at the beginning was totally withdrawn and who, hanging from her left arm, would scream if separated—say to me after a year and a half of treatment: "My family has become richer, our life is fuller now, the sister, father and I have become so much more resourceful and creative! It is amazing how *you* could see the personality of my daughter and I couldn't. I had too much hate for the difficulties, too slow the way, too unknown the nasty and other bad feelings."

So, emotionally withdrawn babies *can* start looking at their mothers, relate to them, want to be held, want to enter into the dynamics of relationships when they are sufficiently equipped—whether by nature or by therapy. This means that mothers and caregivers must attune to the level the baby can receive them. Then, the cradle for thinking, feeling, relating, and communicating can be carefully and slowly constructed following the specification of each baby's make-up.

Rolo was overwhelmed by all the interpersonal dynamics and noises in the household, but these factors may not have been the only cause. There very well could be other circumstances: the intergenerational transmission of the internal occupants of the mother's mind, factors not necessarily in relationship to the father of the child, but other characteristics related to circumstances at the time of birth or those having to do with the grandmother's impact in their lives. But the success of the treatment centred squarely on the inner workings and extensions of the Eternal Triangle. And while I do feel that this configuration is fundamental in relationships, I have to go further to help concretely in cases of withdrawn babies. The sensorial capabilities of babies have to be such that they can perceive the mother as a whole, to find the mother's eyes and integrate them into a mother's face . It is very difficult for emotions to develop if a relationship is not established.

CHAPTER TEN

Helping toddlers to communicate: infant observation as an early intervention

Maria Rhode

My aim in this chapter is to describe the use of infant observation as an early intervention for children at risk of autistic-spectrum disorder, as well as some of the preliminary findings of a pilot study intended to investigate its effect.[1] Vignettes from observations are cited in order to illustrate some of the interactions taking place between toddlers, their family, and the observer, and some speculations are offered about how the observer may facilitate communication between the children and their families.

This intervention focuses on preverbal communication, even more perhaps than on the development of language. It is now well known (e.g., see Hobson, 2002; Trevarthen, 1979) that language arises out of the matrix of nonverbal communication between the infant and its caregivers. When all goes well, babies and their parents intuitively read each other's cues, share each other's feelings, and build up increasingly complex and sophisticated sequences of communication. These include the familiar games of infancy such as peek-a-boo and, during the course of the second year of life, culminate in speech.

However, babies can be unresponsive, for a wide variety of different reasons; their signals may also be difficult to read. It is hard to imagine any experience that could be more devastatingly undermining and invalidating for parents. In the case of babies who are later diagnosed as autistic, many parents report feeling from the beginning that something was wrong without being able to pinpoint it. Indeed, as Muratori and Maestro have documented (see chapter 3), it is often not easy to distinguish, on the basis of home videos made in the first year of life, those babies who are later diagnosed with autism from those who are not. It is only gradually that distinguishing signs are beginning to emerge, as discussed in several chapters in this volume (see also Acquarone 2004). In these circumstances, it is little wonder that parents can often feel doubly invalidated: by their baby's lack of responsiveness, and by doubts—their own as well as those of professionals—about the accuracy of their own perceptions. These are circumstances that the presence of a sensitive, non-intrusive observer can do much to alleviate.

Infant observation as part of mental health training

Infant observation was originally developed in 1948 by the psychoanalyst Esther Bick, as a central component of the training for child psychotherapists that she founded at the Tavistock Clinic in London (Bick, 1964). It now forms part of the training of many mental health professionals (see Sternberg, 2005). It is also greatly valued by professionals, such as teachers, who wish to develop the insight and reflectiveness they bring to their work. Papers on various aspects of infant observation are published in the *International Journal of Infant Observation*, and a number of books and collections of papers have been devoted to the topic (e.g., A. Briggs, 2002; S. Briggs, 1997; Haag, 2002; Miller, Rustin, Rustin, & Shuttleworth, 1989; Reid, 1997a).

The observer visits a family once a week at a mutually convenient time, ideally from birth onwards, though this will, of course, depend on when a visit becomes manageable for the family. The observer's aim is to understand something of what it feels like, for the baby as well as for other family members, as relationships unfold within the ordinary events of everyday life. Of course, the beginnings of a life are never ordinary. Observers inevitably find that their emotions are deeply stirred by the miracle of birth, by the baby's vulnerability, by the parents' devotion and struggles that are part of the demanding task of child-rearing, and by the siblings' feelings of love and jealousy (M. E. Rustin, 1989). Learning to pay attention to these emotions, and to think about them instead of acting on them, is an important part of what makes infant observation such a valuable training experience.

Bick's injunction to observers was that they should always put the family's needs and feelings before their own, and that they should interfere as little as humanly possible in the family's routine (Haag, 2002). This is not to say that it is possible or desirable to be a "fly on the wall": that in itself would be a kind of interference, since it is not natural human behaviour. But the observer must be reflective about her[2] own contribution to the observation and accommodate to the parents' practical and emotional needs. The observer makes notes as soon as possible after the observation; these should include as much detail as possible, as well as her own feeling responses. However, any attempt to conceptualize is deliberately left to the seminar group in which the observations are presented, so that observation and theory are purposely distanced from each other.

Helpful implicit messages

Infant observation conducted in this way conveys a number of important messages to the family. The first is that someone is consistently interested in everything the baby does, as well as in everything the parents say. Parents generally love talking about their babies, and they appreciate the observer's genuine interest, particularly since it is free of any claim to "know", let alone to "know better". Many mothers with new babies can feel cut off from their previous activities and relationships. Although they may form new friendships with other parents, they can sometimes feel that their baby's development, which to them is so absorbing, is of limited interest to friends from the past. The regular visit of an adult concerned with the minutiae of the baby's life can be welcome and reassuring. So, too, can the observer's openness to the full range of the parents' feelings about the baby: happiness and pride as well as exhaustion and resentment, frustration and fears for the future alongside fulfilment and love.

Another important message is that the observer will fit in with the family, will put their needs first, and will not be put off by behaviour that might be problematic in other circumstances. The observer's consideration for the parents' needs conveys her respect for them and for the importance of their task in modulating their children's feelings, even when they are under pressure themselves and suffering from lack of sleep. If the mother misses an appointment, the observer will not react punitively: if the parents have not found time to get dressed, or if the older child's toys are all over the floor, the observer will not be critical. At a time when the encounter with a new, vulnerable baby reawakens the parents' own infantile anxieties, support from their own parents is particularly welcome. Often, however, grandparents have other claims on them, and professionals, no matter how helpful, do not have the time simply to witness the baby's development but must, rather, focus on a specific problem. The observer's stance shows that she realizes the importance of ordinary events and the power of the feelings that can be associated with them.

The birth of a new family member unavoidably brings with it the disruption of previous family patterns and some degree of strain on relationships. Part of the observer's task is to learn to take in and respond to the actions, words, and feelings of all members of the family, even though she is primarily there to focus on the baby. Inevitably this is difficult, and she will not always succeed. However, the very fact that she continues to struggle, and that her behaviour expresses the conviction that there is room for many viewpoints, can be helpful to a family on its way to reconstituting itself to include an additional member.

These are some of the factors that contribute to the helpful effect of an observer's presence. Although infant observations were intended as a learning experience for the observer, writers from Bick (1964) onwards have noted that those parents who choose to have an observer—and, of course, not all families would—tend to feel supported by the experience. (In a way, this is not really surprising: most mothers find that it is easier to cope with their children when another adult is present, even if that person is not offering any practical assistance.) Out of this recognition has grown the applied use of infant observation with specifically therapeutic aims.

"Therapeutic" infant observation

In some infant observations, unforeseen difficulties mean that the observer deliberately takes on a more therapeutic role. For instance, the parents of a baby who was failing to thrive had difficulty in making use of the professional help offered, but they responded well when the observer took up the potential seriousness of the child's condition (Wedeles, Grimandi, & Cioeta, 2002; Williams, Grimandi, & Cioeta, 2002). The observer's role changed to that of participant observer: her observations and her feeling response now served as information on which she relied in order to respond directly to the baby and "interpret" the baby's cues for the parents. The child stopped refusing food, and family relationships were much improved. When the observer had to leave, the parents asked for another participant observer to take over.

Therapeutic infant observation has been applied in a number of different settings and for varying problems, largely in France and in South America. Its systematic use was pioneered by Didier Houzel, a French psychoanalyst and professor of child psychiatry who integrated it into the regional child psychiatry services in Brest and, later, in Caen (Houzel, 1989, 1999). He stresses the usefulness of the method on a number of counts. It is minimally intrusive, and the fact that it is based on home visits means that families can be reached as soon as a problem is detected. This includes those families who, for whatever reason, would not be able to make use of formal, clinic-based appointments, though the experience of improvement during the observation may encourage families to support such treatment later if it is still necessary. Houzel underlines the cost-effectiveness of therapeutic infant observation when compared to outpatient treatment: observations can be carried out by psychiatric nurses or generic mental health workers who have had the experience of doing a conventional infant observation, as long as they have adequate access to supervision seminars in which to discuss their observations and to process their own feeling responses. Even when observers visit a family twice weekly and attend two supervision seminars a week, the intervention package costs less than outpatient treatment by professionals with lengthier trainings. Once-monthly appointments are offered with the supervising psychiatrist for the parents to discuss their child's development and any concerns they may have.

This intervention is offered to babies with failure to thrive or who are thought to be at risk of communication disorders, both by Houzel's team and by that of Pierre Delion, a psychoanalyst and child psychiatrist who formerly worked in Angers and is now a professor of child psychiatry in Lille (Delion, 2000a). Good outcomes are reported, and the package remains part of district child-psychiatry provision.

Bianca Lechevalier, who has written widely on the psychoanalytic treatment of children with autism, has described a successful outcome to the observation of a baby with West's syndrome (Lechevalier, Fellouse, & Bonnesoeur, 2000). This is a degenerative convulsive disorder in children that is associated with an abnormal EEG and, often, with autistic behaviours; it is generally treated with cortisone. The baby discussed by Lechevalier was observed from the age of 7 months; six months later, his EEG was normal, and his subsequent development proved satisfactory. Lechevalier is careful not to suggest that all cases of West's syndrome would respond like this. However, even one such well-documented case has obvious far-reaching implications, both practically and theoretically.

Successes have also been reported for the use of therapeutic infant observation in cases where the family's capacity to care for a baby was compromised, whether because of a life-threatening illness of the child (Cardenal, 1998) or because of long-standing transgenerational diffi-culties that had led to previous children being taken into care (Delion, Libeau-Manceau, Péan, & Petit, 2000).

Houzel (1999) has proposed that three main qualities of the ob-server contribute to the therapeutic effect of a participant infant obser-vation. The first is her "perceptual" receptivity—that is, her capacity to pay attention to details and sequences of behaviour that are later made sense of in the seminar. The second is emotional receptivity: it hardly needs belabouring that children flourish through the provision of sympathetic attention. The observer can serve as a model to parents because of her receptivity both towards them and towards the baby: they can begin to feel, if they did not already, that they and their child are worth paying attention to, over and beyond the professional at-tention that others give to their child's problems. Parents soon begin to tell the observer things they have noticed about their child, even if they did not do so previously: they begin to realize how precious is their own gift of attention. Perhaps the most important factor, in Houzel's opinion, is what he calls unconscious receptivity—that is, the observer's openness to communications at the deepest level, beyond what can be achieved through an effort of will. It is because the ob-server will need an opportunity to process and formulate impressions and reactions that she is not consciously aware of that the provision of a seminar or of individual supervision is such an essential part of this intervention. Equally, the observer's conscious feeling response is often very painful, particularly if a child is ill or if the observer wit-nesses miscommunications between parents and children and does not cut herself off from the distress that each one suffers. Where this is the case, a time for discussion is essential if the observer is to be able to conceptualize the interactions she becomes part of and to consider how best to respond.

Design of the pilot study

In view of the encouraging reports I have cited, it seemed urgent to pilot a study of the facilitatory effects of infant observation on chil-dren at risk of autistic-spectrum disorder. One could expect that such a study should provide two kinds of information. On the one hand, it would furnish much detail about the development of at-risk children, of the kind yielded by "ordinary" infant observations of babies who turn out by chance to have features characteristic of the autistic spectrum such as the avoidance of eye contact (Cowsill, 2000; Reid, 1997b; Somerville, 2000). The systematic observation of a number of children within the same diagnostic grouping (M. J. Rustin, 1997) should allow fresh understandings to emerge through the application of systematic methods of qualitative analysis. On the other hand, the use of commonly accepted instruments to frame such a study would permit one to say whether a *prima facie* case existed for a systematic study on a larger scale and with a comparison group.

At present, no commonly accepted measures exist for the diagnosis of autistic-spectrum disorder in children below the age of 15 months, though clinicians agree on danger signals, including muscular hypo- or hypertonicity and withdrawal from social contact (Acquarone 2004) (see also chapter 6). Systematic efforts to validate these are well advanced (see chapters 3 and 5). A new scale (Greenspan, 2005) discriminates between children with communication problems and those with other difficulties, though it has not as yet been validated against diagnostic tools used in the second year of life, such as the Autism Diagnostic Observation Schedule (ADOS: Lord et al., 1989) or the Checklist for Autism in Toddlers (CHAT: Baron-Cohen et al., 1996) (see also chapter 5). The ADOS is valid from the age of 15 months; the CHAT has a window of validity between 16 and 20 months. We decided to use the CHAT in this pilot study, since it is a simple screening measure designed to be used by primary-care workers; it takes some 20 minutes to administer and includes a brief parent questionnaire as well as direct observation of the child, centring on the capacity for gaze-monitoring, for proto-declarative pointing, and for representational play. Although the sensitivity of the CHAT is very low (it picks up only 27% of the children found to have autism at the age of 3½ years), it produces virtually no false positives. Of 12 children (in a sample of some 16,000: Baron-Cohen et al., 1996) who had developed none of the three capacities tested and thus fell in the high-risk category of the CHAT at age 16–20 months, 11 were diagnosed as autistic at the age of 3½ years; the only one who was not showed residual expressive-language delay. This absence of false positives makes the CHAT an excellent screening tool, though the age of 22 months or so seemed to us regrettably late to begin a therapeutic infant observation for children suffering from a condition that is so difficult to modify.

We decided also to observe the toddlers—first, before the start of the intervention and then a year later—during two minutes when the mother left the room, and then on her return. This separation–reunion task was inspired by the Strange Situation Test (Ainsworth & Wittig, 1969), a means of assessing a child's attachment status, which is carried out in a laboratory and rated from a video-recording. We carried out the procedure in the child's home and without a video, which made it less stressful for mother and child. The child's attachment status was assessed from the research assistant's notes made during the separation/reunion.

Several measures were used for the mother (and will in future be used for fathers, too, where possible). Mothers were asked to supply standard demographic information and to fill in the Goldberg General Health Questionnaire, which provides a measure of anxiety. In addition, they were given a semi-structured interview about their experience of pregnancy, birth, and the child's early development. Finally, the short form (Slade, Aber, Berger, Bresgi, & Kaplan, 2003) of the Parent Development Interview (PDI) was administered before and after the intervention. This interview provides a measure of the parent's capacity to think about their child's feelings and motivation: it is scored for reflective functioning, but without those questions about the parent's own past that form part of the Adult Attachment Interview. Such questions could upset a vulnerable group of parents and might be misunderstood as implying a causal connection between the parents' past and their child's difficulties.

The following summarizes the sequence of stages in the project:

1. Participants are contacted through workers in primary care who may have concerns about the child's capacity to communicate or who may have been alerted by the parents.

2. Families are visited by the project coordinator, who explains the intervention, answers any questions, and obtains informed consent.

3. A research assistant visits to administer the CHAT (twice), the separation–reunion task, the demographic questionnaire, the Goldberg General Health Questionnaire, and the semi-structured interview on the parents' experience of the birth and early history.

4. The parent worker visits to administer the PDI, which can provide a good way of accessing themes likely to be important in parent work. [This work provides an opportunity for the parent(s) to

discuss any issues arising out of the observation, as well as any concerns they may have in relation to their child.]

5. The intervention now begins, comprising weekly visits by a participant observer and fortnightly visits from the parent worker. We had originally expected to offer monthly parent support, but this proved too little and was increased to fortnightly.

6. At the end of the year, the parent worker again gives the PDI, and the research assistant returns in order to readminister the Goldberg General Health Questionnaire and the separation–reunion task.

7. When the child reaches the age of 3½ years, an independent psychiatric interview is arranged if one has not already been put in place by the statutory services.

Some preliminary findings

So far, only three children have been offered the programme, partly with the aim of piloting the measures and of discovering how best to deliver the intervention. (For example, we needed to establish whether monthly parent work was sufficient or whether the frequency needed to be increased to fortnightly.) Of these, only one child, Adam, of those assessed during the window of validity for the CHAT remained in London for the whole year of the intervention. This child was in the high-risk category of the CHAT and statistically had an 11-in-12 chance of receiving a diagnosis of autism at 3½ years. However, the psychiatrist found no signs of autistic-spectrum disorder when Adam was 3½, despite "a very worrying early history". Instead, there remained some residual expressive-language delay, though emotional, nonverbal communication was excellent, including social referencing. According to the CHAT, the chances of such an outcome are only 1 in 12.

In addition, this child's attachment category, as rated on the separation–reunion task, had changed over the year from Avoidant to Secure, and the mother's anxiety level, as measured by the Goldberg General Health Questionnaire, had been reduced by half.

Another of the children was contacted at the age of only 12 months. He had avoided eye contact with his mother since birth and was showing some pronounced stereotypic movements, which is rare at such a young age. Though 12 months was too young for the CHAT, we proceeded with the intervention, as the mother was very anxious for this to start at once, and we felt that, from an ethical viewpoint, we could not refuse. In this case, too, the child's attachment category

we could not refuse. In this case, too, the child's attachment category changed from Avoidant to Secure, and maternal anxiety was reduced by half; no problems were found when the child was reassessed by the paediatrician at the end of the intervention. More particularly, normal eye contact with the mother had been established, and language development was age-appropriate.

In spite of the very small numbers in this pre-pilot, we therefore feel encouraged to proceed with the pilot project, particularly in view of the 1-in-12 chance, according to the CHAT, that the boy who completed the intervention would have been diagnosed as suffering only from expressive-language delay. Our intention is to recruit a further six children in the high-risk category of the CHAT, all of whom would have the intervention. The very high likelihood of a later diagnosis of autism for such children would make it possible to gauge from a small number whether a *prima facie* case had been made for a more extended study with random allocation and an untreated comparison group.

The process of the intervention

I would now like to offer some speculations as to what may be taking place in the course of the intervention, and what functions may be fulfilled by the observer and parent worker. In order to do this, I shall offer some illustrative vignettes drawn from all the observations.[3]

The vicious circle of discouragement

Babies and toddlers who have a particular vulnerability, whether neurological or emotional, require even more responsive handling than other children if they are to reach their full potential. Young children at risk of autism are no exception to this. However, their own lack of responsiveness and difficulty in tuning in to other people can sometimes make parents and professionals feel exhausted and discouraged. Their hopefulness can be undermined, and they can become less able to respond to what are often minimal cues. In this way, a vicious circle can be set up that adds to problems in communicating that may already be present, much as Sinason (1986) has proposed that the "primary handicap" of some learning disabilities may be aggravated by the "secondary handicap" arising from the child's way of coping with the condition.

I would like to give two examples of this. The first is from my pre-liminary visit to Mr and Mrs C and their son Andrew, who, in fact, did not complete the intervention because they moved away.

Andrew was sitting on his mother's lap while I explained what the project would entail, and he held out his arms in the direction of his father, who was watching the television while the other children played nearby. I commented that Andrew seemed to want to go to his father. Both Mr and Mrs C disagreed: they thought Andrew was gesturing to go out the door, though this was, in fact, at right angles to the direction of Andrew's outstretched arms. I said that obviously I had only just met them and Andrew, whereas they had known him all his life, but that I would not have hesitated to assume that Andrew was reaching out towards his father. His parents remained convinced that this was not so: Andrew would never reach out towards either of them.

It is clear that this attitude would be likely to interfere with the way family members could relate to each other.

The other example concerns Adam, the little boy in the high-risk category of the CHAT who completed the intervention with the good results I have indicated.

During the research assistant's first visit, before the observation and parent work began, she was distressed to witness how difficult it was for mother and child to get together, though both were try-ing. Adam's mother, who had just returned to the room, went to lift Adam down from the window seat. Adam protested, wriggled out of his mother's grasp, and climbed down himself. He looked at his mother, who had gone to sit on the sofa, and then climbed onto her knee. The research assistant wrote:

"I was expecting him to cuddle, but instead of putting his arms around his mother's neck, Adam reached behind her and put his fingers behind the sofa. His mother's arms remained by her sides on the sofa. Adam pulled out a little soft toy, then used his moth-er's shoulders to lever himself onto the arm of the sofa. He tried to edge round the door, then gave a terrible scream, as though he were stuck. His mother told him to come back inside, and he did. . . . He came over to the sofa where his mother was still sitting, put his head into the sofa next to her, and fretted some more. His mother sighed and tried to pick him up. Adam howled, struggled out of her arms, pushed his face into the sofa cushions, and really cried out. . . . He got down and pushed my papers onto the floor, then hurled himself onto the carpet and cried loudly. As his cries got more determined, his mother said, 'This is normally when he starts banging his head. I try and pick him up and he pushes me away.' She then said, 'Come on, Adam, are you coming up?' She sounded tender but exhausted. She sat Adam on her lap so that they were facing each other, and they had a brief, but very touching cuddle. I felt very moved and relieved. Almost immediately, Adam pulled back from his mother and climbed off the sofa, becoming absorbed in a toy."

This extract shows how hard it was for Adam's mother to persist in offering him comfort, in view of the many experiences of rejection she had suffered. Equally, Adam did not ask for the affection and comfort he so clearly yearned for. His mother had to persevere in the face of his discouraging behaviour. To the research assistant's huge relief, the "very touching cuddle" did happen—but almost immediately Adam interrupted it and distanced himself.

In contrast, this is what happened at the end of the separation–re-union task after a year's intervention:

While mother was out of the room, Adam pointed at an aeroplane outside the window. The research assistant agreed: "Yes! An aero-plane!" . . . Adam watched the plane and called out, "Bye!" as it moved across the sky. He looked back at the research assistant, then said "Bye!" "See!" and "Oh!", finally calling "Bye" more softly as he waved at the plane. . . . He went over to the table, handed the assistant a pen, and pointed to a letter that his mother had written on a piece of paper. He said, "Mu! Mu! Mum!" a bit anxiously, and the research assistant felt that his mother was very much on his mind. He drew a mark on the paper and said "Mu!" in a brighter tone; the research assistant said that that was where Mummy had done her writing. Adam said "Yeah" in a sing-song way. . . . At that moment, his mother and elder brother came back. Adam sat up im-mediately on hearing their voices, . . . looked round at his mother, pointed at the research assistant, and made some excited noises. Then he made an "all gone" gesture with his hands. He picked up a ruler with wild animals on it, made an exaggerated "Oooh" sound, and looked up at his mother, smiling. He took the ruler over to her, and she acknowledged it in an affirming way. He then began pointing out the bricks, pen, and paper to his mother, chattering excitedly as he did so. The research assistant wrote:

"He seemed really pleased to be showing his mother the things he had been doing while she was out of the room. His mother nodded and said 'Yes' as Adam pointed the things out to her. It felt as though they were really coming together and communicating even though a physical distance remained between them. Adam suddenly made a loud roar at his mother, which was done playfully but which also felt a little precarious. She returned the roar. Adam looked at the ruler and roared again, smiling. His mother roared back, and it felt as though a game were taking place."

After a somewhat edgy interlude with his elder brother, Adam crawled over to his mother and lay down at her feet. He looked up at his mother, who clapped her hands. Adam reached his hands up towards his mother, who bent down and lifted him up by his hands. They stood for a moment holding hands and looking at each other. Adam glanced round at his elder brother, then turned back to his mother, fell on his knees and buried his head in her tummy. The research assistant wrote:

"Mother's body became concave, as though making room for Adam. I was very moved at the sight of their togetherness. Adam lifted up his head and reached up his arms and his mother gathered him up onto her lap for a cuddle. Their necks were locked together and their arms wrapped round each other in a strong embrace. Adam looked up at the fan behind him and made urgent 'uh, uh' noises, which suggested that he wanted to share his interest with his mother, who looked around at the fan with him. He slid off mother's knee, looking round at me and his brother while keeping hold of her hand, then ran out of the room to chase the cat."

At this stage, Adam is able to communicate with the research assistant about the plane that goes away like his mother ("Bye") and to refer to his absent mother by means of the paper on which she had been writing. When mother comes back, Adam "tells" her what he had been doing. He can now deal with a mishap (the fallen ruler) by exaggeration, which suggests that he now understands the pretend mode. It is also as though he were remembering and reproducing a helpful adult reaction: this comforting internalized voice supports him, and he smiles up at her as though sharing the reference. The sudden, slightly precarious roaring communicates something about a sudden irruption of anger, but it remains appropriately contained within a game, quite unlike the painful interaction between him and mother the year before. It is striking how closely Adam's mother follows his communications. Later, when they find each other for a cuddle, it is not suddenly broken off as it was in the previous instance. Then, Adam's attention was immediately distracted by a toy; this time, he shares with his mother his interest in the fan. He then looks at his brother and the research assistant while keeping hold of mother's hand, before running off to pursue his own interests. It is as though he had begun to feel that there was room to include everybody.

Interestingly, Adam showed many instances of social referencing very early during the observation: he looked round in the direction of the observer, as though to make sure she was paying attention or to check her reaction. This is particularly striking because, according to the CHAT (which he had been given twice, at intervals of a week) he was not capable of following someone else's gaze. It is not unduly surprising that he should have shown more of his capacities when he was receiving someone's undivided, empathetic attention. However, we must remember that the prognostic validity of the CHAT is linked not to what a child *can* do in optimal circumstances, but to what he or she *does* do when tested. The implication must be that at least some children in the high-risk category of the CHAT have capacities they do not show. One of the questions for the pilot study will be how many of the children this applies to.

A related important point is that both Adam's mother and the observer had difficulty in noticing, remembering, and believing in Adam's capacities. His mother often described him as being unable to do something that the observer witnessed him doing. However, she could sympathize with the mother, since she had the same difficulty, though she often needed the supervision sessions to realize this. For example, very early in the observation Adam produced a word: he imitated the observer, who had just said "Ta" when he handed her a toy. But it was difficult fully to take the implications on board: months later, the observer, just like Adam's mother, was asking herself why he didn't speak. It was as though Adam powerfully put over a picture of himself as someone incapable, so that it was difficult even for the observer to trust the evidence of her own ears. This again would lead to a vicious circle. A number of authors (e.g., Brazelton, Koslowski, & Main, 1974; Papousek, 1992) have documented the importance of parental expectations for early language development. The parents' assumption that early vocalizations are intended as words, as are their responses to them, plays a vital role in the normal process by which words develop out of sounds. Any factors—physical or emotional—that undermine the parents' confident expectations will be likely to have far-reaching effects.

Observation and parent work

How might Adam's striking transformation have come about? I shall offer only a few suggestive vignettes, together with some speculations. I do not go into any detail here about the parent work, except to say that it was an essential component of the intervention and that monthly visits proved to be insufficient. The parent worker provided support of any kind that seemed necessary or appropriate, including, at times, liaison with nurseries or with social services.

The optimal degree of communication between observer and parent worker touches on difficult boundary issues. On the one hand, teamwork could be a source of strength: the families rightly assumed that both workers knew each other, and this seemed to be experienced as a helpful example of two people cooperating to support the parents and children. Some information—such as the child's first word or first day at nursery school—obviously had to be shared in the interests of common sense. On the other hand, the parent worker had access to factual and biographical information that sometimes seemed unhelpful for the observer to know. Some kinds of knowledge could have provided an adult understanding of the parents' behaviour that was not available to the child and, in that way, could have interfered with the observer's emotional sharing of the child's experience. For example, the father in one of the families often suddenly left the room in the middle of an interaction in a way that made the observer—and, quite possibly, the child—feel abruptly cut off for no understandable reason. She could not have responded to this as fully as she did if she had known the cause of this behaviour, which was related to a recurrent urinary infection. (Later, the father began to tell his daughter when he was going to leave the room.)

Functions of the observer

The following is a discussion of some of the functions of the observer in a therapeutic observation, as distinct from the less active role in an observation carried out for training purposes.

• *Receiving, containing, and validating/verbalizing communications
from both parents and children*

Firstly, and perhaps most importantly, the observers were witnesses. This applied to all of Houzel's levels of receptivity—perceptual, emotional, and unconscious. Many of the functions that I suggest the observers fulfilled were variations on this fundamental role of witness. While this may seem quite a modest function, it has profound implications on an existential level. The presence of a witness who is empathetic and non-judgemental provides validation of a person's point of view; of his or her emotional experience; and, ultimately, of his or her existence. As Winnicott (1967) described in his paper on the mirror role of mother and family, it is himself that the child sees reflected when he looks into his mother's face. This experience, Winnicott argues, is the foundation of the child's sense of self. It can then be built on through the internalization of experience in ways that have been described by psychoanalysts from Freud, Abraham, and Klein onwards.

Sometimes, so as not to intrude, the observers remained silent witnesses. At other times, however, they might put into words what they had seen or experienced, particularly when parents and child seemed to need "interpreting" to each other. Observers might use words to reflect the experience of parents and child ("It can feel really difficult sometimes"; or, "That's right, Mummy's gone into the kitchen"; or "You want Mummy to see that you like the music from that toy"). At other times, they might engage the child by means of actions, particularly imitation. Children with communication disorders readily respond to being imitated—something that many different programmes of intervention make use of—but they do not themselves imitate spontaneously in the way that other children do. In the course of these observations, the children began to imitate the actions of the observer, who had imitated them: it is as though, once they had felt their own actions had been witnessed and reflected, they could begin to take the adult as a model.

Sometimes the observer had to validate an experience, not by naming it in parents or child, but by tolerating it emotionally herself (Bion, 1962). For example:

Six months into the observation, Adam was watching television. He put his drink down on the table, making a noise. The observer imitated the noise, tapping the table with her hand. Adam looked at her with surprise and delight, and they enjoyed a brief "rhythm game". The observer put words to the game, saying that she and

Adam were playing together: "Adam is banging with the cup"; "Mrs Y is tapping the table with her hand"; "Now we are doing it together". Adam made lively bubbling sounds and stared at the observer. Then he went back to watching the television. The observer felt very lonely. She tried to attract his attention by moving her head into his line of sight, but it felt mechanical and she stopped. Suddenly Adam pointed to the screen, as though he wanted to share something with her. She said, "Adam wants Mrs Y to share something with him, something on the screen." Adam looked at the observer, then back at the screen, still pointing. She said, "How exciting, Adam and Mrs Y can both watch something at the same time", and Adam laughed delightedly.

In this example, a game developed when the observer imitated Adam; however, he then broke off the contact, just as he had with his mother in the first separation–reunion sequence. The observer had to tolerate feeling lonely and unable to do anything about it, just as one might assume both Adam and his mother had felt. This seems a good example of the process of emotional containment, in which, as Bion (1962) described, the mother's or therapist's capacity to tolerate an emotion communicated by the infant or patient makes the emotion less overwhelming. It also provides an example of someone who can sustain and think about a feeling and thereby make it meaningful. In this vignette, the observer's function of containment is immediately followed by Adam's pointing out something on the screen: an instance of the capacity for joint attention, which the observer validates to Adam's delight.

- *Making links between parents and child*

The observers would often "interpret" parents and children to each other: "You want Mummy to see you hold the dolly"; "He likes being close to you"; "Mummy will be pleased with what you've done". This applied largely to positive situations that might otherwise have been overlooked. It links with the next function.

- *Embodying a third-party/regulatory function*

Describing and fostering an interaction between parent and child sends the message that the observer welcomes it, even though she is not directly involved. This is an essential aspect of what Britton (1989) has termed the "third position", that of someone who observes a relationship. He suggested that this position was the foundation of self-reflectiveness, of the capacity to "observe oneself while being oneself". Equally, the observer might act to set boundaries, in this way embodying a paternal function that regulates the distance between mother and child. Some of the parents would set limits verbally, but they might give up in exhaustion when it was necessary to actively enforce them. If the mother, for instance, asked the child to stay inside the room and the child did not respond, the observer might support the mother by closing the door. She would make a point of verbalizing the reasons: "I'm closing the door because Mummy wants you to stay inside."

• *Facilitating the inclusion of all people present*

This function, in turn, follows on from the previous one: the underlying message is that there is room for more than one person, and that it is possible to tolerate waiting one's turn. Alvarez (1997) has described mothers who have the capacity to keep their children in mind even when they are temporarily concentrating on something else—for example, turning the page of the book the child is looking at, in-between cooking the dinner or talking to their husband. These mothers can also allow their children to follow their own interests: they do not feel invalidated by not always being in the forefront of the child's concerns. Alvarez has suggested that these maternal qualities can support the child's own capacity for turn-taking and for trusting that thoughts, as well as people, can wait their turn without disappearing and can therefore be organized in meaningful patterns. Besides attending to more than one person, observers actively drew parents or siblings into a game or other interaction that had begun between themselves and the child.

• *Modulating separations*

Modulating separations was a particularly important function of the observer: Adam's response to the first separation–reunion task gives the flavour of his early response to separations. Some of the components of the observer's modulating function included:

Registering and witnessing the child's feelings: this might be a matter of noticing that, after the mother had gone out of the door, the child went to it and stood there looking forlorn. At the beginning of the observations, the child often gave no sign of this once the mother came back. Because the observer did not herself leave the room, she provided an ongoing background of continuity. Sometimes simply speaking to the child's distress could have a dramatic effect:

> Adam always went rigid and screamed when he was put in the car seat, so much so that the family went out much less than they wanted to. The observer found herself talking emphatically about how much he hated it. To her amazement as well as his mother's, Adam calmed down and allowed himself to be strapped in, and this was consolidated over the following weeks. An important factor was that Adam's mother had appealed to the observer to witness his behaviour and that he would have felt they were supporting each other.

Referring verbally to the absent mother: this is a way of supporting a mental and emotional link to her. The children began to follow the observers' example and to refer to people who had left the room, as Adam did in the second separation–reunion vignette.

Tolerating the reasons for mother's absence: this conveys the message that things happen according to a coherent, meaningful pattern—for instance, saying "Mummy's gone to unload the washing machine".

Experiencing aloneness and rejection: this could be seen, for example, in the vignette of Adam in front of the television. Later in the observation, when Adam and his mother were linking up more, the observer was often in the position of the one who was left out or left behind in the room. In other observations, observers sometimes felt left out of what was being discussed with the parent worker, who often had similar feelings themselves. It is not surprising that the experience of being excluded should be so important in relation to children who do not readily respond in understandable ways.

Conclusions

Observation plus parent work seems a promising early intervention for children at risk of communication disorder, even when they have reached the relatively late age of 22 months. It may be particularly appropriate for those cases where the "vicious circle of discouragement" has gone so far that simply encouraging the parents to follow the child's lead, as in the "Watch, Wait and Wonder" approach[4] (DeGangi

& Greenspan, 1997; Muir, 1992; Muir, Lojkasec, & Cohen, 1999) may be not be practical. The feature that distinguishes therapeutic infant observation is the central importance of the observer's emotional and unconscious receptivity (Houzel): her function of being available to receive and process experiences, like loneliness, that are often painful. An additional advantage is the fact that parents do not need to change their routine or attend a clinic.

Notes

1. Partners in this study are Maria Rhode (lead investigator), David Simpson, Judith Trowell, Margaret Rustin, Martin Bellman, and Elizabeth Nevrkla. We gratefully acknowledge the financial support of the Winnicott Trust and the Tavistock Institute of Medical Psychology.

2. Although most observers are female, there are some male observers. For ease of exposition, feminine pronouns are used in this chapter.

3. I would like to express my thanks to the observers and the research assistant (Agathe Gretton, Liz Stevenson, Jenifer Wakelyn, and Rebecca Hall) for permission to cite illustrative examples from their work.

4. I wish to thank Victoria Blincow for information on Watch, Wait and Wonder.

PART **IV**

THEORETICAL CONTRIBUTIONS

CHAPTER ELEVEN

Me, you, and the others:
on being born emotionally

Stella Acquarone

T here is a difference between being born physically and being born emotionally—one you can see, the other you must feel. The following scenario is a thought experiment and theory on the cause of autism.

What if a baby is born physically but not emotionally?

To do this thought experiment we must explore, with the aid of psychoanalytic tools, the sort of complex problems and behaviours presented by those caught in the autistic spectrum. We must bear in mind prior research and case studies to support and challenge our thinking. The result of the experiment will be the construction of a general theory about the birth of autistic behaviour.

Background to the theory

A persistent curiosity as to what is *causing* distress, coupled with professional experience in *treating* the distressed, has seen my focus over the years gradually shift from treatment to research—exploring ways to avoid the distressing outcomes altogether. It is in this spirit of persistent curiosity that I present my theory.

While the Oedipus complex (the passionate emotions of preferred love for the parent of the opposite sex) gets activated early on in life, what I call the "autistic complex" (the inability to experience passion due to being born physically but not emotionally) may get activated even earlier. In the autistic complex, the tendrils of genetics, physiology, and the environment race ahead, interacting, interplaying, and intertwining in the incessant demands of growth and development, but the emotional strand—so crucial in the formation of relationships—is stunted and left behind, with devastating consequences.

How can this happen? For many years, I have been exploring the impact that the other occupants of mother's mind make on her baby's emotions. In other words, how does the general psychodynamics of "me, you, and the others" affect a baby's emotional development, and how, in particular, does a baby's emotional makeup be such that the other occupants of mother's mind could be felt as unbearable? Francis Tustin (1972) conceptualized a "nest of babies . . . as the fantasy that he (the patient—the child who is receiving my therapeutic milk) is in competition with predatory rivals on the other side of the 'breast' who want to snatch the nipple away from him—to take away his chance of life and sustenance" (p. 174). In this context, the nest of babies she refers to are other imagined patients—*predatory rivals,* she calls them. Furthermore, she goes on to say that these "feelings of rivalry . . . appear too early in life with a premature awareness of bodily separateness from the satisfying object of his needs". Obviously, in Tustin's opinion, babies must be emotionally able to handle being separated from mother if they are ever to be able to handle physical separation.

So how is it that children in Tustin's practice could feel the other occupants in mother's mind as *predatory rivals*? This idea involves an awareness of others in mother's life, which Houzel (2001) discusses at length as *sibling rivalry*. He locates rivalry as a "more primitive and much more relentless version than its Oedipal counterpart." If Houzel's sibling rivalry were another way of talking about a baby's premature rivalry with the other occupants of mother's mind, *we would have a very primitive and very powerful inhibitor of emotional development!* Houzel goes on to say: "By placing heterosexual and homosexual object relations into a libidinal context, Oedipal rivalry and the ambivalence of affect it implies enables the individual to find a way out of this kind of conflict that, in the Pre-Oedipal situation of primitive sibling rivalry, would have been impossible." Were he an infant–parent psychotherapist specializing in autistic behaviour, Houzel would have been very close to discovering that the autism complex comes before the Oedipus complex and that finding a way, on their own, out of a premature rivalry with the others in the mother's mind during the formation of interpersonal relationships *is impossible*. In other words, babies caught in this pre-oedipal conflict are trapped in the autistic spectrum.

It is my opinion that, in some babies, the awareness of others in mother's affections cannot even be conceived of, since it is impossible for these babies to see themselves as separate or distinct from mother. There is not even a "me" or a "you". To even experience the feeling of rivalry, the unborn self must already have started developing the mind and the symbiotic "me, you, and the others" (or the pre-me and pre-you mental and emotional existence).

This transition of moving from the autistic complex to the Oedipus complex might feel tricky and dangerous, particularly if a premature rivalry is fuelling the transition. The infant—already feeling vulnerable—may feel broken apart rather than merely separate. Having recently been one with the container (the womb), it now exists separately, unprotected from an onslaught of sensory and emotional data. Because the infant does not allow the mother in (due to lack of recognition of her as separate or to an inability to compete with her "other occupants"), the mother cannot hold, integrate, or help her baby process the array of incoming sensations. The baby with a fragile self might want or need the whole of the mother's mind, undivided by other loyalties or loves; in not getting her exclusively, no passionate experience is shared between mother and baby, and the triangular relationship is in jeopardy. Emotional malfunctioning can then start occurring at different levels.

I wonder whether the emotional malfunctioning now caught in the avalanche of events occurring in the family does not allow for the proper integration of everything that needs to be integrated for primary relationships to emerge. With relationships failing to emerge, a deterioration sets in, and it, too, gets carried forward to the point where it touches the parents' deep guilt over their shared sexuality, triggering the "damaged-child" syndrome (a deep fear of having produced a strange mind and a strange being). The lack of an attachment to a safe person leads the baby into vicious circles of rage, panic and fear, and constant seeking of self-soothing. Seen from the outside, these self-soothings make their baby seem aloof. They seem to be in limbo, looking inward to a place where they and their mother were one in the womb, where they were looking at their hand and playing with the umbilical cord; or, now born, they are actively looking for knobs that are openings to secure places. From the inside, the infant/child is still floating, and, because changes to this limbo state might be felt as terrifying, they never stop looking for stable hooks.

Some might feel as if they are falling. These babies or children enter into oblivion when they masturbate, but it is without great passion—they can go on for ever and be unaware of the presence of others or the social repercussion of their self-soothing. As in all of their passionless doings, like their fascination for cracks and doors, they soothe without lust. Perhaps this attraction to their cracks and other cracks is a fascination not only of the crack, but of the aspect of two together: their buttocks, mother–father, mother–siblings, mother–other. Do they feel lost in the space between mother and others? Do they feel they fall from awareness, love, and care if they do not get them unilaterally?

For ordinary babies, the presence of father or another adult helping and supporting their mother or caregiver gives rise to complex new feelings to accommodate. And ordinarily, according to Houzel, this oedipal rivalry and the ambivalence of affect it implies enables ordinary babies to find a way out of their conflicts. They feel their space alone, observe the couple in front of them or in the mind of the mother, allowing for the integration or reintegration of their own identity. For some babies, this process is calming; for other babies it is not. Instead, it seems to be the source of fear, resentment, and anxiety. To go to their own self-soothing movements, or the quiet world of their hands, or air, or their body in a kind of automatic self-reliance, produces the opioids necessary to calm themselves, regardless of who or what is happening at that time, leaving the parents depleted, perplexed, and impotent of feeling love or sharing any passionate encounters with them.

It seems to be apparent that babies who are born physically but not emotionally tend to retract from meaningful passionate relationships with their parents. Mahler, Pine, and Bergman (1975) thought that this process was a normal phase of development. I disagree, since it only happens to some vulnerable babies who might become autistic later on. Trevarthen and other neuroscientists have for thirty years demonstrated the central role that parents and reciprocity play in the development of primary relationships. Maiello (2001) showed us how the "frozen" child can reactivate previous traumatic experiences, and if the mother "thaws" emotionally and accompanies the child to external human qualities without fear, they can together defuse the frightening distress and the mother's childhood or pregnancy trauma.

Bearing all this in mind, I shall explore if and how it is possible to introduce the passion, enjoyment, and fun of relationship to these difficult-to-reach babies.

The theory

The psychoanalytic theory of autism is based on the assumption that communicating as a process starts with the psychological acceptance of a physical fact: at birth, the one becomes two. Pre-autistic babies may resist communicating with others because, at their deepest levels, communicating represents their own admission that they and their mother are two and not one, and, because they cannot bear this reality (or even the thought of this reality), they refuse to acknowledge it or deal with it—even if they sense it. So, the first part of the theory is an undeniable reality:

> At birth, the baby is forced to integrate a physical fact: that they and their mother are not one, but two. Neither the mother nor the baby has a choice about this.

The birthing process is a physical separation that is obvious, intractable, and irreducible. What is not obvious, not as intractable, and perhaps not irreducible is the is the second part of the theory:

> At birth, the baby is also forced to integrate a psychological fact: that they and the mother are not one, but two. Either or both the mother and the baby may or may not choose to accept this as a psychological fact.

The psychological birth and its inevitable recognition—the former "we" is now an "I" and a "you"—is not obvious, not as intractable, and perhaps not irreducible as the is physical birth. In other words, psychological separation may be so unbearable for either or both the mother and baby that they refuse to acknowledge the separation by refusing to communicate. The third part of the theory deals with the "others":

> The baby soon is forced to integrate a psychodynamic fact: that the mother's mind is full of "others" rivalling what the baby may have thought to be an exclusive relationship. The one has now become three, and any communication or interaction is felt as unbearable.

Resisting communicating is an unconscious resolve. Consciously, pre-autistic babies cannot process communication with others because to do so would cause them to violate an unconscious resolve they have placed over their deepest fear: they are no longer one with the "other". Not communicating with others is a deeply felt state that self-soothes. The lack of intimacy and the need to regain/maintain this state could explain the retraction into themselves.

Theory discussion

One aspect that researchers, observers, and clinicians encounter in studying babies and the infant–parent relationship is the baby's inbuilt impulse for passionate encounter (Trevarthen, 2001). Even in their dreamy state, newborns will move their lips and touch their hands with eagerness, finding themselves and achieving some comfort or satisfaction. In a state of imbalance, they instinctively search for balance. They find that their mouth is the limit between the inside and outside: for food, for making sounds, and in the satisfaction of the great new need that hunger brings. Their hands are nearby, the smells around, sensations of cold, wet, light—even gravity calms by its familiarity, as the holding required to control the weight is comforting and provides another sense of security. All that is familiar is comforting.

To cope with this dizzying array of new sensations, experiences, and reactivations of prenatal awareness plus the primitive pull of inner resources to satisfy new needs, the mother helps with her available maternal reverie and once again becomes one with her baby, holding her baby in her arms and holding the scattering attention. The baby usually shows an array of passionate reactions and experiences that can be shared and felt with excitement by both mother and father. Researchers like Trevarthen (2001) and Panksepp (2001) explore and explain the positive effect made in the brain of babies resulting from the full-body, mental, and emotional processes of involvement. This process of involvement can take babies and their mothers to a realm that transcends the here-and-now, taking them into a state of coherent expected satisfaction not unlike the state reached in the sexual encounter of two adults. Little wonder that psychoanalysts consider sexuality central to libidinal development and recognize its expression in different manners and in all phases in the baby's development.

As therapists we need to envisage the all-body synchrony, and we must maintain an awareness throughout that though the mother and baby seem bodily separated, they may carry on as if one, as if the same blood is coursing through both bodies, as if, across the air, minuscule particles anchored in both of them will not let go. Any gain that might eventually accrue from separation and independence is offset by the immediate loss of a kind of relationship where neither sight nor words mattered so much. In fact, I can envisage that every passionate encounter is related to the recovery of that deep, private intimacy a pregnant mother shares with her unborn child. She and her child are both the need and the object of satisfaction, whether the need and the object is a part of the mother (e.g., her breast, smell, voice, etc.) or part of a more structured representation of her, including all external and internal aspects of her. This is from an infant observation:

> "Adam is 2 weeks old, and he stops crying the minute the mother picks him up. Mother takes him to the sofa and sits down and both look comfortable and snug. The observer is very touched by the sight and wishes to paint it to preserve in memory what is observed, thinking that Adam is very lucky in having such a lovely mother who understands without words his needs of proximity and being held . . . it looks like a blissful union."

What happens, however, when the difference from internal life to external becomes unbearable? When all the new experiences cannot be held in the arms of the mother, or contained in her mind? When gravity is felt as terrifying because of the fear of falling? When hooked by the pain or gnawing feeling of hunger rather than satisfaction, because of the struggle with the experience of being fed—the difficulty, or sore breasts, or milk spilt? Each impediment or enlargement of experience is felt differently: encountering new voices of the family adds to feelings of anxiety rather than of pleasure; having clothes on feels uncomfortable; independence is dreaded or forced upon when not mentally and emotionally ready—the list is as long as experience itself. Protective, inbuilt behaviours kick in, the withdrawal into sleep increases, the cutting-off or dissociating becomes prolonged, the crying or fussing appears constantly, self-calming techniques are rapidly developed or found by regressing to previous memories.

So, in the midst of all these upheavals and having to find regulation or balance or dispose of terrors, where is the passion, fun, and joy between mother and baby? Where is that exhilarating feeling of coming together, being understood, and enriching each other? How can passion, fun, joy, and that exhilarating feeling manifest itself?

When none of these loving, sensual libidinal charges are present in the relationship, the feelings will be scattered unintegrated and seemingly strewn around. Drawings of autistic teenagers and children show this scattering of scribbles of part objects strewn around the paper without structure. As treatment progresses, however, the same bits start getting integrated into a spiral or a border. You can see this

Figure 11.1.   Beginning sessions.

Figure 11.2.   After the establishment of a relationship.

progression, for example, in the drawings made by Sinclair, a 15-year-old (Figures 11.1, 11.2).

Likewise, the little autistic toddler and pre-autistic baby in their aloofness seem to be looking around, interested in the particles silhouetted by rays of sunlight and hanging in the air (Tyndall effect) not passionately anchored to anything or anybody. Not yet having been born emotionally, they cannot find a "me, you, and the others", and progress can be made only by restarting the process.

Case study

Jonas, an 8-month-old, cried incessantly in front of any face and—always covering his head and ears—he would continue to rock until all was quiet and he was alone. Once in silence, he would blow in the air and put his hands up, enchanted with the string of mobiles; or he would stare at the string of his dummy, immobile—it was the string that that captivated him, not the objects tied to it. Mother and father were very worried since they could not socialize with him, and he made guttural strange sounds even when crying, as if entertaining or comforting himself.

Patiently, in the meetings with father and mother, we waited and waited behind the screen of Jonas's cot. We talked about their anxieties about him, about not forcing him to accept us, about it being the opposite technique of the one they had used so far, one including him rejecting us. Mother talked about feeling guilty and terrified: did I think she was breeding an autistic child? What did she do so wrong? How can she help him? She talked about putting the radio on loud and of taking him to the big shops on Oxford Street for him to get used to people. She asked herself: Why she should accept him like that? She wondered if it was her fault as a "bad mother", yet she spoke also of being a "good mother" to her younger siblings when her father abandoned the family. Paranoid anxieties started building up, and she started hating her unresponsive baby, and the more the time passed the more her discomfort and fear started to blind her towards her distancing baby.

In the sessions, mother developed an angry transference with me and voiced her sense of despair at the work with the co-therapist. Father directed his anger at the practical implications that living with Jonas placed on his life: the continuous turmoil at night, the exhaustion, the isolation of not going out. He shared his fear about his son's development and concerns for his future. While sitting, letting the parents' inner fears and frustration emerge, we waited too for their son to emerge, waited for Jonas to come out of his hiding and peep at us.

In Session 7, with only Jonas, mother, and me present, Jonas started peeping in the direction of our voices. Mother was getting worried again about not seeing any progress, and I didn't have any more ideas about the situation. I wanted to wait more and more, continuing our long sessions in the quietness of the room. Jonas started looking cautiously again and again. I mentioned to him the fact that we were so quiet today and that mother was on her own, without father. He started playing with a piece of string. I mentioned his entertainment being close-in with mother, remembering good calm times, and how difficult it was for him to share her. The following sessions, mother was again by herself and we were quiet, waiting for Jonas to play with the string, and we commented again about being just with mother and how difficult it was to share her, how he wanted her only for himself, all of her—no others, no separations, no waiting. He carried on now on mother's lap and being held tightly, enjoying her in a sensuous way, and starting possessing her with touches and kisses. Mother was so overwhelmed that she just let it be, until she made a fleeting comment to me—and that made Jonas very angry, and he hid inside her cardigan. We continued with the talk about not wanting to hear my voice and to feel one with mother, like long ago.

These sessions lasted three more months until he was able to walk around and explore. He was timid and cautious, always referencing back to mother but smiling coyly at me. In the meantime, he had gone from being unable to cope or relate to the world to understanding at some level the pain and misery of parting with the quiet place of denying both his mother's and his own existence. We could contemplate together a mother who could have others in her life as well as him. When he could allow himself real proximity to his mother and her internal occupants—mainly her husband and others—he began to build a relationship with her externally, and eventually he could tolerate a relationship with others. The talking to him and about him and others allowed him to be able to feel the passionate encounter of losing mother and having her, the joy of being able to share her and the pain of not having her for himself, of perhaps identifying with others who, too, struggle with coping with other difficulties and taking care of themselves and the objects of their love.

What is this numbness generated between babies like Jonas and their mothers? Is it shyness? A lack of symbolic imagination? Why did it appear when mother was with other people? How was mother colluding in this process? Was it impossible for her to empty her mind and heart for her baby's benefit? Could she? Did he want to be inside mother, inside her head, inside her heart? How could he go forward with the father constantly around? If autistic babies ever start the process of integrating their experiences, they smile and look others directly in the face when they play with their mouth or genitals or whatever is in their mind that they are in communication with, like a nice daydream, for instance.

Case discussion

In Jonas we see more a negative aspect of mirroring, where, as Sartre described, other people can be felt as hell. Jonas transforms the people who look at him into objects so he can make them a part of his inner world. He does this because he does not want to lose himself in the perception of somebody else. For Jonas, being perceived by others feels like being sucked into a world without control. But without others—even if they are felt as hell—we cannot exist, for, Sartre says, "we need other minds to mirror our own; we need other minds to tell us the qualities of our own existence; and we need other minds to tell us that we exist at all". But what if Jonas is surrounded by absurd caregivers, or they are forced to live in an absurd world? Sartre tells us that it is *nauseating*. (Sartre was a year old when his father died and his grieving mother moved to her parents' home.) Development work has to be restarted from the very beginning, so that "me, you, and the others" can be found and the mother seen and shared in her totality. If mothers cannot be accepted as separate and shared, their babies can get lost in existential dilemmas: they have trouble existing and being and keeping their identity safe because they can neither separate nor share. By not accepting the triangulation of "me, you, and the others", they refuse to participate in it. Development pushes them into the negative aspect of mirroring, as opposed to the more familiar Winnicottian positive aspect in which infants see a reflection of themselves as being seen and admired by mother.

To restart development from the beginning, the therapist had to allow her maternal reverie in the countertransference to let time pass and allow Jonas the time to re-enter the familiar state of being in the womb, hearing voices but not seeing. What happens in the time that passes while the therapist takes in the ongoing split or dilemma of the autistic baby or child? During this time, we allow the process to take form within us, and we make sense of what is going on. The relationship of the maternal reverie might allow for empathy to exist in a physiological/psychological dynamic:

> Benign and partial fusional situations are represented by instinctive and natural compenetrations in areas in which mucus membranes and liquid secretions constitute the somatic parallel to the battle of the preconscious: an area of transit between inside and outside, of contact between temperatures and moods, of acquaintance and between the known and the unknown, of exchange between the I and the You, of pleasure and constitution of the "We". [Bolognini, 2004]

When therapists dare to immerse themselves in the symbiotic relationship of the infant–parents triangle and put words to possible fears, it helps both the infant and the parents. As Houzel (2004) claims, "every one of us has a black hole somewhere deep within our personalities, at the umbilical cord of our being". Reaching and touching this part enables us to understand—and helps not to collude in denying—what is happening. To be sure, the process can be frightening for the therapist; this is when the team plays an important role in holding not only the family, but the therapist as well.

Conclusion

So, returning to the original question of our thought experiment: what if a baby is born physically but not emotionally?

Wouldn't the outcome look like autism?

CHAPTER TWELVE

Developmental and autistic aspects of vocalization

Maria Rhode

Words are not just symbols: they are sensory constructs with rhythmical and musical properties. These two aspects of language are perhaps most fruitfully integrated in poetic diction, which relies on the sound of words to produce a bodily and emotional impact just as their meaning produces a mental impact. Clinical work, on the other hand, and particularly work with autistic children, allows us to study the disjunction between form and meaning, or sound and sense. In normal usage, as in the stages documented by developmental researchers (Schore, 1994; Stern, 1985; Trevarthen 1998b), the rhythmical and musical aspects—which Meltzer (1975) has described as the song-and-dance level—provide a foundation for the semantics of speech. In contrast, children with autism will often experience words concretely rather than symbolically, as something that can be physically lost from their mouth. They may then attempt to deal with these fears by using the physical aspects of words in the service of self-soothing rather than of communication.

Many factors will interact to allow sounds produced by the mouth to be used communicatively. For example, most parents react to their babies' early vocalizations as though these were intended as words: without this expectation and response, language development can be impaired (Brazelton, Koslowski, & Main, 1974; Papousek, 1992). The children can themselves contribute to the adults' low expectations. For example, the observer who visited Adam's family as part of the project I have described in chapter 10 recorded his parents' frustration at his failure to speak. Some months into the observation, when Adam was becoming increasingly communicative on a nonverbal level, she wondered herself, "Why doesn't the child talk?" In fact Adam had talked, at the very beginning of the observation: the observer had said "Ta" to him when he gave her a toy, and he had answered, "Ta". The emotional context was one of reciprocity, and Adam's "Ta" was clearly not echolalic. However, his capacity for this kind of developmental imitation came and went; the many disappointments and frustrations that his delayed development of communicative capacities brought with it made it very difficult for adults to believe in what he could sometimes do, to remember it, and to expect it to happen again. It is easy to see how a vicious circle could be set up and reinforced.

Another centrally important factor, of which I shall give an example later, concerns the question of how far the child expects to be understood. Where this expectation is strong, words can feel like a way of getting through emotionally and eliciting a response. Where the expectation of understanding is weak, words can feel like something that is concretely lost from the mouth. This is particularly important in autism, where, as Tustin (1972) discovered, there is a central experience of a mouth that is broken or lost.

Language and the body

Psychoanalytic workers as well as developmentalists have linked the musical, rhythmical properties of language to the intact sense of a bodily self. For example, Tustin has described the extreme anxieties about bodily fragmentation often conveyed by children with autism, who may be afraid of losing parts of their body, of liquefying or spilling out, of burning or freezing. This work has been developed by Geneviève Haag (1985), who has documented the fears that children with autism can have of coming apart down the midline—as one little boy asked her, "Are my buttocks properly stuck together?" I have myself treated a girl with a diagnosis of (fairly mild) Asperger's syndrome who dragged her leg behind her at the end of a session and explained, quite matter-of-factly, "It's come off." Anxieties of this kind can be counteracted by repeated experiences of reliability, of experience that is patterned rhythmically like a steady heartbeat—what one of Tustin's (1986) patients called the "rhythm of safety". Autistic children's responsiveness to music is well known; child psychotherapists, even non-musical ones, find themselves instinctively singing in sessions, emphasizing syllables in a regular beat as in nursery rhymes, or using what Trevarthen (1979) has called "motherese". Children who do not have autism and may speak fluently and communicatively, but who need to work on the fundamental, primitive levels I have been describing, may make contact by tapping out a rhythm in sessions. The therapist "answers" by tapping the same rhythm in response and, later, perhaps, introducing a variation to build up a "conversation". This is what Meltzer has termed the "song-and-dance" level of language, which he thought encompassed the most profound emotional communications between mother and infant (Maiello, 2000; Meltzer, 1975). Such psychoanalytic formulations link readily with knowledge about the importance of mutual regulation of the right hemisphere of the brain occurring between mother and infant at the beginning of life (Schore, 1994), since this hemisphere seems to be concerned with emotion and music more than with cognition. Equally, studies by Trevarthen and Malloch (2000) have documented the precise rhythmical and musical attunement of vocalizations by mother and baby. They can be notated as a musical score with a regular bar length occupying an amount of time that is characteristic of fundamental autonomic bodily rhythms. All these lines of work converge on the fundamental connections between language, emotion, and the sense of bodily integrity.

Central to this sense of bodily integrity is the possession of an intact, undamaged mouth. The psychoanalyst Esther Bick (1968) proposed that the baby's sense of a cohesive self, bounded by an intact skin that is experienced both on the physical and mental levels, derived from repeated experiences of being responded to both emotionally and physically. In her view, the experience of the nipple or teat in the mouth, together with the caregiver's focused attention, was quintessentially suited to drawing together all the different domains of the baby's experience and, in this way, to supporting the sense of cohesion. This sense of cohesion is the opposite of fears of spilling out, falling forever, and so on. Frances Tustin's work with children with autism further focused attention on their experience of having a mouth that was broken and damaged, particularly when they realized that the source of sensation and satisfaction during feeding was something that was not part of their own body: that they were not self-sustaining. This seemed to be a catastrophic experience that left them, as her little patient John described it, feeling that their mouth was "a black hole with a nasty prick" (Tustin, 1972). A patient of my own talked about an impending separation in terms of damage to both his skin and his mouth: "Poor mouth; poor skin", as he said before a holiday break (Rhode, 1997b).

The "Theatre of the Mouth"

Psychoanalytic authors who were not primarily concerned with autism have stressed the importance of the mouth in normal development. The title of Spitz's (1955) paper, "The Primal Cavity", highlights the fundamental role of the baby's experience of the mouth. (It is important to stress that he does not write about experiences in the mouth as though they were divorced from relationships: Spitz was one of the first to emphasize the importance of the mother's face and of eye contact between mother and infant). As we all know, older babies routinely find out about objects by exploring them with their mouths: the mouth is one of the prime points of contact between the baby and the outside world, and a whole world of meaning can be located there.

For example, Augusta Bonnard (1960) proposed that babies could learn about orientation in space, well before they were able to turn over, by moving their tongue inside their mouth to discover up and down, left and right. She distinguished between this developmental kind of exploration and the self-stimulation that can be provided by sucking or chewing the tongue or cheeks and that can serve to deflect the baby's attention from the outside world and the relationships it offers. This is the kind of self-stimulation that Tustin later described in her autistic patients.

Perhaps the most comprehensive statement of the mouth's function as a bridge between internal experience and the outside world is provided by Meltzer's formulations on the "Theatre of the Mouth" (Meltzer, 1986). In his view, the mouth is the first theatre in which meaning is generated through the child's interpretation of the shape, texture, and taste of food (within the context of an emotional relationship); of the feel of mouthed objects; and of the sensory properties of words. These functions of the mouth, he suggested, are later divided between the hands, which allow the manipulation of objects in the outside world for various purposes including play, and the internal world of dreams, in which personal meanings are elaborated.

Such formulations suggest ways of understanding some kinds of speech impairments that might otherwise be puzzling. For example, workers in a variety of fields come across children who write but do not speak: the problem seems to be to do with the production of words in the mouth rather than with the capacity for symbolic functioning. Morton Gernsbacher (2005) has described her son's out-standing verbal sophistication and high intelligence, in spite of which extreme dyspraxia—particularly oral dyspraxia—prevents him from speaking. The psychoanalyst Karl Abraham (1916) treated a mute 17-year-old patient who, he said, was unable to use his mouth to speak with because he was far too busy using it for other things. These other things included sucking his tongue and cheeks—practices that today would be thought of as autistic. The voice itself can serve as a source of reassuring sensory stimulation, quite apart from its proper function as a medium of communication. Several child patients of my own (e.g., Rhode, 1997a) did not use their voice to speak with but to produce a loud, resonant, and piercing vibratory noise. They seemed to use this sensory stimulation in order to reassure themselves about the integrity of their mouth, particularly in contexts that might have made them anxious. Examples included situations in which they were frightened of falling, or others, like going to the lavatory, in which they might have been worried about losing bodily contents (see also Laznik, 1995b, 2000b).

Sometimes children with autism distort words in ways that seem random but turn out to make sense in terms of the Theatre of the Mouth.

> For example, 4-year-old Robert, who had come with his family for his first assessment session, constantly repeated "wzz-ztt, wzz-ztt, wzz-ztt". He climbed on the table and mimed losing his footing near the edge. Then he began to play with an old-fashioned tel-ephone with a dial. He rotated the dial as far as it would go, then released it and watched intently as it revolved until it came up against the metal stopper. I said how important it was that the stop-per was there, so the dial didn't just carry on spinning, and used my voice to mirror the trajectory of the dial being released from its final position and moving "downwards" until it came up against the solid stopper: "Aaahhh-uh". Robert then startled me by saying clearly: "What's that?" I realized that his earlier "wzz-ztt" was, in fact, a contraction—"What's that?" with the vowels left out.

I would understand this vignette as suggesting that Robert was fright-ened of open spaces he could fall into (like falling off the edge of the table). He seems to have been reassured by the firmness of the metal stopper on the telephone dial and by the way my voice mirrored the dial spinning through space but coming up against the stopper and being held by it. This, I think in retrospect, helped him to manage the space in his mouth that has to be tolerated to generate a vowel sound. "What's that?" is, in fact, a perfectly reasonable question to ask in the new situation in which he found himself.

Conversely, when children with autism begin to speak, they may leave out consonants, so that syllables consisting only of vowels can seem to run into each other (e.g. Haag, 1984). Sometimes this can seem like a magical way of eliminating boundaries, as though this could be done by eliminating the boundaries between syllables. For example, a boy with autism who had begun "speaking" in vowels combined this with pinching and scratching the skin on my hand, as though the dividing "membrane" between syllables were the equivalent of the skin membrane (Rhode, 1995). Haag has noted that children who are beginning to establish a complete body image and to feel confident that both sides of their body are in place sometimes reflect this in the structure of their babbling: they begin to produce the symmetrical di-syllables that are characteristic of early language development "(ma-ma", "ba-ba", "da-da", and so on).

In case some of these vignettes seem far-fetched, I would like to cite an example from a little boy of 18 months who was developing normally. He was introduced to a visibly pregnant woman whose name, he was told, was Meg. Pointing at her, he said, "Mummy Egg!" (Rhode, 1995). Obviously, he did not construe her name as being in any way arbitrary: he took it as conveying, by its structure, important information about her condition, with the initial M denoting Mummy and the "-eg" sound "meaning" "egg". As in the previous clinical examples of the "Theatre of the Mouth", the "shape" of a word serves as the bearer of meaning.

The expectation of understanding

The following vignette illustrates how holding back words can create the illusion of being in control, particularly in relation to unprocessed experiences of loss. A second vignette, by way of contrast, shows how a child's babbling was transmuted into a communicative "word" within a context in which she expected to be understood.

The first example I wish to cite concerns Baby Jenny, who had a particularly close relationship with her mother in the first weeks of her life. Mother then returned to full-time work quite suddenly: the observer felt that the loss of ongoing intimate contact with her baby was too painful for her to be able to make the transition in any way that was not all-or-nothing. Jenny did not take well to being looked after by relatives, and, when an au pair took over, things got worse. She had been strikingly vocal: now she was silent. The au pair obviously felt invalidated by her behaviour, and the observer witnessed a particularly painful, teasing interaction between them when Jenny was 10 months, which ended with Jenny banging her head hard against the wall and shouting, "Mummy!" This use of words was quite exceptional: at her 18-month check, Jenny was found to be developing normally in respect of everything except her language, which was described as severely retarded. She was still not speaking at the age of 4 years, when her mother became sufficiently worried to decide that she wanted to stay at home and "teach" her to speak. They must have managed to re-establish the emotional connection between them, as Jenny was soon talking age-appropriately.

The observer—like another in a similar situation (Kaplan, 1998; Wedeles, Grimandi, & Cioeta, 2002; Williams, Grimandi, & Cioeta, 2002)—speculated on the importance of control: perhaps, she thought, Jenny felt as though she could assert some degree of mastery by literally allowing nothing to escape her lips. This links with the despair she sometimes seems to have felt about being heard. Jenny's unusual recourse to speech at a point of crisis, when she was literally beating her head against a wall, brings to mind the behaviour of some children with autism who do speak when they are desperate.

I must stress that this vignette is not meant to imply anything so crude as the supposition that children with autism do not speak because their mothers have gone back to work. This is obviously non-sense. What it does illustrate, I believe, is that children who are not autistic may sometimes hold back their words as a way of trying to establish some measure of control—in this case, of words leaving their mouth—as an illusory, magical way of dealing with emotional loss.

By way of contrast, here is an observation of a little girl of 8 months whose mother was absent for long periods, but who "found her voice" in order to communicate about her to sympathetic adults (Cristinelli, 1997):

Nina had been at a day nursery from a very young age when her mother returned to work. She had a good rapport both with her keyworker and with the observer, who had been struck by Nina's enjoyment of each new developmental opportunity. She relished new kinds of food, vocalized enthusiastically, and seemed to be making the most of her interactions with other children as well as with adults. This observation shows her for the first time transforming babbling into communicative words. She caught the adults' eye in a way that showed that she both expected and wanted them to get the message—a clear example of what Trevarthen (1998b) calls secondary intersubjectivity.

Nina, at 8 months 2 weeks, watches children playing with a very realistic doll baby. She vocalizes in a crescendo of emotion: "Ma . . . ma . . . mamama!" and establishes eye contact with both the observer and her keyworker. The observer notes that both she and the keyworker feel very moved. Nina crawls over to the keyworker, who picks her up and cuddles her.

Cristinelli's reading of this event was that the children's play with the doll reminded Nina of a mother with a baby, and hence of her own mother. The emotional atmosphere was such that neither observer nor keyworker had any doubt about what the child wanted them to understand. Far from losing her voice in her mother's absence, Nina was able to transmute babbling into speech thanks to her expectation of being understood. That is: words that left her mouth would elicit understanding and an appropriate response, rather than leading to concrete loss and impoverishment.

Factors in Adam's language development

The therapeutic observation of Adam, the toddler at risk of autism I referred to in chapter 10, provided illustrations of a number of important factors relating to the capacity to use language.

First, as I have already noted, Adam was able to imitate the occasional word within a context of emotional reciprocity from the very beginning of the observation. Equally, from the beginning he showed the capacity for social referencing when he was the focus of someone's undivided attention. However, his unresponsive behaviour at other times was sufficiently discouraging so that neither his parents nor the observer could fully appreciate the implications of what he was sometimes able to do, or even remember it, let alone expect him to do it again and therefore support his patchy capacities. This illustrates the importance of emotional factors for the full expression of a child's communicative competence.

Another important emotional factor in Adam's language development concerned the degree to which he identified with the language
production of people who were important to him. For example, at one
stage he began to speak into a toy telephone, imitating his mother
who was herself speaking on the telephone. He very deliberately demonstrated this for the observer, who had for many weeks sought to
engage him in imitative games. It was as though he were showing her
that he could take the important step of following his mother's example, and that he could expect her to support this.

Finally, Adam had a considerable developmental spurt when he
was reunited with people he saw regularly, and from whom he had
been separated during a holiday break. This developmental spurt involved increased mastery in the use of his dummy and ball, as well as
the beginning of two-word sentences. One could see these capacities as
being related in terms of Adam's growing confidence that things—the
ball and the dummy—could be retrieved, just as absent people could
be found again. That would imply (as in the case of Jenny) that, with
increasing security, the child feels more able to let go of his words.

Concluding remarks

I have touched on a few of the factors among the many that affect the
production of speech: theories concerning syntax, for instance, are
beyond the scope of this chapter (see Pinker, 1994), and I have not
discussed theories of language development based on a cognitive approach, such as theory of mind (Baron-Cohen, Leslie, & Frith, 1985),
or on a relational perspective (Hobson, 2002). My focus has been on a
psychoanalytic approach to anxieties about bodily integrity and how
these affect whether the mouth can be employed for speech. I have
suggested that the use of language reflects primitive bodily anxieties,
often staged in the Theatre of the Mouth, and that work supporting the
integration of these anxieties can promote more integrated speech and
can allow inbuilt capacities for relatedness and the use of language to
come into play.

Note

Some of this material was previously published in M. Rhode, "Sensory Aspects
of Language Development in Relation to Primitive Anxieties." *International Journal
of Infant Observation*, Vol. 6 (2004): 12–32, and is reproduced by permission.

Conclusion

The case for training, early screening, early treatment, and further research

Stella Acquarone

This book shows the efforts to understand certain kinds of families who have infants with distancing or rejecting behaviours who sometimes become withdrawn toddlers and later may be diagnosed in the autistic spectrum.

This book has ended. But the journey has just begun. From further research, training, assessment, and treatment will come new conferences and new books. This is just the first volume in a widening set, a growing body of knowledge that extends our ability to reach *earlier* for better outcomes.

But the journey—as difficult as it may be—will be worth the effort. It is estimated that the lifetime cost of an autistic in the UK is now up to £2.5 million. In the UK alone, 1,280 babies born each year are headed towards a life with autism. With 640,000 births every year and 1 in 100 of them (if left untreated) becoming autistic (Baird et al., 2006), the total lifetime cost to society *just for babies born this year* is £218.5 million: [(640,000 ÷ 100) x £2,500,000] ÷ 73.2 years (the average life expectancy of males in the UK in 2001).

The social cost is more institutions and a greater use of social services. The family cost is a stretching of family resources—and more divorces. The cost to the autistic is not being able to relate to the family, the experience of inner neglect, isolation, and, what is more obvious, lack of signs of happiness.

As you have read in the preceding chapters, advances in medical, biological, developmental, and psychological sciences have enabled us *to recognize the signs of autism in infants and to intervene early*. Steady progress made in all the disciplines addressing what is now referred to as the "autistic spectrum" is showing a convergence on psychoanalytic early intervention as the "sweet spot" in treatment and prevention. The cost of early intervention—relative to the costs of autism—is small. Even an intensive early intervention can cost as little as £25,000.

Henry Massie presented a history of research into signs of alarm of autistic behaviour. His own investigations have been with home videos from birth of children who became autistic at the age of 4 years. More contemporary research followed the same technique. The work of Colwyn Trevarthen, Catherine St Clair, and Laurent Danon-Boileau has given us a greater understanding of detailed behaviour in normal infants, and they hypothesize on what home videos tell us about the internal model of processing thoughts and emotions in the baby who becomes autistic. Filippo Muratori and Sandra Maestro described their findings from their work in identifying markers of autistic behaviour.

All these signs are invaluable for the clinicians, not just to detect or treat, which they may not be trained to do, but certainly to follow up and refer early—at a time when it is easier to help, when there is still little damage in the morale of the family .

The psychoanalytically informed early-intervention approaches presented here are less well known than behavioural approaches, yet they show great benefit for the parent–infant relationship in the case of attachment difficulties of another kind from the classical conceptualization. The latter is more related to the pattern (according to their experiences) that the parents transmit to their infant. We propose here that there is yet another kind of attachment difficulty derived from the fragility of the infant in coping with the external world or with the infant's sensations and formation of mental representations. This fragility is difficult or impossible to attach to their loving/caring parents. It is to this complication in their relationship that we address an approach based on psychoanalytic psychotherapy.

As with any psychoanalytic practice, the approach needs a great deal of training, whatever the background of the practitioner. We are all involved in finding and putting together the tools and information required to intervene early with these infants and their parents. The problem arising from this particular difficulty is relating to others, and one of the "others" is also the person who is providing treatment! This is why the psychoanalytic approach is more delicate and why extra skills are needed by the practitioner.

We are doing research with individual clinical cases that are followed up—both the treated and, where parents did not agree to treatment, untreated cases. We do not have control studies because human beings cannot be replicated; however, each case is submitted to individualized and careful thinking. The result is hopeful, because we see a marked increase in patients' integration of experiences and the capacity to relate to people. The infants develop cognitively without stereotypic movements and with speech and feelings that can be expressed. What is fascinating is the speed of recovery at 6 and 9 months, compared with 2½ year-olds—and even more with 5-year-olds onwards.

In the intervention approaches presented here, the family benefits: by the acknowledgment of an inner world in the different members of the family, each with different emphasis; and by the internal transformation of the mother/parents, or with the baby.

Any after-the-fact observer could say that perhaps to intervene early is an alarmist approach and could only frighten parents. However, to increase the knowledge about each other can only help relationships, and there is also the possibility of avoiding the terrible diagnosis of autism.

Even though this is the end of this book, it is the beginning of new thinking about real possibilities open to eradicate one, if not many, of the disorders and mental illnesses in childhood. Early screening and specific early interventions hold out that promise. They certainly show a promising way forward. Early intervention is to communication difficulties what immunization is to infectious illnesses or what medical screenings are to contagious and fatal diseases.

Whether autism is in our nature or nurture, there is a lot we can do about it in the pre-autistic stage.

REFERENCES

Abraham, K. (1916). The first pre-genital stage of the libido. In: *Selected Papers on Psycho-Analysis*. London: Hogarth Press, 1927 (4th impression, 1949).

Acquarone, S. (1992). What shall I do to stop him crying? *Journal of Child Psychotherapy, 18* (1): 33–56.

Acquarone, S. (2004). *Infant–Parent Psychotherapy: A Handbook*. London: Karnac.

Adrien, J. L., Lenoir, P., Martineau, J., Perot, A., Hameury, L., Larmande, C., & Sauvage, D. (1993). Blind ratings of early symptoms of autism based upon family home movies. *Journal of American Academy Child Adolescent Psychiatry, 33*: 617–625.

Ainsworth, M. B., & Wittig, B. A. (1969). Attachment and exploratory behaviour of one-year-olds in a Strange Situation. In: B. M. Foss (Ed.), *Determinants of Infant Behaviour, Vol. 4* (pp. 111–36). London: Methuen.

Alonim, H. (2002a). "Early Signs of Autism." Paper presented at the Conference on Early Signs of Alarm and What Can Be Done, organized by The Centre for Child Mental Health and The School of Infant Mental Health, London (31 May).

Alonim, H. (2002b). *Post Treatment Social Integration of Children with Contact and Communication Disorders*. Rosh Pinna, Israel: The Mifne Centre.

Alonim, H. (2004). The Mifne Method, Israel: Early intervention in the treatment of autism/PDD: A therapeutic programme for the nuclear

242   REFERENCES

family and their child. *Journal of Child and Adolescent Mental Health, 16* (1): 39–43.

Alonim, H. (2005). "Infants at Risk—Attachment Disorders: Diagnosis and Treatment." Paper presented at the Conference on the Early Signs of Autism in Infants, School of Infant Mental Health, University College, London (11–12 July).

Alvarez, A. (1992). *Live Company: Psychoanalytic Psychotherapy with Autistic, Borderline, Deprived and Abused Children.* London: Routledge

Alvarez, A. (1997) (with Furgiuele, R.). Speculations on components in the infant's sense of agency: The sense of abundance and the capacity to think in parentheses. In: S. Reid (Ed.), *Developments in Infant Observation: The Tavistock Model.* London: Routledge.

Alvarez, A., & Reid, S. (1999). *Autism and Personality.* London: Routledge.

APA (2000). *Diagnostic and Statistical Manual of Mental Disorders, DSM-IV* (4th edition, Text Revision). Washington, DC: American Psychiatric Association.

Apter, A., Farbstein, I., Spiegel, R., & Vograft, Y. (2001). *Retrospective Evaluation of an Intensive Method of Children with PDD, Schneider Children's Medical Center, Israel.* Rosh Pinna, Israel: The Mifne Centre.

Ayers, M. (2003). *Mother–Infant Attachment and Psychoanalysis: The Eyes of Shame.* New York: Brunner-Routledge.

Baird, G., Cass, H., & Slonims, V. (2003). Diagnosis of autism. *British Medical Journal, 327* (7413): 488–493.

Baird, G., Charman, T., Baron-Cohen, S., Cox, A., Swettenham, J., Wheelwright, S., & Drew, A. (2000). A screening instrument for autism at 18 months of age: A 6 year follow-up study. *Journal of the American Academy of Child and Adolescent Psychiatry, 39*: 694–702.

Baird, G., Simonoff, E., Pickles, A., Chandler, S., Loucas, T., Meldrum, S. D., & Charman, T. (2006). Prevalence of disorders of the autism spectrum in a population cohort of children in South Thames: The Special Needs and the Autism Project (SNAP). *The Lancet, 368* (9531): 210–215.

Bakeman, R., & Adamson, L. B. (1984). Coordinating attention to people and objects in mother–infant and peer–infant interaction. *Child Development, 55*: 1278–1289

Baranek, G. T. (1999). Autism during infancy: A retrospective video analysis of sensorimotor and social behaviors at 9–12 months of age. *Journal of Autism and Developmental Disorders, 29*: 213–224

Baranek, G. T. (2002). Efficacy of sensory and motor interventions for children with autism. *Journal of Autism and Developmental Disorders, 32* (5): 397–422.

Baron-Cohen, S., Allen, J., & Gillberg, C. (1995). Can autism be detected at 18 months? The needle, the haystack, and the CHAT. *British Journal of Psychiatry, 168*: 158–163.

Baron-Cohen, S., Cox, A., Baird, G., Swettenham, J., Nightingale, N., Morgan, K., Drew, A., Charman, T. (1996). Psychological markers in the detection of autism in infancy in a large population. *British Journal of Psychiatry, 168* (2): 158–163.

Baron-Cohen, S., Leslie, A. M., & Frith, U. (1985). Does the autistic child have a "theory of mind"? *Cognition, 21*: 37–46.

Barthélémy, C., Adrien, J. L., Roux, S., Garreau, B., Perrot, A., & Lelord, G. (1992). Sensitivity and specificity of the Behavioral Summarized Evaluation for the assessment of autistic behaviors. *Journal of Autism and Developmental Disorders, 22*: 23–31

Bauman, M. L., (2005). *The Neurobiology of Autism*. Baltimore, MD: Johns Hopkins University Press.

Beebe, B. (1982). Micro-timing in mother–infant communication. In: M. R. Key (Ed.), *Non-Verbal Communication Today*. The Hague: Mouton.

Bentata, H. (2001). *Sirènes et chofar: Incarnation mythique et rituel de la voix.* Paris: L'Harmattan.

Bick, E. (1964) Notes on infant observation in psychoanalytic training. *International Journal of Psychoanalysis, 45*: 184 –188. Also in: A. Briggs (Ed.), *Surviving Space: Papers on Infant Observation*. Tavistock Clinic Book Series. London: Karnac, 2002.

Bick, E. (1968). The experience of the skin in early object relations. *International Journal of Psychoanalysis, 49*: 484–486.

Bion, W. R. (1957). Differentiation of the psychotic from the non-psychotic personalities. In: *Second Thoughts: Selected Papers in Psychoanalysis*. London: Heinemann [reprinted London: Karnac, 1984].

Bion, W. R. (1959). Attacks on linking. In: *Second Thoughts: Selected Papers in Psychoanalysis*. London: Heinemann [reprinted London: Karnac, 1984].

Bion, W. R. (1962). *Learning from Experience.* London: Heinemann.

Bion, W. R. (1967a). *Second Thoughts: Selected Papers in Psychoanalysis*. London: Heinemann [reprinted London: Karnac, 1984].

Bion, W. R. (1967b). A theory of thinking. In: *Second Thoughts: Selected Papers in Psychoanalysis*. London: Heinemann [reprinted London: Karnac, 1984].

Boddaert, N., Chabane, N., Hervais, H., Good, C. D., Bourgeois, M., Plumet, M.-H., Barthelemy, C., Mouren, M.-C., Artiges, E., Samson, Y., Brunel-lee, F., Frackviak, R. S. J., & Zilbovicius, M. (2004). Superior temporal sulcus anatomical abnormalities in childhood autism: A voxel-based morphometry MRI study. *NeuroImage, 23*: 364–369.

Bollas, C. (1987). *Psychoanalysis of the Unthought Known*. New York: Columbia University Press.

Bolognini, S. (2004). *Psychoanalytic Empathy*. London: Free Association Books.

Bolognini, S. (2005). "Narcissism in Adults." Paper presented at the Institute of Psychoanalysis, London.

Bonnard, A. (1960). The primal significance of the tongue. *International Journal of Psychoanalysis, 41*: 301–307.

Boszormenyi-Nagy, I. (2005). Intensive family therapy as process. In: I. Boszormenyi-Nagy & J. L. Framo (Eds.), *Intensive Family Therapy*. New York: Harper & Row.

Boucher, J., Lewis, V., & Collins, G. (1998). Familiar face and voice matching and recognition in children with autism. *Journal of Child Psychology and Psychiatry, 39* (2): 171–181.

Bowlby, J. (1969). *Attachment and Loss, Vol. 1: Attachment*. New York: Basic Books.

Brazelton, T. B. (1992). *Touchpoints*. New York: Addison-Wesley; London: Viking, 1993.

Brazelton, T. B., Koslowski, B., & Main, M. (1974). The origins of reciprocity: The early mother–infant interaction. In: M. Lewis & L. A. Rosenblum (Eds.), *The Effect of the Infant on Its Caregivers*. London: Wiley Interscience; New York: Elsevier.

Briggs, A. (Ed.) (2002). *Surviving Space: Papers on Infant Observation*. Tavistock Clinic Series. London: Karnac.

Briggs, S. (1997). *Growth and Risk in Infancy*. London: Jessica Kingsley.

Britton, R. (1989). The missing link: Parental sexuality in the Oedipus complex. In: J. Steiner (Ed.), *The Oedipus Complex Today*. London: Karnac.

Bruner, J. (1983). *Child's Talk: Learning to Use Language*. New York: W. W. Norton.

Bruner, J. S. (1990). *Acts of Meaning*. Cambridge, MA: Harvard University Press.

Bryson, S. E., Rogers, S. J., & Fombonne, E. (2003). Autism spectrum disorders: Early detection, intervention, education, and psychopharmacological management. *Canadian Journal of Psychiatry, 48* (8): 506–516.

Buhler, K. (1934). *Sprachtheorie: Der Darstellingsfunktion der Sprache*. Jena: Fischer.

Burnham, D., Kitamura, C., & Vollmer-Conna, U. (2002). What's new, Pussycat? On talking to babies and animals. *Science, 296*: 1435.

Bursztejn, C., Baghdadli, A., Lazartigues, A., Philippe, A., & Sibertin-Blanc,

D. (2003). [Towards early screening of autism.] *Archives of Pediatrics, 10* (Suppl. 1): 129s–131s.

Cardenal, M. (1998). A psychoanalytically informed approach to clinically ill babies. *International Journal of Infant Observation, 2*: 90–100.

Charman, T. (2003). Why is joint attention a pivotal skill in autism. *Philosophical Transactions of the Royal Society London B, Biological Sciences, 358*: 315–324

Courchesne, E. (2003). *Unusual Patterns of Brain Development in Autism.* University of California.

Courchesne, E., Carper, R., & Akshoomoff, N. (2003). Evidence of brain overgrowth in the first year of life in autism. *Journal of the American Medical Association, 290*: 337–344

Courchesne, E., Chisum, H., & Townsend, J. (1994). Neural activity dependent brain changes in development: Implications for psychopathology. *Development and Psychopathology, 6*: 697–722.

Courchesne, E., Townsend, J., & Saitoh, O. (1994). The brain in infantile autism: Posterior fossa structures are abnormal. *Neurology, 44*: 214–223.

Cowsill, K. (2000) "I thought you knew": Some factors affecting a baby's capacity to maintain eye contact. *International Journal of Infant Observation, 3*: 64–83.

Cristinelli, C. (1997). *The Forerunners of Language during Weaning: Observation of Children during Their First Year of Life.* Unpublished MA Dissertation in Psychoanalytic Observational Studies, Tavistock/University of East London.

Cullere-Crespin, G. C. (2002). De la langue autistique à la langue maternelle. L'histoire de Bob. In: *Bilingüisme: incidences subjectives et épistémogènes* (pp. 51–57). Paris: Cahiers de l'ALI.

Danon-Boileau, L. (2005a). *Children without Language: From Dysphasia to Autism.* Oxford: Oxford University Press.

Danon-Boileau, L. (2005b). "Early Signs of Posture and Communication: The Mother's Reaction." Paper presented at Conference on the Early Signs of Autism in Infants, School of Infant Mental Health, University College, London (11–12 July).

Darwin, C. (1872). *The Expression of Emotions in Man and Animals.* London: Fontana, 1999.

Davidovitch, M., Glick, L., Holtzman, G., Tirosh, E., & Safir, M. P. (2000). Developmental regression in autism: Maternal perception. *Journal of Autism and Developmental Disorders, 30*: 113–119

Dawson, G., Ashman, S. B., & Carver, L. J. (2000). The role of early experience in shaping behavioural and brain development and its implications for social policy. *Developmental Psychopathology, 12* (4): 695–712.

Dawson, G., Munson, J., & Estes, A. (2002). Neurocognitive function and joint attention ability in young children with autism spectrum disorder versus developmental delay. *Child Development, 73*: 345–358.

DeGangi, G. A., & Greenspan, S. I. (1997). The effectiveness of short-term intervention in treatment of inattention and irritability in toddlers. *Journal of Developmental and Learning Disorders, 1*: 277–298.

Delion, P. (2000). The application of Esther Bick's method to the observation of babies at risk of autism. *International Journal of Infant Observation, 3*: 84–90.

Delion, P., Libeau-Manceau, M., Péan, M.-C., & Petit, D. (2000). "L'Impact des carences affectives chez l'enfant." Paper presented at the Conference of the Child and Adolescent Division of the Tavistock Society of Psychotherapists, Larmor-Plage, Brittany (29 August–2 September).

DeLong, R. (2004). Autism and familial major mood disorder: Are they related? *Journal of Neuropsychiatry and Clinical Neuroscience, 16*: 199–213.

DiLalla, D. L. (1990). Age of symptom onset in young children with Pervasive Development Disorders. *Journal of the American Academy of Child and Adolescent Psychiatry, 29*: 863–872.

Doussard-Roosvelt, J. A., Joe, C. M., & Bazhenova, O. V. (2003). Mother child interaction in autistic and nonautistic children: Characteristics of maternal approach behaviors and child social responses. *Development and Psychopathology, 15*: 277–295.

Dupoux, E., & Mehler, J. (1990). *Naître humain.* Paris: Odile Jacob.

Dzikowski, S. (1993). *Ursachen des Autismus.* Weinheim: Deutscher Studeinverlag.

Edelson, S., & Rimland, B. (2003). *Treating Autism: Parent Stories of Hope and Success.* San Diego, CA: Autism Research Institute.

Fernald, A., & Kuhl, P. K. (1987). Acoustic determinants of infant preference for parentese speech. *Infant Behavior and Development, 10*: 278–293.

Fernald, A., & Simon, T. (1984). Expanded intonation contours in mother's speech to newborns. *Development Psychology, 20* (1): 104–113.

Fraiberg, S. (1982). Pathological defenses in infancy. *Psychoanalytic Quarterly, 51* (4): 612–635.

Freud, S. (1900a). *The Interpretation of Dreams. S.E.,* 4.

Freud, S. (1905c). *Jokes and Their Relation to the Unconscious. S.E.,* 8.

Freud, S. (1912–13). *Totem and Taboo. S.E.,* 13.

Freud, S. (1915c). Instincts and their vicissitudes. *S.E.,* 14.

Frith, U. (1989). *Autism: Explain the Enigma.* Oxford: Blackwell.

Gernsbacher, M. (2005). "Learning Communities and Learning Relationships: Older Children and Adults with ASD." Panel presentation at the

Annual Conference of the Interdisciplinary Council of Developmental and Learning Disorders, Tysons Corner, Virginia (12 November).

Gervais, H., Belin, P., Boddaert, N., Leboyer, M., Coez, A., Sfaello, I., Barthelemi, C., Brunelle, F., Samson, Y., & Zilbovicius, M. (2004). Abnormal cortical voice processing in autism. *Nature Neuroscience, 7* (8): 801–802.

Gori, R. (2002). *Logique des passions.* Paris: Denoël.

Grandin, T., & Scarttino, M. (1986). *Emergence: Labelled Autistic.* Tunbridge Wells: Costello.

Greenspan, S. (2005). *The Greenspan Social-Emotional Growth Chart.* San Antonio, TX: Psychological Corporation-Harcourt Assessment.

Greenspan, S., & Wieder, S. (1999). A functional developmental approach to autism spectrum disorders. *Journal of the Association for Persons with Severe Handicaps, 24*: 147–161.

Greenspan, S., & Wieder, S. (2005). *Engaging Autism: The Floor-Time Approach to Helping Children Relate, Communicate, and Think.* Boston, MA: DaCapo Press/Perseus Books.

Gutstein, S. E., & Sheely, R. K. (2002). *Relationship Development Intervention with Young Children: Social and Emotional Development Activities for Asperger Syndrome, Autism, PDD and NLD.* London: Jessica Kingsley.

Haag, G. (1984). Réflexions sur certains aspects du langage d'enfants autistes en cours de démutisation. *Neuropsychiatrie de l'Enfance, 32*: 539–544.

Haag, G. (1985). La mère et le bébé dans les deux moitiés du corps. *Neuropsychiatrie de l'Enfance, 33*: 107–114.

Haag, G. (n.d.). *Réflexions de psychothérapeutes de formation psychanalytique s'occupant de sujet avec autisme.* Unpublished manuscript.

Haag, M. (2002). *A propos et à partir de l'oeuvre et de la personne d'Esther Bick, Vol. 1: La méthode d'Esther Bick pour l'observation régulière et prolongée du tout-petit au sein de sa famille.* Paris: Livre Autoedition.

Hobson, P. (1993). *Autism and the Development of Mind.* Hove: Lawrence Erlbaum.

Hobson, P. (2002). *The Cradle of Thought.* London: Macmillan.

Hockfield, S., & Lombroso, P. J. (1998a). Development of the cerebral cortex: IX. Cortical development and experience: I. *Journal of the American Academy of Child and Adolescent Psychiatry, 37*: 992–993.

Houzel, D. (1989). Un mode d'approche thérapeutique de l'autisme et des psychoses infantiles précoces. Les traîtements à domicile. In: G. Lelord, J. P. Muh, M. Petit, & D. Sauvage (Eds.), *Autisme et troubles du développement global de l'enfant.* Paris: Expansion Scientifique Française.

Houzel, D. (1999). A therapeutic application of infant observation in child psychiatry. *International Journal of Infant Observation*, 2: 42–53.

Houzel, D. (2001). The "nest of babies" fantasy. *Journal of Child Psychotherapy*, 27 (2).

Houzel, D. (2004). The psychoanalysis of infantile autism. *Journal of Child Psychotherapy*, 30 (2): 225–237.

Humphries, T. (2003). Effectiveness of pivotal response training as a behavioral intervention for young children with autistic spectrum disorders. *Bridges*, 2 (4): 1–10.

Hutt, C., & Ounsted, C. (1966). The biological significance of gaze aversion with particular reference to the syndrome of infantile autism. *Behavioural. Science*, 11: 346–356.

Kanner, L. (1943). Autistic disturbances of affective contact. *Nervous Child*, 2: 217–250.

Kaplan, H. (1998). *Bridging the Gap. Early Feeding and Abrupt Weaning: Language Delay as a Means of Adaptation*. Unpublished MA Dissertation in Psychoanalytic Observational Studies, Tavistock/University of East London.

Kerem, D. (2003). *Effect of Music Therapy on Communicative Interactions among Deaf Toddlers following Cochlear Implantation*. PhD thesis, lborg University, Denmark.

Klein, M. (1945). The Oedipus complex in the light of early anxieties. In: *Love, Guilt and Reparation and Other Works*. London: Hogarth Press, 1975.

Kobayashi, R., Takenoshita, Y., Kobayashi, H., Kamijo, A., Funaba, K., & Takarabe, M. (2001). Early intervention for infants with autistic spectrum disorder in Japan. *Pediatrics International*, 43 (2): 202–208.

Lacan, J. (1964). *Séminaire sur les quatre concepts fondamentaux de la psychanalyse* (pp. 210–215). Paris: Seuil.

Laznik, M. C. (1995a). Les effets de la parole sure le regard des parents, fondateur du corps de l'enfant. In: D. Brun (Ed.), *Les parents, le pédiatre et le psychnalyste*. Paris: Editions P.A.U.

Laznik, M. C. (1995b). *Vers la parole. Trois enfants autiste en psychanalyse*. Paris: Denoël.

Laznik, M. C. (2000a). La théorie lacanienne de la pulsion permettrait de faire avancer la recherche sur l'autisme. *La Célibitaire* (Autumn–Winter): 67–78.

Laznik, M. C. (2000b). La voix comme le premier objet de la pulsion orale [The voice as first object of oral drive]. *La Revue Psychanalyse et Enfance du Centre Alfred Binet*. Paris.

Laznik, M. C. (2004). Marine, trois ans et demi, présentant un risque d'autisme. In: *Aspects cliniques et pratiques de la prévention de l'autisme. Cahiers de PRÉAUT, No. 1.* Paris: L'Harmattan.

Lechevalier, B., Fellouse, J.-C., & Bonnesoeur, S. (2000). West's Syndrome and infantile autism: The effect of a psychotherapeutic approach in certain cases. *International Journal of Infant Observation, 3*: 23–38.

Lord, C., Rutter, M., Goode, S., Heemsbergen, J., Jordan, H., Mawhood, L., & Schopler, E. (1989). Autism diagnostic observation schedule: A standardized observation of communicative and social behaviour. *Journal of Autism and Developmental Disorders, 19*: 185–212.

Lord, C., Rutter, M., & LeCouteur, A. (1994). The Autism Diagnostic Interview Revised—ADI/R. *Journal of Autism and Developmental Disorders, 24*: 335–349.

Losche, G. (1990). Sensorimotor and action development in autistic children from infancy to early childhood. *Journal of Child Psychology and Psychiatry, 31*: 749–761.

Lovaas, I. (1987). Behavioral treatment and normal educational and intellectual functioning in young autistic children. *Journal of Consulting and Counseling Psychology, 55*: 3–19.

Loveland, K. A. (2005). Social-emotional impairment and self-regulation in autism spectrum disorders. In: J. Nadel & D. Muir (Eds.), *Emotional Development* (pp. 365–382). Oxford: Oxford University Press.

Maestro, S., Casella, C., Milone, A., Muratori, F., & Palacio-Espasa, F. (1999). Study of the onset of autism through home-movies. *Psychopathology, 32*: 292–300.

Maestro, S., & Muratori, F. (2002). Les films familiaux. *Le Carnet Psy, 75*: 35–36.

Maestro, S., Muratori, F., Barbieri, F., Casella, C., Cattaneo, V., Cavallaro, M. C., Cesari, C., Milone, A., Rizzo, L., Viglione., V., Stern, D., & Palacio-Espasa, F. (2001). Early behavioural development in autistic children: The first 2 years of life through home movies. *Psychopathology, 34*: 147–152.

Maestro, S., Muratori, F., & Cavallaro, M. C. (2002). Attentional skills during the first 6 months of age in autism spectrum disorders. *Journal of American Academy of Child and Adolescent Psychiatry, 41*: 1239–1245.

Maestro, S., Muratori, F., & Cavallaro, M. C. (2005). How young children treat objects and people: An empirical study of the first year of life in autism. *Child Psychiatry and Human Development, 35*: 383–396.

Maestro, S., Muratori, F., Cavallaro, M. C., Pei, F., Stern, D., Golse, B., & Palacio-Espasa, F. (2002). Attentional skills during the first 6 months of age in autism spectrum disorder. *Journal of the American Academy of Child and Adolescent Psychiatry, 41*: 1239–1245.

Maestro, S., Muratori, F., & Cesari, A. (2005). Course of autism signs in the first year of life. *Psychopathology, 38*: 26–31.

Mahler, M. (1968). *On Human Symbiosis and the Vicissitudes of Individuation.* New York: International Universities Press.

Mahler, M., Pine, F., & Bergman, A. (1975). *The Psychological Birth of the Infant: Symbiosis and Individuation.* London: Karnac, 1985.

Maiello, S. (2000). "Song-and-dance" and its developments: The function of rhythm in the learning process of oral and visual language. In: L. M. Cohen & A. Hahn (Eds.), *Exploring the Work of Donald Meltzer: A Festschrift.* London/New York: Karnac.

Maiello, S. (2001). Prenatal trauma and autism. *Journal of Child Psychotherapy, 27* (20): 107–125.

Mars, A. E., Mauk, J. E., & Dowrick, P. (1998). Symptoms of pervasive developmental disorders as observed in prediagnostic home videos of infants and toddlers. *Journal of Pediatrics, 132*: 500–504.

Massie, H. (1978a). Blind ratings of mother–infant interaction in prepsychotic and normal infants. *American Journal of Psychiatry, 135*: 1371–1374.

Massie, H. (1978b). The early natural history of childhood psychosis. *Journal of the American Academy of Child Psychiatry, 14*: 683–707.

Massie, H., & Campbell, B. K. (1983). The Massie-Campbell scale of mother–infant attachment indicators during stress (ADS scale). In: J. Call, E. Galenson, & R. Tyson (Eds.), *Frontiers of Infant Psychiatry* (pp. 394–412). New York: Basic Books.

Massie, H., & Campbell, B. K. (1984). The Massie-Campbell Scale of mother-infant attachment indicators during stress (ADS scale). In H. Massie & J. Rosenthal, *Childhood Psychosis in the First Four Years of Life* (pp. 253–282). New York: McGraw-Hill.

Massie, H., & Campbell, B. K. (2006). *The Massie-Campbell Scale of Mother-Infant Attachment Indicators During Stress (ADS Scale).* Van Nuys, CA: Child Development Media.

Massie, H., & Campbell, B. K. (2007). *The Attachment During Stress Scale (ADS Scale)* (available at: www.adsscale.com).

Massie, H., & Rosenthal, J. (1984). *Childhood Psychosis in the First Four Years of Life.* New York: McGraw-Hill.

Meltzer, D. (1975). Mutism in autism, schizophrenia and manic-depressive states—the correlation of clinical psycho-pathology and linguistics. In: D. Meltzer, J. Bremner, S. Hoxter, D. Weddell, & I. Wittenberg, *Explorations in Autism.* Strath Tay: Clunie Press.

Meltzer, D. (1986). Concerning the perception of one's own attributes and its relation to language development. In: *Studies in Extended Metapsychology*. Strath Tay: Clunie Press.

Meltzer, D., Bremner, J., Hoxter, S., Weddell, D., & Wittenberg, I. (1975). *Explorations in Autism*. Strath Tay: Clunie Press.

Midence, K., & O'Neill, M. (1999). The experience of parents in the diagnosis of autism: A pilot study. *Autism, 3* (3): 273–285.

Miller, L., Rustin, M. E., Rustin, M. J., & Shuttleworth, J. (Eds.) (1989). *Closely Observed Infants*. London: Duckworth.

Minuchin, S. (1978). *Families and Family Therapy*. Cambridge, MA: Harvard University Press .

Mottron, L. (2004). *L'autisme. Une autre intelligence*. Belgium: Mardaga.

Muir, E. (1992). Watching, waiting and wondering: Applying psychoanalytic principles to mother-infant intervention. *Infant Mental Health Journal, 13*: 319–328.

Muir, E., Lojkasec, M., & Cohen, N. (1999). Observant parents: Intervening through observation. *International Journal of Infant Observation, 2*: 11–23.

Mundy, P., & Crowson, M. (1997). Joint attention and early social communication: Implication for research on intervention with autism. *Journal of Autism and Developmental Disordorders, 27*: 653–676.

Mundy, P., & Neal, R. (2001). Neural plasticity, joint attention and autistic developmental pathology. *International Review of Research in Mental Retardation, 23*: 139–168.

Murray, L. (1992). The impact of post natal depression on infant development. *Journal of Child Psychology and Psychiatry, 33* (3).

Murray, L., Cooper, P. J., Wilson, A., & Romaniuk, H. (2003). Controlled trial of the short- and long-term of psychological treatment of postpartum depression. *British Journal of Psychiatry, 182*: 420-427.

Murray, L., & Trevarthen, C. (1985). Emotional regulation of interactions between two-months olds and their mothers. In: T. Field & N. Fox (Eds.), *Social Perceptions in Infants*. Norwood, NJ: Ablex.

Nagy, E., & Molnar, P. (2004). Homo imitans or Homo provocans? Human imprinting model of neonatal imitation. *Infant Behavior and Development, 27* (1): 54–63.

Ninio, A., & Bruner, J. S. (1978). The achievement and antecedents of labelling. *Journal of Child Language, 5*: 1–15.

Ogden, T. (1992). *The Primitive Edge of Experience*. London, Karnac.

Osterling, J., & Dawson, G. (1994). Early recognition of children with autism: A study of first birthday home videotapes. *Journal of Autism and Developmental Disorders, 24*: 247–257

252   REFERENCES

Osterling, J. A., Dawson, G., & Munson, J. A. (2002). Early recognition of 1-year-old infants with autism spectrum disorder versus mental retardation. *Development and Psychopathology, 14*: 239–251

Panksepp, J. (2001). The long-term psychobiological consequences of infant emotions: Prescriptions for the twenty-first century. *Infant Mental Health Journal, 22* (1/2).

Papousek, M. (1992). Parent-infant vocal communication. In: H. Papousek, U. Jürgens, & M. Papousek (Eds.), *Nonverbal Vocal Communication*. Cambridge: Cambridge University Press.

Phillips, J., & Schuler, A. (2005). *Outcome of Interventions with Children with Autistic Spectrum Disorders*. Unpublished manuscript, Department of Special Education, San Francisco State University.

Piaget, J. (1936). *The Origins of Intelligence in Children*, trans. M. Cook. New York: International Universities Press, 1952.

Pinker, S. (1994). *The Language Instinct*. New York: Morrow.

Prechtl, H. (1963). The mother–child interaction in babies with minimal brain damage (a follow-up study). In: B. M. Foss (Ed.), *Determinants of Infant Behaviour II*. New York: Wiley.

Rascovsky, A. (1971). *Niveles profundos del psiquismo*. Buenos Aires: Editorial Sudamericana.

Ratey, J. (2001). *A User's Guide to the Brain*. London: Abacus.

Reid, S. (Ed.) (1997a). *Developments in Infant Observation: The Tavistock Model*. London: Routledge.

Reid, S. (1997b). The development of autistic defences in an infant: The use of a single case study for research. *International Journal of Infant Observation, 1*: 51–79.

Reissland, N., Shepherd, J., & Cowie, L. (2002). The melody of surprise: Maternal surprise vocalizations during play with her infant. *Infant and Child Development, 11*: 271–278.

Ridley, M. (2003). *Nature versus Nurture: Genes, Experience and What Makes Us Human*. London: Fourth Estate.

Rhode, M. (1995). Links between Henri Rey's thinking and psychoanalytic work with autistic children. *Psychoanalytic Psychotherapy, 9*: 149–155.

Rhode, M. (1997a). Going to pieces: Autistic and schizoid solutions. In: M. Rustin, M. Rhode, A. Dubinsky, & H. Dubinsky (Eds.), *Psychotic States in Children*. Tavistock Clinic Book Series. London: Duckworth.

Rhode, M. (1997b). The voice as autistic object. In: T. Mitrani & J. L. Mitrani (Eds.), *Encounters with Autistic States: A Memorial Tribute to Frances Tustin*. Northvale, NJ: Jason Aronson.

Rhode, M. (2004). Infant observation as research: Cross-disciplinary links. *Journal of Social Work Practice, 18*: 283–298.

Rhode, M. (2005). Mirroring, imitation, identification: The sense of self in relation to the mother's internal world. *Journal of Child Psychotherapy, 31* (1): 52–71.

Rogers, S. J. (1996). Brief report: Early intervention in autism. *Journal of Autism and Developmental Disorders, 26*: 243–246.

Rogers, S. J. (2004). Developmental regression in autism spectrum disorders. *Mental Retardation and Developmental Disabilities Research Reviews, 10*: 139–143.

Rogers, S. J., & DiLalla, D. L. (1990). Age of symptom onset in young children with pervasive developmental disorders. *Journal of the American Academy of Child and Adolescent Psychiatry, 29*: 863–872.

Rogoff, B. (2003). *The Cultural Nature of Human Development*. Oxford: Oxford University Press.

Rosenthal, J., Massie, H., & Wulff, K. (1980). A comparison of cognitive development in normal and psychotic children in the first two years of life from home movies, *Journal of Autism and Developmental Disorders, 10*: 433–444.

Rustin, M. E. (1989). Encountering primitive anxieties. In: L. Miller, M. E. Rustin, M. J. Rustin, & J. Shuttleworth (Eds.) (1989). *Closely Observed Infants*. London: Duckworth.

Rustin, M. J. (1997). What do we see in the nursery? Infant observation as laboratory work. *International Journal of Infant Observation, 1*: 93–110. Reprinted in: *Reason and Unreason: Psychoanalysis, Science and Politics*. London: Continuum.

Sacks, O. (1973). *Awakenings*. London: Picador, 1991.

Sacks, O. (1995). *An Anthropologist on Mars*. New York: Vintage Books.

Sallows, G., & Graupner, T. (2005). Intensive behavioral treatment for children with autism: Four-year outcome and predictors. *American Journal of Mental Retardation, 110*: 417–438.

Sartre, J.-P. (1955). *No Exit*. New York: Random House.

Sauvage, D., Faure, M., Adrien, J. L., Hameury, L., Barthélémy, C., & Perrot, A. (1988). Autisme et films familiaux. *Annales de Psychiatrie, 4*: 418–424.

Schore, A. N. (1994). *Affect Regulation and the Origin of the Self: The Neurobiology of Emotional Development*. Hillsdale, NJ: Lawrence Erlbaum.

Schore, A. N. (1996). The experience-dependent maturation of a regulatory system in the orbital prefrontal cortex and the origin of developmental psychopathology. *Development and Psychopathology, 8*: 59–87.

Schore, A. N. (1998). The experience-dependent maturation of an evaluative system in the cortex. In: K. H. Pribram (Ed.), *Brain and Values: Is a Biological Science of Values Possible?* Mahwah, NJ: Lawrence Erlbaum.

Schultz, R. T., Grelotti, D. J., Klin, A., Kleinman, J., Van de Gaag, C., Marois, R., & Skudlarski, P. (2003). The role of the fusiform face area in social cognition: Implications for the pathobiology of autism. *Philosophical Transactions of the Royal Society of London, Series B: Biological Sciences, 356* (1430): 415–427.

Seligman, K. (2005). Chronicles in autism. *San Francisco Chronicle Magazine,* 13 November, pp. 11–16.

Sigman, M., Dijamco, A., Gratier, M., & Rozga, A. (2004). Early detection of core deficits in autism. *Mental Retardation and Developmental Disabilities Research Reviews, 10*: 221–233.

Sinason, V. (1986). Secondary mental handicap and its relationship to trauma. *Psychoanalytic Psychotherapy, 2*: 131–154.

Slade, A., Aber, J. L., Berger, B., Bresgi, I., & Kaplan, M. (2003) (with Mayes, L., Target, M., & Blatt, S.). *Parent Development Interview Revised: Short version (PDI-R2-S)."* Unpublished protocol.

Snyder, A., Bossomaier, T., & Mitchell, D. J. (2004). Concept formation: Object attributes dynamically inhibited from conscious awareness. *Journal of Integrative Neuroscience, 3*: 31–46.

Somerville, G. (2000). "Everybody's dead": The observation of an infant with autistic features. *International Journal of Infant Observation, 3*: 39–63.

Spensley, S. (1995). *Frances Tustin: Makers of Modern Psychotherapy.* New York: Routledge.

Spitz, R. (1955). The primal cavity. *Psychoanalytic Study of the Child, 10*: 215–240.

Stern, D. (1971). A microanalysis of mother-infant interaction. *Journal of the American Academy of Child Psychiatry, 10*: 501–517.

Stern, D. (1977). *The First Relationship: Infant and Mother.* London: Fontana.

Stern, D. (1985). *The Interpersonal World of the Infant: A View from Psychoanalysis and Developmental Psychology.* New York: Basic Books.

Sternberg, J. (2005). *Infant Observation at the Heart of Training.* London: Karnac.

Stern-Bruschweiler, N., & Stern, D. (1989). A model for conceptualizing the role of mother's representational world in various parent-infant therapies. *Infant Mental Health Journal, 10* (3): 142–156.

Teitelbaum, P., Teitelbaum, O., Nye, J., Fryman, J., & Maurer, R. G. (1998). Movement analysis in infancy may be useful for early diagnosis in autism. *Proceedings of the National Academy of Sciences, 95*: 1392–1397.

Thoman, E. B. (1975). How a rejecting baby affects mother-infant synchrony. *Ciba Foundation Symposium, 33*: 177–200.

Tinbergen, N., & Tinbergen, E. (1983). *Autistic Children: New Hope for a Cure*. London: Allen, & Unwin.

Tomatis, A. A. (1977). *The Conscious Ear*. Barrytown, NY: Station Hill Press.

Trevarthen, C. (1979). Comunication and cooperation in early infancy: A description of primary intersubjectivity. In: M. Bullowa (Ed.), *Before Speech: The Beginnings of Human Comunication* (pp. 321–347). London: Cambridge University Press.

Trevarthen, C. (1998a). *Children with Autism: Diagnosis and Interventions to Meet Their Needs* (2nd edition). London: Jessica Kingsley.

Trevarthen, C. (1998b). The concept and foundations of infant intersubjectivity. In: S. Braten (Ed.), *Intersubjective Communication and Emotion in Early Ontogeny* (pp. 15–46). Cambridge : Cambridge University Press.

Trevarthen, C. (2000). Autism as a neurodevelopmental disorder affecting communication and learning in early childhood: Prenatal origins, post-natal course and effective educational support. *Prostoglandins, Leucotrines and Essential Fatty Acids, 63* (1/2): 41–46.

Trevarthen, C. (2001). Intrinsic motives for companionship in understanding their origin, development and significance for infant mental health. *Infant Mental Health Journal, 22* (1–2): 95–131. (Special Issue: Contributions from the Decade of the Brain to Infant Mental Health, ed. A. Shore.)

Trevarthen, C. (2003). Intersubjectivité chez le nourrisson. Recherche, théorie et application clinique. *Devenir, 15* (4): 309–428.

Trevarthen, C. (2004). How infants learn how to mean. In: M. Tokoro & L. Steels (Eds.), *A Learning Zone of One's Own* (pp. 37–69). SONY Future of Learning Series. Amsterdam: IOS Press.

Trevarthen, C. (2005a). Action and emotion in development of the human self, its sociability and cultural intelligence: Why infants have feelings like ours. In: J. Nadel & D. Muir (Eds.), *Emotional Development* (pp. 61–91). Oxford: Oxford University Press.

Trevarthen, C. (2005b). First things first: Infants make good use of the sympathetic rhythm of imitation, without reason or language. *Journal of Child Psychotherapist, 31* (1): 91–113.

Trevarthen, C. (2005c). Stepping away from the mirror: Pride and shame in adventures of companionship. Reflections on the nature and emotional needs of infant intersubjectivity. In: C. S. Carter et al. (Eds.), *Attachment and Bonding: A New Synthesis* (pp. 55–84). Dahlem Workshop Report 92. Cambridge, MA: MIT Press.

Trevarthen, C., & Aitken, K. J. (2001). Infant intersubjectivity: Research, theory and clinical applications. *Journal of Child Psychology and Psychiatry, 42* (1): 3–48.

Trevarthen, C., Aitken, K. J., Papoudi, C., & Robarts, J. Z. (1998). *Children with Autism: Diagnosis and Interventions to Meet Their Needs* (2nd edition). London: Jessica Kingsley.

Trevarthen, C., Aitken, K. J., Vandekerckhove, M., Delafield-Butt, J., & Nagy, E. (2006). Collaborative regulations of vitality in early childhood: Stress in intimate relationships and postnatal psychopathology. In: D. Cicchetti & Cohen (Eds.), *Developmental Psychopathology, Vol. 2: Developmental Neuroscience* (2nd edition, pp. 65–126). New York: Wiley.

Trevarthen, C., & Daniel, S. (2005). Disorganised rhythm and synchrony: Early signs of autism and Rett syndrome. *Brain and Development, 27:* 25–34.

Trevarthen, C., & Hubley, P. (1978). Secondary intersubjectivity: Confidence, confiding, and acts of meaning in the first year. In: A. Lock (Ed.), *Action, Gesture, and Symbol* (pp. 183–229). London: Academic Press.

Trevarthen, C., & Malloch, S. N. (2000). The dance of well-being: Defining the musical therapeutic effect. *Nordic Journal of Music Therapy, 9:* 3–17.

Tronick, E. Z. (Ed.) (1982). *Social Interchange in Infancy: Affect, Cognition and Communication*. Baltimore, MD: University Park Press.

Tronick, E. Z. (2005). Why is connection with others so critical? The formation of dyadic states of consciousness: Coherence governed selection and the co-creation of meaning out of messy meaning making. In: J. Nadel & D. Muir (Eds.), *Emotional Development* (pp. 293–315). Oxford: Oxford University Press.

Tustin, F. (1972). *Autism and Childhood Psychosis*. London: Karnac, 1995.

Tustin, F. (1981). *Autistic States in Children*. New York: Routledge.

Tustin, F. (1986). The rhythm of safety. In: *Autistic Barriers in Neurotic Patients* (2nd revised edition). London: Karnac, 1994.

Van Rees, S., & Leeuw, R. de (1987). *Born Too Early: The Kangaroo Method with Premature Babies*. Video. Heythuysen, The Netherlands: Stichting Lichaamstaal.

Vargas, D., Nascimbene, C., Krishnan, C., Zimmerman, A., & Pardo, C. (2004). Neuroglial activation and neuroinflammation in the brain of patients with autism. *Annals of Neurology*, epub., November (DOI: 10.1002/ana.20315).

Volkmar, F. R., & Cohen, D. J. (1985). The experience of infantile autism: A first-person account by Tony W. *Journal of Autism and Developmental Disorders, 1:* 47–54.

Volkmar, F. R., & Pauls, D. (2003). Autism. *The Lancet, 362*: 1133–1141

Wedeles, E., Grimandi, S., & Cioeta, M. (2002). "From Traditional Observation to Participant Observation in the Case of an Infant Who Was Failing to Thrive." Paper presented at the Third International Conference
for Teachers of Infant Observation, Tavistock Clinic, London (March).

Welch, M. (1983). Retrieval from autism through mother–child holding. In:
N. Tinbergen & E. Tinbergen, *Autistic Children: New Hope for a Cure* (pp.
322–336). London: Allen & Unwin.

Welch, M., Welch-Horan, T., Anwar, M., Anwar, N., Ludwig, R., & Rug-
giero, D. (2005). Brain effects of inflammatory bowel disease in areas
abnormal in autism and treatment by single neuropeptides secretin
and oxytocin. *Journal of Molecular Neuroscience, 25*: 259–274.

Werner, E., & Dawson, G. (2005). Validation of the phenomenon of autistic
regression using home videotapes. *Archives of General Psychiatry, 62*:
889–895.

Werner, E., Dawson, G., Osterling, J., & Dinno, N. (2000). Brief report.
Recognition of autism spectrum disorder before one year of age: A
retrospective study based on home videotapes. *Journal of Autism and
Developmental Disorders, 30*: 157–162.

WHO (1993). *The ICD-10 Classification of Mental and Behavioural Disorders:
Diagnostic Criteria for Research*. Geneva: World Health Organisation.

Williams, G., Grimandi, S., & Cioeta, M. (2002). "From Traditional Observation to Participant Observation in the Case of an Infant Who Was
Failing to Thrive." Paper presented at the Bick Centenary Conference
on Infant Observation, Krakow (August).

Wing, L. (1996). *The Autistic Spectrum: Guide for Parents and Professionals*.
London: Constable.

Wing, L., & Gould, J. (1979). Severe impairments of social interaction and
associated abnormalities in children: Epidemiology and classification.
Journal of Autism and Developmental Disorders, 9: 11–29.

Winnicott, D. W. (1956). Primary maternal preoccupation. In: *Through Paediatrics to Psychoanalysis*. London: Hogarth Press, 1975.

Winnicott, D. W. (1958). *Through Paediatrics to Psychoanalysis*. London:
Hogarth Press.

Winnicott, D. W. (1967). Mirror-role of mother and family in child devel-
opement. In: *Playing and Reality* (pp. 111–118). London: Routledge,
1971.

Wolke, D., Rizzo, P., & Woods, S. (2002). Persistent infant crying and
hyperactivity problems in middle childhood. *Pediatrics, 109*: 1054–
1060.

Young, R. L., Brewer, N., & Pattison, C. (2003). Parental identification of early behavioural abnormalities in children with autistic disorder. *Autism*, 7 (2): 125–143.

Zilbovicius, M. (2004). *Les autistes ne reconnaissent pas la voix humaine.* Interview conducted by F. Maxime & E. Lecluyse, "Les chercheurs de l'année 2004". *l'Express en ligne*, 20 December (available at http://www. lexpress.fr/info/sciences/dossier/recherch/dossier.asp?ida=430986).

Zwaigenbaum, L., Bryson, S., Rogers, T., Roberts, W., Brian, J., & Szatmari, P. (2005). Behavioral manifestations of autism in the first year of life. *International Journal of Developmental Neuroscience*, 23 (2–3): 143–152.

INDEX